A PERFECT GOD *created*

AN IMPERFECT WORLD *perfectly*

30 Life Lessons from

Kids Kicking Cancer

Defeat Stress
to Live Longer and Better

BY RABBI G.

Rabbi Elimelech Goldberg
Founder and International Director
Kids Kicking Cancer
Clinical Assistant Professor Department of Pediatrics
Wayne State University School of Medicine

Kids Kicking Cancer Office
27600 Northwestern Highway
Southfield, Michigan 48034
248–864–8238
www.kidskickingcancer.org

Editor: Eric Schramm
Graphic Design: Pennie Barbel
Photo Credits (Amber & Rabbi G.): Joshua Schwartz
Book Layout: ©2014 TheBookMakers.com
Meditation Voice Recording: Reid Mclellan (Hello World)
Meditation Music: Spencer Hall (Hudson Edits)
Book Layout by York Expert Book Services

A Perfect God Created An Imperfect World Perfectly / Rabbi G. —1st ed.

Hard Cover ISBN 978-0-9863583-0-2
Trade Paperback ISBN 978-0-9863583-2-6
eBook ISBN 978-0-9863583-1-9

Contents

Dedicated to Ruthie
My partner on this amazing journey

In the Beginning

I had the privilege of serving a congregation for almost twenty years before I resigned my rabbinical position to teach karate. Although a lot of people change jobs in mid-life, the journey from Orthodox rabbi to *sensei* is not all that common. In fairness, I did not exactly leave my pulpit to create the classic karate school, or *dojo*. Instead, many of the lessons I teach are in hospitals and clinics. My students are little boys and girls diagnosed with cancer. While we do practice kicking and punching, our studies mainly focus on the power of our inner light to break through the stressors of pain, fear, and anger. My new pulpit still focuses on the soul, but now the congregants are the little patients in pediatric hospitals and clinics across the globe. For me, this has been a very personal mission. My first mentor was our beautiful little girl, diagnosed with leukemia a week before her first birthday.

Martial arts is a fascinating amalgam of self-awareness, introspection, movement, and energy that emphasizes the melding of mind, body, and spirit. It doesn't matter whether one calls this energy "chi," "ki," "tenaga dalam," "prana," "neshama," "light," or "soul"—the theme remains the same. Each of us contains a very powerful force that can positively affect our lives and those around us. This is particularly fascinating to me because it mirrors so much of the mystical underpinnings of the Biblical literature I am accustomed to.

Children who have been given a difficult medical diagnosis can especially feel victimized by their disease. Martial arts provides a great methodology for allowing sick boys and girls to see themselves as victors more than as victims. Many of our students find that coming in contact with their inner energy empowers them significantly when dealing with their struggles.

In 1999, I started the Kids Kicking Cancer program in response to the amazing benefits I found that martial arts, meditation, and breathing techniques have for those in great pain and stress, particularly children. As the program began to develop, parents, doctors, nurses, and many others began to comment on the changes they saw within the boys and girls who had joined our classes. These adults were nothing short of mesmerized as they witnessed kids utilizing a technique for taking control of pain, fear, and anger. In addition, the children, some as young as three years old, became natural teachers of these very methods. Our mantra, "Power, Peace, Purpose," a phrase the children yell as they do their martial arts, describes this flow of power that creates inner peace. When asked, "What's your purpose?" they yell out, "To teach the world!" It turned out that the more purpose our young little heroes felt, the less pain they reported. Before long, we were having the children teach adults with cancer and other serious illnesses. But the broad applicability of what the children were demonstrating only became clear when we elicited serious interest from companies large and small in learning our breathing techniques and meditations. CEOs and human resource managers told us they also wanted their employees to take control of their stress, fear, pain, and anger. And so, for the last five years, we have been invited to give seminars across the globe to Fortune 500 companies on how to use a very simple technique to reconquer our brains and our lives. Ninety-seven percent of the participating adults surveyed described the presentation as having had "a profound influence" on their lives. I will take some credit for putting the slides together. But the real teachers in the program are the children of Kids Kicking Cancer—some as young as three years old.

The purpose of this book is to share with you the wisdom of these children and the techniques that have changed their lives. The thirty chapters are intended as a platform to allow you access to a powerful world of awareness and focused response. Leading wellness experts have described our relaxation and focus techniques as "unique," "very effective," and "the best stress-busting tools out there." The second half of the book contains simple exercises, associated with each chapter that one can read or download to watch and listen to. And because this book is uniquely attached to our website, every time that you engage in an exercise, you are not only teaching your brain to defeat stress; you are also letting our little heroes know that you are watching them. You will live longer and they, knowing how their purpose in life has been enhanced, will feel less pain. Welcome to our family.

Stress May Be Your Most Dangerous Adversary

Stress kills. You know it, and yet you may be doing very little to address this hazard. Unlike arsenic, guns, or guillotines, chronic secretions of stress chemicals kill you rather slowly. Your heart, lungs, muscles, and body tissue become long-term victims to the perils of your high-pressure life, raising your blood pressure, causing vital muscles to spasm, and lowering your immunological capacity to fend off disease. In olden times, forty-year-olds were senior citizens. Life was short. The negative impact of stress was not as noticeable. Today, when seventy is the new forty, stress has become the new gunslinger in town, and, whatever your age, you're in the line of fire.

If all stress did was kill you, it would only be half as bad. However, the accompanying tightness of pain, fear, and anger all chip away at your ability to take control of your life. Stress destroys your relationships and your opportunities, and it diminishes you as a person. Living with the chronic fears of "what if?" fills the few healthy years you have with the "fight or flight syndrome," a term coined by Walter Cannon at Harvard at the turn of the last century. Dr. Cannon focused on people "blowing up" from the stress response and on how it impacts the body negatively. You know that feeling of "losing it" due to stress, and so do the people around you whom you affect and who affect you. Your ability to serve as parent, spouse, teacher, employer, worker, or friend is significantly diminished by the ongoing chemical assault that stress wages on your brain. Perception is mired, communication is challenged, and your influence on the world around you becomes negatively impacted. The chronic secretions of glucocorticoids from the adrenal gland make your physical pain worse while potentially shaping you into a conduit of emotional pain to the people around you—ironically, often those whom you care about the most. Stress is the painfully off-key harmony to that old song, "You Always Hurt the One You Love."

We often make the mistake in believing that we are the sole authors of our life's script. Children, perhaps because they are so young, know they are not in control. As adults, however, we need to take responsibility for our actions, and yet the strain when something goes wrong and the fear of failure produce the unhealthiest chemical cocktails in our bodies. The neurological stress response to the "what ifs" and all the far-flung responsibilities in our lives is not much different from the body's discovery of necrotic or dying tissue. The blaring alarm bells of stress drown out the effective orchestration of our rational and calm responses. Over time, it also makes us sick. The more we think we need to be solely responsible for writing the scripts of our lives, the less power we have to really live it.

We know that smoking is bad for you, sunbathing is bad for you, and too much caffeine is bad for you—but don't worry, because that's bad for you, too!

"A Perfect God Created an Imperfect World Perfectly" means that a greater power has strategically placed bumps in our road as important opportunities for our growth. That message, coupled with a focused, empowered mind/body response, can help you train your brain to take control and to best respond to the myriad problems you face. It will allow you to live longer, live better, and, perhaps most important, live with purpose. For you will soon notice, as our children do, that as you respond to pain, fear, and anger with light, power, and focus, others will notice, and you too will be teaching the world around you. And when you allow yourself to relax those stressors, you become the most effective "you" that you can be!

The word for breath in the Bible is *neshima*. It derives from the very same root as the word *neshama*, which means "soul." In the world of the Kabbalah, or Jewish mysticism, the right breath can connect you to enormous spheres of power and well being. On a neurological level, learning how to use your breath to move your body and your body to control your breath can effectively act as a brake on the chemical stress levers within you. Our little martial artists will teach you to identify the moment you are coming under attack and respond to that threat without stress, fear, pain, and anger. Your effectiveness in your life choices will be based on the higher parts of your thinking mind rather than the lower, terribly ineffective responses of the primal brain. The more you retain control, the greater your ability to eliminate negative stress from your life and the lives of those around you. It starts with your breath.

If three-year-old children can do it, you can too!

LESSON 1

Bernard

OPTIMISM

> *Conquering stress begins with the knowledge that you can. The first thing to remember is that the battle for control of your life is rooted in optimism. Even if you find yourself on a road not of your own choosing, you have the power to grab hold of the steering wheel of life and point yourself where you need to go. The children of Kids Kicking Cancer are usually too young to drive, but they are successful in controlling pain because they believe they can control it. Having already experienced much disappointment and challenge in their young lives, they learn that optimism is very important. However, they define it in a way you may not expect. Lesson 1 is their definition of optimism, and how it changes them. It can change you, too.*

It was a dreadful winter day, even by Michigan standards. The early morning sunlight quickly vanished behind giant blustery clouds that shed their load of hard snow with incredible speed, churning up a slippery blanket below. Had it been a school day, children would have awakened with a smile informed by the expectation that school would be canceled. But this was a Sunday, and a special one at that. For the children of Kids Kicking Cancer it was the day they had been invited by the Macomb Area Optimist Club to an end-of-the-year holiday party. The prudent thought was to call it off.

An early call to the Optimist leadership indicated that they were . . . optimistic. It was too late to cancel the party, and in any case there was not enough time for us to contact our parents and staff. Somewhere, I thought, there must be a Pessimist Club. That would be for optimists with experience. And it was clearly my experience talking here: there was no way that the majority of our kids would be at the party. It was going to be a huge disappointment for children whose lives of chemotherapy, radiation, surgeries, and pain were already filled with disappointments. The snow outside was anything but bright.

After a very long and difficult drive, I arrived at the school where the party was to be held. Despite the accumulation that had already blanketed the parking lot, the shapes underneath the falling snow clearly indicated the presence of cars, and a lot of them. That day the parents became real optimists and felt it was imperative that nothing was going to stop them from getting to the school and celebrating together. There would be enough time later to be stuck at home or in the hospital. Now the school gym was packed. The smiles inside were melting the frozen tundra outside.

It was a fun event, with clowns, activities, food, and prizes. For those of us who travel to the hospitals and clinics with these kids, it was especially beautiful. Toward the end of the event, I noticed that one of our children, a ten-year-old boy named Bernard Johnson, was being pushed in his wheelchair toward the microphone by his twin sister, Brittany. With a smile, the Optimist MC gave Bernard the microphone. All the activities surrounding us stopped as this little boy began to speak. "Hi, my name's Bernard," he started. "And I want to thank all of the people here for making such a fun party for us. You are really very nice. And I really want to thank all of Kids Kicking Cancer for being part of our family. They care so much for us and teach us some really important stuff." As I looked around at our staff of martial arts therapists, there wasn't a dry eye to be found. Bernard had been with us for almost a year and a half. His mom had abandoned the family when he was very young. Bernard's dad died a little after Bernard and Brittany's eighth birthday. When they were nine, their uncle passed away. That was the same year Bernard was diagnosed with an inoperable brain tumor that had already robbed him of the ability to walk. It was slowly stealing the rest of his body.

Bernard was not letting any of that get in the way of what he had to say. "And I want to teach you what we do in Kids Kicking Cancer," Bernard proclaimed in a loud voice. "You can breathe in the light which is your essence and blow out the darkness. You can do this no matter what is going on in your life."

It wasn't easy to take the microphone after Bernard, to speak to four hundred people who had just been lifted off the floor by a ten-year-old who could not even pick up his own feet. I tried to arrange my thoughts, opening with greetings to our families and thanks for the many volunteers, which allowed me enough time to compose the next words as a message to the Optimist Club members. It was eventually to become Kids Kicking Cancer's message to the world.

"Optimism," I said, "does not mean that everything is going to be great. It means that we can respond to everything with greatness. That is what we just heard from Bernard and what we regularly learn from the children you see here today."

The story of Kids Kicking Cancer is about greatness. It is also a very practical guide for every person on this planet who will inevitably face challenges in his or her life—in other words, everyone. While it is perfectly natural to respond to the ups and downs of your existence with stress, anger, and pain, the heroic response that these children live and teach by example provides incredible insight and practical tools for conquering those stressors. When you take control of your life and make decisions without the cloudiness of stress, you are able to reach the highest levels of effectiveness and purpose. You become a teacher!

Before we leave chapter 1, I would like to introduce you to your first student: your brain. If you ever stopped and thought about what you were thinking, you would notice a cacophony of feelings, sounds, distractions, and every once and a while, if you're a member of my generation, the theme song from *Gilligan's Island*. (Remember the "three hour tour"?) Very often we get "mugged" by our brains and, despite our best intentions, end up with negative, nagging, sometimes silly thoughts that we recognize as counterproductive. There is actually a section of the brain called the default-mode network that is activated when you have distracted thoughts and that occupies a significant part of your neural circuits. You are hard-wired to be unfocused.

In the book of Genesis, the Biblical patriarch Jacob is described as having a battle with an angel. According to many commentators, this encounter represents a significant internal conflict. It was a struggle that led to Jacob receiving an additional name, "Israel," meaning one who has done battle in both the earthly and heavenly spheres. This struggle, however, is not limited to one individual. Every one of us has thoughts, feelings, and sensations that we know are bad for our soul, our health, our family. These unwelcome intruders into our psyche damage our potential to positively impact this world. What you may not realize, however, is how simple it is to teach your brain to identify stressful negative thoughts and to remove them.

As a big fan of classical music (I grew up on Elvis), I have arranged this book like a symphony. A theme is introduced, followed by several variations leading to a finale that will help you produce reflections of light and remove thoughts of darkness. The uplifting crescendos are the stories of children who demonstrate this inner power magnificently. The entire score has been composed with simple tools that you can use to integrate positive energy into your life over a period of one month. And the climax occurs when you recognize that others around you are learning the lessons of our little heroes from you. The second half of this book provides QR codes that will connect you to thirty audio meditations. If you don't have a smart phone scanner, you can go to our website (www.kkcbook.org) to download the audio file there. When prompted enter the number 1613. The audio meditations are also printed out for those people who are more visual learners as well as for anyone who might have a challenge getting to the website. If you don't know what a website is, you probably have no stress in your life, so don't start worrying about it now.

Many people get uptight when they hear the word "meditation," believing it's an escape from reality or that it requires yogi-like powers to achieve. Other people associate it with Eastern religions that they are not comfortable with. In truth, meditation has a profound impact on your brain and goes all of the way back to the Bible. Many recent studies have shown that contemplative neuroscience (the medical term for the study of meditative techniques) has significant impact on treating depression, lowering chronic pain, creating healthier bodies, improving social relationships, and even growing a greater volume of brain tissue in the prefrontal cortex (the part of the brain that rationally allows you to problem solve and achieve great goals). In the Bible, meditation was an important ingredient in prophecy, an essential calm and inner sense of well-being. As you proceed through these short exercises, you will find how easy it is to take control. Over time you will turn your brain into a great student, and before you know it you will be ready to take on your next teaching assignment: family, friends, co-workers, and anyone else around you. Just let them know that you learned it from our kids.

Sara Basya

OUR DAUGHTER, HER SCRIPT

We tend to think that we alone write the script about our lives, and we imagine the ways we want our lives to unfold. But when things don't go the way we imagined, it creates fear, anger, frustration, and disappointment. It also creates a lot of stress. There comes a point when it is important to realize that we don't really write the scripts in our lives, at least not all by ourselves. Our greatness, however, is determined by how we respond to that script.

The journey that led to the creation of Kids Kicking Cancer is very personal. It began with a mountain. It was the twenty-fourth of October, 1980. On Friday mornings I would give my Yeshiva University students in Los Angeles a lecture about the weekly Biblical portion that we were to read in the synagogue the next day. These young men were just a few years younger than I, and we had formed a very close bond.

The Jewish calendar divides the entire Five Books of Moses into weekly portions that are read in part during the week and in entirety on the Sabbath morning. This particular week we were studying the binding of Isaac, the near sacrifice of Abraham's precious and long-awaited child on Mount Moriah. I directed my students to focus on the heroic nature of Abraham's task in light of the fact that God himself had issued the command. What other response could the first patriarch of the Jewish people have given? "Let's do lunch"? "I'll have my people call your people"? These phrases had not yet been created. Nor would such a delaying tactic have been an appropriate response to the Master of all creation. Abraham had to take his son up that mountain. It wasn't a multiple-choice question. What was the greatness of his heroic response? It lay in how he walked up that hill.

The binding of Isaac took place immediately before the death of Sara, our matriarch. Isaac was thirty-seven years old at that time, not the little boy often envisioned in paintings. He was directed by his father to help prepare for what would have seemed a festive offering to God. Isaac had no reason to assume otherwise. It would have been a celebration with Abraham's son walking up the mountain singing and dancing. And, as the Bible writes, "The two of them walked as one." Thus Abraham found the strength to put aside his own set of feelings and, despite the enormity of the tragedy that lay ahead, found the faith to walk up that mountain singing and dancing.

The key to greatness was not, I explained to my students, that we are given overwhelming challenges. Heroism is all about how we respond to those challenges. Abraham, facing the most unthinkable task, maintained a very deep faith even as he continued to march up that mountain. Interestingly, Isaac interrupts their climb with a question: "Behold, here is the fire and the wood"—materials easily available at the Home Depot of Canaan—"but where is the lamb for the offering?" Without hesitation, Abraham responds in a manner that, according to the syntax of the Biblical text, allows Isaac to understand that he himself is to be the sacrifice. This is followed by the repetition of the phrase, "And the two of them walked as one." Isaac was thus ascending the path up the mountain knowing that he was approaching his death and that Abraham was bidden to do the unthinkable, and yet they were walking as one. They traversed that mountain singing and dancing together. Despite their mutual awareness of the overwhelming darkness that lay ahead, they found the strength to focus on the light. At the age of twenty-four years I was transmitting a lesson of profound faith and conviction, and I felt that I myself understood it.

A few hours later, I was summoned to the administrative office to take an urgent phone call from my wife, Ruthie. It is hard to remember that there was a time when all phones were attached to walls or sat on desks. Ruthie was adamant that although we had just taken Sara Basya, our beautiful little girl, to the pediatrician two days before, we had to take her back again, as soon as possible. Knowing that my schedule that day was tight and that the doctor had already diagnosed a bad virus that was going around, I tried to protest. It didn't work. Mothers know. There was something really wrong.

This little smiling blonde girl was born on the sixth of November, 1979. She did something to me that no one else could do. She turned a young man into a father. Watching your baby sleep, smile, cry, or begin to laugh is one of the most transformational experiences. To me, each day was miraculous and despite the sleepless nights, the dreams of my little girl growing up occupied every part of my being. Sara Basya was a Daddy's girl; more accurately, I was wrapped around her little finger.

My wife's concerns won out and we took Sara Basya back to the doctor for a blood test. We went home afterward, and then our phone rang. No one is immune from that phone call. No matter how carefully we prepare our portfolios or double-check our to-do lists, that one phone call that can change your life is never far away. The doctor was on the line, and the results were not good. "We have to rule out leukemia," he told us in a not very reassuring voice. "Bring her back to the hospital now." More than thirty years later, I can still feel the ground opening up beneath us. Los Angeles has had its share of tremors and earthquakes, but nothing ever felt like this. The human brain is equipped to shield us from pain; we are blessed with a certain numbness so that we can continue to walk forward even through the most wrenching darkness. I remained numb from that phone call until the following morning, when at 9:45 am the X-ray technician walked into our room. "The doctors want another picture of her spleen. Would you bring your daughter down to the X-ray room?" Hospital basements are not designed to look as pleasant as the spaces above, and this one was absolutely dreadful. When we reached what felt like the dungeon of diagnostic machinery, the technician turned to me. "We are a little short-staffed today. Do you mind fastening her arms and legs to the table?" It was now 10:00 am on our Sabbath, when all the synagogues in Los Angeles were reading the story of Abraham binding the arms and legs of his child to the altar. He probably did not use Velcro. And yet everything else felt the same. I remembered what I had taught my students just hours before. *We are given these journeys to find the strength to walk up the mountain singing and dancing.*

I quickly realized that it is a lot easier to give a lecture than to live its message.

Sara Basya's diagnosis of ALL (acute lymphocytic leukemia) is the garden variety of what today is a very curable disease. Her white blood count and her age did not bode well for her thirty years ago, however. The next year's cycles of remission and relapse, of hospitalization due to fevers that her small body was not equipped to handle, of the devastating impact of chemotherapies and radiation, were nothing compared to the eventual bone marrow transplant. Before the diagnosis we used to worry if her pacifier fell to the ground. (There's no "five second rule" for your first child.) Now we were filling her body with chemicals so dangerous they had to be prepared in hooded bins so as not to burn the skin of the people administering them. Our world was turned upside down.

In the midst of all of this madness, however, our beautiful blue-eyed and once blonde little girl showed a spirit that belied her youth. At just under two years of age she would tell the doctors at UCLA, "No medication today, please." She would kiss the doctors after they held her down for particularly painful procedures and tell the five-year-old kids in the clinic not to cry. What was most remarkable was that as her skin was sloughing off and she was having the most horrible reactions to the overly toxic chemo and radiation of the bone marrow transplant (almost none of the kids survived the transplants in those days), she would lie on top of me and pat me on the shoulder and assure me, "It's okay, Abba ['daddy' in Hebrew]. I love you."

Sara Basya passed away on November 19th, 1981. It was two weeks after her second birthday. Approximately eight years later, I found myself the rabbi of a synagogue in Southfield, Michigan, a great community whose warmth makes up for the frigid winters. One day I received a call from a gentleman passing through town who was collecting money for one of the very first pediatric oncology summer camps. I thought it was a great idea, having a personal awareness of what the children and their families go through. I volunteered to write a check and help this fellow identify others who would be willing to join in the effort as well. Instead, I was stunned when Rabbi Simcha Scholar told me that he didn't call me for my check. He wanted me to direct the camp. (I have a camping background.) "You are completely out of your mind," I told him. "Every little girl is going to be my daughter. My wife and I can't go there." But Rabbi Scholar is quite a salesman. It takes just a few minutes to make a child laugh, he said—even those with cancer—and then they are just kids again. He was right. Ruthie and I worked the camp for twelve years.

It was at Camp Simcha (which means "joy" in Hebrew) that I came across a pediatric reality that I now lecture about in medical circles across the globe. If an adult screams in the middle of a painful procedure, usually the doctors will stop and figure out another way to do it. If children scream, the medical team often holds them down even tighter.

The infirmary at Camp Simcha was like a little hospital in the woods. One day I walked into the chemo room to see a five-year-old boy held down by two nurses, with a third clutching a very large syringe to put into this boy's port in his chest. He was screaming and struggling. This child was from Texas, far away from Mom and Dad and the doctors he was used to. The nurses were great, but the child refused to be distracted or bribed. He was too afraid, and his chemo wasn't negotiable.

In the old days it was medically accepted that there was a pain center in the brain. Today, with the use of functional MRIs we have evidence of an entire neuro-matrix of pain reception. Included within the fray are the parts of the brain that register fear, anger, despondency, and other emotional parameters; the more afraid or angry, the greater the pain. Conversely, brain scans indicate that people who sense a purpose to their struggles experience less pain.

Josh from Texas was anything but calm. The fears of a different environment, combined with his all-too-practiced familiarity with pain, promised a horrific experience. I walked into this agonizing scene just as the nurse was ready to plunge the syringe into his chest amidst his harrowing screams. The situation was so counterintuitive to me—the nurses trying to help this little boy while at the same time terrifying him—that I suddenly heard myself shout, "Wait!" Everyone in the room stopped struggling at once. Even Josh stopped screaming. They all looked at me. I had no clue what I was going to say next. "Give me five minutes with this boy," I heard myself request. The nurses were happy to leave, and the young patient looked at me as if I had been the governor who had just stayed his execution. I walked over to him and said, "I'm a black belt." Frankly, that doesn't mean much, but to Josh, it was clearly a "wow!" sort of thing. "Do you want me to teach you some karate?" I asked. He almost jumped off the table. Did he somehow intuit that learning karate meant he could exercise power on his own? "In the martial arts," I began, "pain is a message that you don't have to listen to. You can bring in this amazing karate energy and blow out the pain." He was interested. Five minutes later we were doing a simple Tai Chi breathing technique together. Then the nurses returned. He and I continued the breathing exercise. Twenty minutes later one of the nurses pulled out the needle from his chest. Josh looked up at her. "Did you do it yet?" he asked.

At that moment, Kids Kicking Cancer was born.

Very few of us have accurately predicted the scripts that play out for ourselves. We like to believe we can control our lives and the world around us. But the stress that we generate by holding firm to this belief renders us less effective than we can be. Understanding that a perfect God created an imperfect world perfectly allows you to more readily accept your situation. This philosophy more readily allows you to let go of the fear, anger, and pain that flood your brain with stress chemical, clouding your ability to respond with clarity and strength. Ironically, the more you let go, the more you can begin to take control of your life. Your greatness is all about how you respond to the script you are handed. Our children will teach you how to do that—with real power.

LESSON 3

Cathy

POWER, PEACE, PURPOSE

> *Every form of martial arts envisions a medium of power, or chi, that we can harness for use in our lives. But you don't have to be a martial artist to attach to that power from above. We can feel ourselves connecting to an incredible energy simply by creating an image of light traveling inside our bodies. This is not only an antidote for stress; it is a platform for teaching those around you how to live life in a more meaningful and focused way.*

The therapeutic model of Kids Kicking Cancer is the martial arts. Most children believe in the power of karate or the dozens of other disciplines portrayed in movies and on television. There is a deep sense of tradition and respect that permeates the dojo or martial arts studio. The bow that we teach our children is the classical three-step movement of creating a fist to indicate our power. When one hand covers that fist we portray our desire for peace. This is then followed by a motion of bowing as a sign of respect. When the children take these three steps they shout out our mantra, "Power, Peace, Purpose." This is the sound of children ready to fight. For them it is the fight for their lives.

The Kids Kicking Cancer program trains experienced martial artists to be therapists. We give classes in and out of the hospital, intervene in painful procedures with children in clinics, and even work with kids in their homes if they are too sick to get to one of our outpatient classes. We teach children how to use their breath to push out pain, fear, and anger. Our meditations help the boys and girls create "safe places" in their mind and to visualize the destruction of their cancer cells and tumors. What is unique in our methodology is that the children are given tools that they can master rather quickly on their own and use wherever they may be and whenever challenges occur. Moreover, these children embrace the martial arts: they are so eager to be empowered in their upside-down lives. Our wonderful therapists are trained to be flexible and to reach the children, their minds and hearts, wherever they are at that moment. One beautiful little six-year-old named Cathy told our therapist in a New York hospital that she does not like karate. "Well, what do you like?" she was asked. "I like butterflies," Cathy responded. Martial arts, which uses kata or dance movements to mimic confrontation, was perfect for this challenge. Little Cathy learned butterfly dances in which she used her powerful wings to push away her pain and fear.

The unique element of our model is that the children are given purpose. The most common source of despondency among sick children is that their disease has made them so very different from their friends. We allow them to understand that yes, they are different, at least for the moment. But we also teach that when they reach inside of themselves and take control of their darkness with light, they positively impact the lives of so many people around them. That makes them not just different, but powerfully different.

Disease often stops a kid from being a student; we make them a teacher. Kids Kicking Cancer makes it possible for these children to teach adults, not just fellow cancer patients, but people who deal with on-the-job stress at major companies that partner with us. We are also in talks with the Pentagon about having our boys and girls teach soldiers how to breathe in the light and thereby address Post-Traumatic Stress Disorder. That's what the children mean when they proclaim, "Power, Peace, Purpose." They are so powerful that they can teach the world.

"Power, Peace, Purpose" is a message that is as relevant for every adult struggling to pay the mortgage and raise the kids as it is for children battling cancer. It is because our little heroes are going through something so unthinkable for a child that adults stop and take notice of the heroism of these amazing little martial artists. Our warriors sound a clarion call of perspective that inspires us to focus on what is essential and how to create a life of meaning. But the benefits flow in both directions: when the children receive a standing ovation for sharing what they have learned, they feel their purpose. Purpose reduces pain. We thus all have an impact on each other.

Power is the ability to breathe in a great light or energy. Peace is the impact of that energy as it calms the storms of pain, fear, and anger. Purpose is the engine that motivates and leads the other two. When we ask our students, "What's your purpose?" they shout back: "To teach the world!"

Gerard Butler is one of the best-known action heroes in the movies today. Even bigger than his super muscles, however, which he worked hard to perfect for the blockbuster *300*, is his heart. Over the last few years he has been a great supporter of our children, and he has also become a close friend. A few years ago he invited my son Meir and me to the set of *The Bounty Hunter* to meet his co-star, Jennifer Aniston. Jennifer does a lot of work for St. Jude's Hospital and is a very sensitive and caring person. We watched them work from the sidelines as they repeated the same two-minute scene over and over, probably twenty times. All the retakes made watching more than a little tedious, but it gave Gerry an opportunity between takes to introduce us to more people. During a longer break, he sat me down and wanted to review the Kids Kicking Cancer mantra. This wonderful actor is also a deep thinker, and he has spent hours with me assessing ways to make our program more effective. Gerry suggested that we should switch the order of the first two words so that it would be "Peace, Power, Purpose." His thought was that peace is much more important than power. For him as with many of those in his world, power is a readily available commodity. He's an international celebrity who is recognized wherever he goes. But, Gerry noted, the real quest for many famous people is finding that elusive inner peace.

The two of us talked about it for a while. Our organization had already asked our wonderfully generous pro bono patent attorney, Michael Lisi from the Detroit law firm of Honigman, Miller, Schwartz, and Cohn, to secure the trademark for our mantra, and we were not about to change it. But more than that, I explained to Gerry, power before peace makes sense for the children. It's not the power of fame or fortune that he was familiar with. It's a power that makes it possible to have peace. As eleven-year-old Bernard described it, "It's about finding your essence." Bernard couldn't walk, but he had plenty of power. Two years later Gerry sat with Bernard as the movie star made a public service announcement for our kids in Detroit. He asked Bernard when he most uses his martial arts breathing technique. Bernard, ever the teacher, explained that when he wakes up in the morning ready to spring out of bed only to remember that he can no longer stand on his own feet, he can become flooded with some very bad feelings. It is especially then that he remembers his "Breath Brake." He brings in the light and blows out the darkness, powered by the awareness that he is teaching the world. Bernard had to first feel that power to find his place of peace.

In his short life, Bernard excelled at teaching, and his example continues to teach others today.

This is not a book about dying. It is about something much more challenging, living. While we tend to think of our lives in terms of special events—birth, graduations, engagements, marriage, children, and the continuation of the cycle—life is also a continuum filled with challenges, questions, and resolutions. Every moment is the moment of our lives. Every second is an opportunity for greatness. It all begins with finding our true power.

As you turn the pages of this book to learn from and be inspired by our wonderful little teachers, you will learn the practical tools to integrate the message of "Power, Peace, Purpose" into your life. Whatever your source for that higher energy, it is yours for the taking. Reaching upward for this "chi" is a common theme in the martial arts. It is equally popular in the world of spirituality. Bringing in the light to drive out the everyday darkness will allow you to live longer and greater. As you marry this theme to the practical tools that the children teach, you will find an incredible energy to respond to your script with greatness. Knowing that this energy exists is the first step.

Moshe Dovid

THE POWER OF A CHILD

> *Anger is a weakness that you can control. It is also a great indicator of the stress response. By focusing on relaxing your body in the midst of the most maddening of times, you put the brakes on a stress cycle that can leave you powerless to change your situation and your life for the better. In the martial arts we identify anger as an enemy that we must defeat before we can stand up to defend ourselves against any other opponent. First identify the anger as a weakness in order to defeat it before it can control you.*

Before I left my congregation to develop the Kids Kicking Cancer program, I maintained an active counseling schedule. There was one gentleman, let's call him Lenny, who came to my study to inform me that he was leaving his wife and two children. He was overwrought and very anxious because his spouse was continually "abusing" him. It did not take very long to determine that he was the one with an anger issue and was unwittingly responding with outbursts that left emotional scars on everyone at home. To help him identify his anger and begin to take control, I asked him to assign a number from 1 to 10 to describe his wife's "abuse." An example of a 1 would be if she burnt the toast. A 10 would be if she drove the car through the wall of the family room while he was napping on the couch. One day, Lenny arrived at our appointment with a question. "Am I crazy?" he asked. "My wife made a little quip, maybe it was a 2. Something got into me and I started responding like it was an 8 or 9. Am I nuts?" I tried to explain that our brains have one hundred billion cells, each with about one thousand synaptic connections. That's a total of one hundred trillion connections, many of them firing away based on our experiences and memories. Unless a person has a closed head injury, those connections generally remain. Similar memories stick together and trigger each other. It's like a line of trucks gathered at the entrance ramp to a highway. When it's time to move, they all flood onto the highway together. "Your wife," I told him, "made a little joke at your expense. You felt disrespected. It was a 2, but you associated it with the memories of when your father hit you with an 8 or your sister did a 9 to you. Your wife's quip was a 2, but all of your history within that subconscious flooded out and added up to a much bigger number."

Human beings do not respond to life in a vacuum. I know a lot about this, because many of my friends are humans. Every experience in our past triggers the flowing of chemicals in the present, including those neurotransmitters that cause pain, fear, and anger. We re-experience those old emotions all over again. They travel along the same neural pathways as the stressors that do so much damage to our health. These very natural human responses create havoc in our relationships and our world. But there is another possible response. In Kids Kicking Cancer we call it the Heroic Response. The very first step is to realize that we are getting mugged. When we can identify the chemical chain of reactive despair that is flooding our system, we can then bring in the power that will allow us to respond with our souls and not our bodies.

One of the campers at Camp Simcha was a very big boy for an eleven-year-old. His smile was angelic and his good looks made him appear like the perfect child. It was impossible to see that there was a fearsome tumor lurking in his brain. Moshe Dovid Mermelstein, however, was anything but angelic at school. In fact, he had already been sent home several times after getting into fights with other children.

We often hear parents apologizing for their misbehaving children with remarks like, "He's a good boy; he's just tired." What they really mean is that their kid is a monster and they're just waiting to get him married off so they can pass responsibility to a spouse as quickly as possible. But in Moshe Dovid's case, he really was a very good boy. Before the tumor began to cause profound outbursts of anger, he was a model kid and never would consider hurting anyone else. The school understood his situation, but they had the safety of the other children to consider. His parents didn't know what to do. He was getting more and more frustrated that he had become labeled as a "bad boy" and that he had no control over his behavior.

Moshe Dovid loved the idea of the martial arts. My first step in helping this young man was to allow him to identify the anger inside of himself. "It's not you," I tried to assure him. "It's your tumor." "But aren't you your brain?" he asked me. The depth of this question, coming from an eleven-year-old, took my breath away. Somehow I came up with an answer. "No," I said. "Your brain is just an organ of your body, like your liver, lungs, or kidneys. You are not your brain. You are your soul, and that's an amazing light that is inside of you. Your choice in life is to find the power to reach inside of yourself and respond to the challenges of the moment with your soul and not just your body."

Moshe Dovid was an amazing student. He quickly became a teacher. Our first step was to allow him to identify when he was being attacked by "Tom the tumor." He described that the initiation of the anger, although quick, could usually be felt by a tightness in his throat and chest. "Every martial artist," I told him, "needs to be prepared that he might get attacked." That's when we go into action.

Breathing is the only aspect of the autonomic nervous system (the part that works by itself) that we can easily control. The one common denominator of all martial arts is the profound emphasis on breath. "As soon as you begin to feel the tightness in your throat or chest," I instructed Moshe Dovid, "you take a quick and deep breath, blowing it out very slowly. Then you continue to breathe in the air steadily and slowly through your nose, lifting and expanding your body upward with each part of the breath. When your lungs are totally filled up with the air, take in a quick breath of a little bit more. Now, hold that breath for three seconds. As you slowly breathe out through your lips, feel every muscle that you expanded in your body relax and release, until there is no more air left. Then blow out a little bit more and remain with that feeling for a moment." We practiced this. "The next breath you take in, do exactly the same," I continued. "This time imagine the air coming in as a beautiful and powerful light flooding through your body. We don't want to push out this light. In its place we will blow out all the anger, fear, and darkness as we relax every single muscle of our body." In the two weeks of camp that followed, I was able to see my young student work very hard when things didn't go exactly as planned and Tom the tumor was out to throw him into a rage. Increasingly, Moshe Dovid began taking control. By the end of camp season he was lecturing his counselor not to get angry and demonstrating how to dominate the inner demon that we all have in some form or other.

Following camp, Moshe Dovid had to go through many painful procedures. His breathing techniques became very much a part of his routine. On one of these occasions, when his parents asked him if he felt any pain, he responded, "My body is physically here but I am not. I didn't feel anything." Three months after camp, Moshe Dovid's father called me to find out the next time I was going to be in New York, where they lived. He wanted to arrange a meeting with me and his son's neuropsychologist and learning specialist, who wanted to videotape my session with Moshe Dovid. They couldn't believe the change that had taken place in two weeks of camp. Moshe Dovid not only went back to school without hurting the other children; he went back as a teacher.

Many of our children with tumors spring back from their disease and its treatment with great resilience. I have gone to their weddings and celebrated the births of their own children. Unfortunately, Moshe Dovid was not one of those who lived to see those stages of life. I attended his bar mitzvah, which was a very moving event. His tumor continued growing faster than it could be treated. It soon ended his life. And yet Moshe Dovid's power so transcended the fortitude of what anyone could expect from a person of his or any age.

In the Jewish tradition, learning the Bible and the Talmud is a great act of religious observance. Toward the end of Moshe Dovid's life, the tumor was very, very painful and he was confined to bed most of the time because of the medication that made him so tired. One evening, Moshe Dovid called out to his father, "Ta, can you bring me my gemora [volume of Talmud]?" His father walked in with the requested text. "Are you feeling better, Moshe Dovid?" he asked. "No," his son responded, "it's worse. But I remember learning that if you study even though it's hard for you, your reward is that much greater." His father understood. What better time is there to learn than when one is in such terrible pain?

Mastering pain and controlling anger were synonymous for this powerful young man. Using his breath to control his body allowed his soul to reach a level of incredible greatness. For most of us, the triggers of anger, pain, and fear are not tumor-related. But the destructive nature of anger can equally destroy our lives. In community seminars, I tell parents, "If you want your kids not to hear a word you're saying, raise your voice. It works wonders." Angers are stressors that make us ineffective in virtually every area of our lives. Taking a "Breath Brake" and blowing out the tension in our muscles triggered by that anger allows us to stop the stress mechanism. More importantly, it allows us to respond with power. That power is the ability to bring in an amazing light even in the face of the greatest darkness. For Moshe Dovid's parents and so many others, that light is forever.

LESSON 5

Brendan

SOULS ON CHEMO

> *When bad things happen to good people, the world feels less secure and reliable, increasing our feelings of stress. Living in a world of chaos and darkness makes it harder to internalize the light. Our children respond to tragedy with a resolve to reframe their challenges as opportunities that can define their purpose in life and their very being. For us, watching the children is not only inspirational, but can help us reach the heights of human greatness. It is easy to respond to tragedy by asking "Why?" It is far more meaningful to reformulate the question: "How can I grow from this?"*

Every member of the clergy is often confronted with the question "Why?" The death of children significantly intensifies the difficulty. For atheists, convinced that the universe is a series of random accidents, the response is simple: "Why not?" For the rest of us, however, the question persists.

One must allow for the possibility that not every question has an answer fathomable by the human mind. I have studied the responses of many theologians and philosophers, but I don't pretend to understand, much less explain, the infinite. What I can share with you is how much I have learned from our children.

To comprehend the mysteries of life and death, one must begin not with the question "Why do children die?" but "Why are they born in the first place?" Why does a Heavenly Kingdom bestow upon humanity not only joy and comfort but also weakness and destruction and suffering?

When our Kids Kicking Cancer children don't heal, we give them black belts, often in ceremonies in front of hundreds of their family and friends. On the black belt we embroider the child's name on one end. On the other, the words "Master Teacher" stand out. Cancer today is a very treatable illness and pediatric cancers in particular have a cure rate in the neighborhood of 86%. Of course, these cures do not come without physical and emotional scars, but we work hard to empower the children to go beyond their despondency, to cultivate a self-image of victor rather than of victim. We work with thousands of children, however, and we still give out too many black belts.

One of our first black belts was Brendan Filzek. He was seven years old when he started our program. Brendan practiced his karate forms diligently and was very serious about his meditations. It was a good thing, too, because the pains that he faced grew stronger and stronger as one treatment after another failed to halt the growth of the tumor in his head for any significant amount of time. On the one hand, we create a message to the children that they can "kick" their cancer. On the other hand, if the prognosis goes south, we don't want the children to feel that they did not fully put up a fight. On the contrary, we emphasize to those boys and girls that the greater the adversary, the more powerful the martial artist. The key for the kids is that we can respond with light no matter what. And that light is forever.

It was that light that Brendan, his sister, his mother Maureen, and I were holding onto as we sat on their living room floor meditating on the power of Brendan's soul. "I can feel your light, Brendan," Maureen said. "I will miss your cute little 'bod,' but I feel your light with me." Brendan opened up his eyes to look at his mom. I saw a sense of relief on his face. His mother could feel him even if he was at a distance. He knew that they would always be together.

Down the block from the Filzek home was the local public school. Normally shuttered on the weekend, it was brimming on this Sunday morning with hundreds of Brendan's family and friends. The last few days had been really tough on this little boy and he was very tired. The family doubted that he would have the strength to attend his own black belt ceremony, and we were prepared to honor him quietly in his home. Brendan wouldn't hear of it. He was going to be there to receive his black belt no matter how he felt. His father, Doug, carried him onto the stage with his karate uniform enveloping his little body. I helped Doug place Brendan carefully in the seat and we began our ceremony. The principal said a few words and there were some meaningful comments from family. It was then Brendan's turn, but he could no longer speak. His beautiful face was contorted on one side by the massive monster that was taking his life. He had told me the week before what he wanted everyone to know. I was honored to repeat Brendan's words for him:

"I am receiving this black belt because I have defeated my cancer. I am no longer afraid or angry. If anything, I am more connected to God and the people around me." Sensei Jeff, Brendan's teacher, walked onto the stage carrying Brendan's black belt with his name on one end and the words "Master Teacher" on the other. Brendan stood up. He wasn't supposed to. He barely had the strength to sit in a chair. It didn't matter. This was his victory.

I will never be able to find the words to describe the flood of emotions and light, of tears and utter profundity, when this little boy stood up, now wrapped in his black belt, as three hundred people rose to their feet to provide him with the most amazing standing ovation I have ever seen, one week before we buried him with his black belt. There is no other way to describe that moment than as a celebration of victory, of life, and ultimately of a light that is forever. Was it an accident, or did a little boy manage to change the lives of three hundred people just by standing up? Did the fact that God put my daughter, who had such an influence on so many people in our Los Angeles community, into the world for only two years make her life less impactful? I have learned from these children that some lives can be very short in years, but very long in purpose.

Mortality is a central element of the human existential experience; it is ingrained in our psyche from the moment we form our fear of separation and death in childhood. The Bible records that before the Flood, a person could live nearly a thousand years. Social Security probably didn't begin until age 650, and who knows when people began to retire to their condos on the beaches of Southern Mesopotamia? On the other end of the spectrum, consider the life of the adult mayfly, from the order Ephemeropteralts (from the Greek *ephemeros*, meaning "short-lived"). From the moment they exit a very short childhood, mayflies have to engage in mating, creating, and decaying in something close to a twenty-four-hour period. While this puts speed dating in a new light and makes a lifetime warranty seem not so impressive, the life of a mayfly on that day is perfectly normal to them. On their scale, to die two hours early is to be plucked in one's prime; two hours late would be cause for celebration. In the Talmud, a long life is described as *arichat yamim*, which literally translates as "long days." The number of years pales in importance to the value of filling each day with purpose. A perfect God created an imperfect world, perfectly. Too many of our children have short lives, but they can also have long days. Sometimes because they are so young, the power of their days is all the more profound. A soul that finds meaning and strength within trauma can create triumph that impacts the entire world.

Michael and Chaya

WHEN BAD THINGS HAPPEN TO LITTLE PEOPLE

We are too often stuck in a world that highlights our problems. The more our brain focuses on that which seems to be falling apart, the greater the ongoing secretion of stress chemicals that guarantee that they will. For this reason, our children learn to see their challenges as incredible opportunities. By blowing out the tightness of stress, they become master teachers to those around them. And when you learn from our little heroes, you will understand a theme that resonates throughout their lives: "A perfect God created an imperfect world perfectly."

People frequently ask me how I deal with the death of children. The answer is simple: I cry. I often tell our very tough martial arts therapists, "When you stop being able to cry, then you quit." The greatest tragedy to me, however, is not the death of a child after ten years or five years or even two years. These children, in their short time in this world, spread an illumination well beyond their lifespans. They have lived "long days." The greatest tragedy to me is being with a dying nonagenarian who does not have a clue why he or she inhabited this planet. A poet once wrote that one's life is not about the year of birth or the year of death engraved upon the tombstone; it's about the dash between those two dates. There are two-year-old children whose dash continues to influence the world. There are others whose dash never really began, their ninety years like the life of a mayfly.

I cannot reiterate enough that today cancer is a very curable disease, and no age group has made greater progress in beating it than children. Michael Hunt was a student in our very first Kids Kicking Cancer class at Children's Hospital of Michigan in the summer of 1998. He had been diagnosed with a nasty rhabdomyosarcoma and had several of his ribs removed, after which he was fitted with a special mold to protect his torso. His mother asked the doctors if the mold would have to be replaced when he reached the age of twenty and had grown more. The doctors were not concerned by that possibility. They didn't believe that Michael was going to make it to twenty years old. Instead of following that pessimistic assessment, however, Michael kicked his cancer. He is now doing wonderfully in college, getting his degree so that he can teach children, and he serves as an instructor at Kids Kicking Cancer. But even for years before that, Michael has been teaching our students about how he was able to limit his pain medications because his breathing helped him to focus. Our program is filled with these amazing children who, because they have "walked the walk," are superbly equipped to "talk the talk." Michael has been transformed by the program, and now he is helping so many other kids to do what he did.

Even though they are a small minority, there are still too many children whose cancers do not respond to treatment or who are pulled down by numerous ancillary medical challenges. The tragedy of their stories would be greater if we could not share some of their heroism and light. The goal of this book is to transmit not sadness but a powerful, informed, and effective response to the darkness that every one of us faces at some point in our lives. If, as an added bonus, you take the time to give your kids, your spouse, your friends, or whomever else is important in your life that extra hug, then the book has more than accomplished its task. The goal is not to be afraid of death, but to invest in every day of life.

Mortality is not the easiest thing to deal with and thus often leads to denial. The power of death denial is illustrated in a story that takes place in a small church. Putting the fear of heaven into his congregation, a parish priest one particular Sunday morning shouts from the pulpit, "I want you to know that every last man, woman, and child in this parish is going to perish from this earth." In the back of the church, an old man immediately began to grin. Seeing this, and assuming that he was misheard, the priest raised his voice a notch and repeated: "Every single one of you in this parish is going to die!" The older gentleman was now having a hard time restraining himself from laughter. Totally annoyed, the priest now glared at the old man in the back and fixed his vitriol directly on him. "Did you not hear what I said?" he stormed at the old man. "Not one person in this parish is going to survive, and you think that's funny?" "Excuse me, Father," the elderly gentleman chuckled. "I didn't mean to laugh. It's just that I'm not a member of this parish."

It is in the context of facing mortality that the question known as theodicy, or why bad things happen to good people, emerges. Although this question continues to stump many a philosopher, our children are often able to respond like sages.

Chaya Mitchell was a happy and very talented young lady. Her late father, Dr. Grant Mitchell, had been a dear friend of mine and, as a physiatrist, a mentor in my work. Chaya was quite young when her father died of leukemia, and she was now living in Chicago with her mother, siblings, and step-father. After her senior year in high school, Chaya elected to study abroad. It was there that her headaches began. It did not take long before the medical staff sent her for an MRI and then supplied the harrowing report that she had a substantial brain tumor. Chaya returned to Chicago for surgery and was by then in significant pain. When I heard the news, I called Chaya's mother, Jenny, and offered to help teach her daughter the breathing and meditation techniques that we successfully employ with our Kids Kicking Cancer students. "I have already tried going down that road with her," Jenny replied. "I did it so many times with Grant. But she told me that it was not her thing." "I certainly understand," I countered. "But tell her if I could teach her our techniques, she would be an awesome teacher for other children in pain." It didn't take five minutes before Chaya called me back. "Could you come to Chicago to teach me?" she asked. "I want to help other children with cancer."

Chaya did amazingly well with the meditations and breath work, which made her significantly more comfortable even after the surgery. Her type of brain tumor had a protocol that followed the surgery with several weeks of radiation. But in the midst of those radiation treatments, her tumor grew back 150%. She was going to need another surgery, and her pain was back in double dosage.

As I was sitting with Chaya in her home, we had a video camera trained on her face so that she could continue to teach others. Despite the circumstances and the way she was feeling, she had a wonderful smile that day. Her head, now wrapped in a kerchief, was clearly bald, but the beauty of this child was effervescent. "They told me at the hospital that if I keep some of my hair tied up in a rubber band, I could save some," she said. "And it's true; it worked. Look!" At that point, she whipped the kerchief off her head, revealing a large rubber band holding the last ten hairs on her otherwise uninhabited scalp. As the camera focused on Chaya, I asked her, "Could you please tell other people how they can handle adversity in their lives?" For the first time, this child appeared uncomfortable. "I really don't know how to answer that question," she responded slowly. "You see, I've never really had any adversity in my life. Even this brain tumor is just an opportunity for me to grow."

I have a personal rule in Kids Kicking Cancer: I won't cry in front of the children unless they themselves are crying. In this case, I excused myself and walked outside "to make a phone call." I had just heard a teenager answer the question of why bad things happen to good people. She refused to accept her situation as bad. It was just a challenge, and she was standing up to that challenge.

Is the human being a mayfly with a few extra days thrown in, or is there a reason that every one of us goes through the extraordinary challenges of the human condition? If there is a soul, impacted continually by the medium of challenge, then two years, twenty years, or a hundred and twenty years are mere frequencies for experiencing those victories of days.

In the Dearborn Islamic Center, the largest mosque in North America, there is a sign on a wall that reads:, "A perfect God, created an imperfect world, perfectly." I consider it a great honor that underneath it says, "Rabbi Elimelech Goldberg, Founder, Kids Kicking Cancer." Muslims, Jews, Christians, Hindus, Buddhists, or none-of-the-above—all see opportunities for greatness in life's challenges, not merely suffering. Stress can be overwhelming when we feel surrounded by chaos and tragedy. Chaya was proof-positive that we can reframe any situation as an opportunity.

It was one week after our daughter's second birthday when she and I engaged in this same debate. The bone marrow transplant had left her very sick and in significant pain. The only place of comfort that she could find was lying on top of her mother or father. The university where I taught was very considerate and allowed me to lecture only an hour a day just a few days a week (which I did to maintain my sanity) and spend the rest of my time in the hospital. Ruthie was tied up with a newborn at home so I was Sara Basya's primary comforter, willingly serving as our daughter's mattress and pillow. Quite uncharacteristically, on the last day of her life, Sara Basya pushed herself off me. Her eyes were rolling back as she was going into shock. I shook her. "Come back to Abba," I implored. Sara Basya focused on me and with surprising resolve replied, "No." "We can go to the park or the zoo," I suggested, and I quickly rattled off the names of other places she loved and that I had promised we would visit upon leaving the hospital. But at the mention of each place, she responded firmly, "No, no, no." "Well, where do you want to go?" I asked, hoping that I was forgetting the one place that would draw her back. The bed at UCLA was by the window. Our daughter lifted up her arm and pointed to Heaven. "Do you want to go to Hashem [God]?" I hesitatingly asked. To this question she responded with even greater resolve: "Yes." That was not the answer I wanted to hear. "But," I argued, "we need you here, and the Torah says, 'You shall *live* in them [the ways of the commandments].' There is so much to do in *this* world." Even though we had never discussed the concept of the soul returning to Heaven in the event of death, her mind was made up. She was way ahead of me. In my mind, there was no possibility—ever—that our daughter was going to die. I was in total denial. There I was, having a debate with a two-year-old child who was now clutching her bottle in response to my arguments. Suddenly I saw that I was no longer debating with a baby but with an old soul who possessed the most beautiful little body, one that I was begging to remain with her family.

Even as I write these words with tears in my eyes thirty-one years later, I know that her light and her soul are forever. Even after many years, the pain of her loss, as most parents who have lost children will tell you, remains. We would not have it any other way. As we explain to our bereaved families in Kids Kicking Cancer, our job is not to fight the pain but to hold onto our children's light as we continue our lives. We then go back to the breath work that the children have already taught us and emphasize that those breaths are essential in removing the damaging influences from the stress of grief on our bodies. That stress makes it harder to continue being the moms, dads, husbands, and wives that we still need to be. Parents respond very positively to fighting the stressful implications of grief even as we find it impossible to let go of the pain. Learning how to change the stress channels does not require years of counseling. When you counter the stress, you have a greater ability to look beyond the imperfections of our lives and see the opportunities of greatness that are present in those challenges.

We teach thousands of children how to do this. With adults, we just speak a little slower.

LESSON 7

Shachar and Emanuel

AN EXQUISITE ENTANGLED WORLD

> *It is possible to perceive life as a messy amalgam of random events. The metaphor employed by existentialists describes a runaway train hurtling through the darkness with no conductor. This rather stressful view of life can be replaced by one that appreciates the symmetry and miracle of life. Even in the face of our own mortality, understanding the infinite light of our souls and the dimensions of eternity that surround us gives us permission to refocus ourselves without fear. We see children of all ages creating this inner resolve and focus with extraordinary power. With their breath, they are connecting to the infinite.*

As Kids Kicking Cancer expands globally, I find that it is the rule, not the exception, that some connections along the way are made with great serendipity. In 2004, we were blessed with the nation's highest honor in community public health, the Robert Wood Johnson Community Health Leaders Award in Washington, D.C. When we were named one of the finalists for that award, the Robert Wood Johnson Foundation sent out two representatives to see us up close. It turned out that the reason we won was because the assistant director of the program, Ed Chu, was a black belt in Kung Fu and nobody knew it. He quickly grasped the power of the martial arts as a profound medical therapy and helped to propel us to the top.

When we began a partnership that same year with the Detroit Public Schools system, some of our board members felt that we should work through the governor's office. We had some high-level connections in the state capital, and going this route made sense, given that Detroit Public Schools is a tough system to navigate without assistance. Unfortunately, because it was an election year, Governor Jennifer Granholm was often on the road stumping for candidates across the country. As a result, I couldn't get fifteen minutes with her in her office. One day, I found myself on a plane waiting to take off for Phoenix, where I was going to speak at a conference. It was the day of the presidential debate in Tempe, Arizona. The governor walked onto my plane. Of course, I knew this had to be providential. Mid-flight, I introduced myself and briefly explained our situation, and then asked the governor if she preferred to meet inside or out. She chuckled and asked her chief of staff, seated next to her, to allow me to sit down. I then had the privilege of speaking with her for an hour.

I shared a similar story with a young friend of mine, whom I went to visit in Baltimore, Refael Shachar. At seventeen years old, Refael Shachar had gone through many complicated surgeries to remove the tumors rapidly growing in his body. Some of those operations almost killed him. I told my young friend how I had recently travelled from Wisconsin on a flight that had me sitting next to a geneticist from Wisconsin. I have an interest in the young field of epigenetics and eagerly engaged him in conversation. Although the discussion turned into a heated debate about creation and the role of God, by the time we landed we had discovered that we had grown up only a few houses away from each other, and we were singing the PS 95 school song together. After relating this story to Refael Shachar I remarked, "Small world, isn't it?" This young man's body was so filled with tumors that he could barely move his neck. Notwithstanding, he picked up his head to look at me from his electric wheelchair and responded, "No, it is really a very large world. It is just exquisitely managed." Coming from the world that Shachar had known, full of pain and hardship, the remark was not just profound, but overwhelming.

For Shachar and Chaya, a part of life will always be infinite. Fairness cannot be judged in a world that is not completely visible to us. Instead, these children have answered the challenge of theodicy by questioning the placement of the goalposts we call life. Are the boundaries of existence confined only to the dash between birth and death, or is there perhaps a dimension to our being that extends both before and after? Perhaps we do live in a very, very large world that is exquisitely managed; we just can't see the whole thing from here.

Many people refer to Heaven as the "hereafter," but if you listen to them describe their concept of it, you might think they should call it the "thereafter"—some outer dimension beyond Andromeda, as if borrowing from modern cosmology the notion of multiple galaxies in the universe. In contrast, there are those of us who actually do believe in a "hereafter"—it's a dimension that surrounds us with the presence of heavenly souls, despite our limited ability to perceive it.

A former congregant and a good friend, Dr. Julian Nussbaum, who served as the chairman of ophthalmology at Ford Hospital in Detroit, shared with me a conversation he once had with a renowned retina expert that he had brought to the hospital to lecture. After the presentation, Julian and the other doctor had dinner together. With some hesitation, this gentleman opened up with Julian on a personal matter. "You are a religious man," he told my friend. "So I'll tell you something that I can't share with others— they would think I'm totally crazy." Julian didn't know what to expect, but the other doctor didn't wait for him to react. "A number of years ago," he began, "my wife of thirty years passed away. I was in a terrible depression, which I eventually overcame. Three years after her death, she walked into my bedroom in the middle of the night. 'Ed,' she said to me, 'you must go to the emergency room right now and check yourself out.' Despite the clarity of this vision, I'm a scientist and I was well aware that dead people could not be walking around my house dispensing medical advice. My departed wife, however, would not let go. She kept repeating and insisting, 'You have to go to the hospital right now and get yourself checked out.' By two o'clock in the morning I could not deal with this any longer, so I got up and drove down to the emergency room at the hospital. The residents know me and were surprised that I was not there for a patient but wanted to check myself out. 'Put the EKG leads on me,' I told them, which they did. The monitor indicated no abnormal heart activity. 'What are your symptoms?' they asked. 'None,' I replied. At that, the resident phoned upstairs for the psychiatric resident on call. Two o'clock in the morning and I was asymptomatic—they thought I was just nuts. But as they were removing the leads from my chest, I had a massive coronary infarction, right there on the table. It took twenty minutes to revive me in the emergency room. If my dead wife had not forced me to go to the hospital, I would have died at home that night."

Paul Fischer is also a dear friend and a very bright government attorney. His father, Dr. Arthur Fischer, was in the last throes of a terminal illness when I was asked to come to the hospital. Paul's family was gathered there, expressing their love for their dad. I have been privileged to be with many people at the end of their lives. From the shallowness and intervals of Dr. Fischer's breathing, it was clear that he probably had only minutes to live. But despite this and the family telling their father that it was OK for him to leave them, Arthur Fischer was not going anyplace. Each breath looked like a wrestling match. Around midnight, it became clear to me that the family wanted to be alone with him. I took my leave and went home, and in the morning I called the nurse's station to hear the inevitable news. The nurse, who was just finishing her shift, allowed that Dr. Fischer had passed away only moments before. Hearing the incredulousness in my voice—how had he managed to live several more hours?—she shared that she, too, had never seen anything like this. During the week of mourning that followed the funeral, I asked Paul what exactly had happened. How did his father manage to linger so long when it was evident to all that he was only minutes away from death? Paul was a bit uncomfortable telling me at first; he has since given me permission to relate this story.

Several years earlier, Paul was sleeping in his bedroom at home when he was suddenly awakened by the sound of someone walking up the stairs. Since his wife, the only other occupant of the house, was sleeping beside him, the sound of footsteps was anything but welcome. Then he could hear footsteps in the hallway. Fear turned to shock as his mother, who had passed away several years earlier, walked into his room. She leaned over him and said, "Paul, tell Dad to look for me. I will help him across." Paul quickly forgot this apparition, however, and went on with his life. Now, after almost an entire day of watching his father unable to let go but clearly needing to, Paul remembered the message from his mother. He leaned over and whispered in his father's ear, "Dad, look for Mom. She will help you across." "With that," Paul continued, "my father took his last breath."

These two stories, from what I consider very credible sources, are acutely similar to hundreds of other narratives that I have heard through the years. Such anecdotes, however, are usually considered merely anecdotal, someone else's story, until a person experiences what he or she cannot see. Books have been written based on surveys of people who were clinically brain dead and then revived, all describing an experience of transcending their human form and being drawn to a great light of something very powerful and special. This is not a book about the hereafter or the thereafter, however. The light I write about is very much in the here and now. It is generated by children as young as two years old. It is a light that can both illuminate the planet and change your life.

I have hanging in my office a very simple frame that surrounds a calligraphy of the last verse of Psalm 91 in golden Hebrew letters. Translated into English, it reads: "With long days I shall satisfy him and show him My redemption." On the bottom is written, "To the beloved Sara Basya Goldberg from Emanuel." Emanuel Cohen Zedek was a wonderful young scribe who was studying at the university where I was teaching. He was one of the few Cohanim, members of the priestly caste, who had actual documentation tracing his patrilineal ancestry all the way back to Ezra, the priest and scribe known from the biblical book of Ezra, almost 2,400 years ago. Today, genetic coding indicates that the vast majority of Cohanim in fact do descend from a common ancestor. Emanuel had actual documents that had been appended from generation to generation, and that now are held in the Israel Museum. He was from the ancient Jewish community in Iran, previously known as Babylonia. In fact, his father was still there and serving as a leading rabbi. One night, Emanuel ran out of his dorm room, awakened from his sleep in a great fright. He had had a vision of his father in grave danger and felt that he needed to run downstairs to the synagogue to pray for him. Both Emanuel's father and mother had been jailed weeks earlier as the Ayatollah Khomeini's police accused the rabbi of helping local Jews flee the Iranian government and its persecution. It took him three weeks before he found out that his father had been placed in front of a firing squad that very night. Somehow, father and son connected, and Emanuel woke up to pray for his father's life. The horror of that moment in front of the firing squad, however, turned out to be nothing more than an attempt at intimidation, and eventually the family was reunited in Israel.

In the world of quantum physics, there is a process called "entanglement." Einstein described it as the "spooky connection or action between two particles at a distance." Whether by entanglement or some other dimly understood mechanism, Emanuel and his father were connected despite the physical distance between them, with the son able to feel the pain of the father. In Sara Basya's case, my wife Ruthie was always aware of our daughter's situation well before the doctors. She had dreams of Sara Basya being very sick prior to presenting any symptoms. Before we learned of our daughter's relapse, for example, a dream informed Ruthie of exactly what was going to happen, just as it did the next day. It is not unusual to hear of similar connections between parent and child, especially regarding pediatric challenges. Just as Brendan found reassurance that his mother would always be able to feel his light, we too feel an infinite connection with those entangled in our lives. It is not a process without pain, because we are, after all, human. However, it is also not without hope, because within our humanity there is a soul. As little Bernard told the Optimist Club, "It is all about finding our essence." Just as the Hebrew word for soul, *neshama*, comes from the same root as the word for breath, *neshima*, we see in the martial arts that breath allows an incredible "chi," or power, to break through almost anything. It is a great tool because no matter who we are, we all have our something that we need to break through.

As you proceed through the lessons and meditations in this book, learning the special message of Kids Kicking Cancer and their techniques, you are connecting to thousands of amazing little heroes. You are also experiencing the power of the infinite. That is the power we can access as we bring in the light of our breaths. Simply closing your eyes when you inhale and allowing your mind to imagine the air as a great and powerful light is a portal to that energy. We do this constantly in the martial arts. It is a potent force. And as noted, if three-year-old boys and girls can do it, you can, too. Just remember their words: "Power, Peace, Purpose."

LESSON 8

Preston and Martez

THE POWER OF PEACE

> *Pain is a message in our brains that usually alerts us to the presence of necrosis, or dying tissue. It garners so much attention because it triggers a primal survival mechanism. Emotional pain travels very much through the same neurological pathways in the brain as physical pain. It is thus natural to focus on emotional agony with the same attention our brain gives to physical insult. Indeed, there are many times when the pain is a lot worse than the underlying cause, giving license to the sense that "this pain is killing me!" Using your breathing to blow through the pain and relax your muscles will allow you better control and help to reframe your discomfort. You will lower your stress and enjoy living longer.*

Sensei Richard Plowden and I are frequently confused with each other. Although he is about eight inches taller, African American, and a muscular five-time World Karate champion, we otherwise look exactly alike. We certainly share the same heart and love for these amazing children. Richard brings years of experience "getting down" with inner-city youth. His journey to the world of children in pain was merely an extension of the different types of distress that he had worked with for years.

Preston Robinson was seventeen years old and a participant in our Kids Kicking Sickle Cell program. This dreadful disease creates sickle-like shapes in the hemoglobin, turning the blood into a sludge that rams its way through the vascular canals rather than flows. When the bloodstream is occluded and swells the body, the nervous system is triggered to produce such terrible pain that it often takes days of morphine drip to quiet it. On April 24, 2011, Preston was screaming in pain. Morphine was not going to quiet him. This time, however, his distress was not Sickle Cell related. Preston's mother, Melissa, had been murdered. In his agony, Preston had only one thought in his mind: he was determined to kill his mother's murderer, a young man who lived just a few houses away.

Numerous studies have shown that people who live on the lower end of the socioeconomic scale die from natural causes in the United States about ten years earlier than people who are better off financially. The old assumptions were that the quality of health care, differing nutritional regimens, and other lifestyle issues are the most significant culprits. Research indicates, however, that the number one factor accounting for shorter lifespans among impoverished populations is stress. The stress, anger, and pain associated with life in the disadvantaged neighborhoods of America is ongoing and deadly. It kills slowly by forcing the body to remain in fight-or-flight mode significantly longer than it is meant to be.

Preston had every right to own the stress, anger, and pain that was submerging him. Melissa was his mother, his nurse, his guide through a maze of adversity. And now she was dead. Sensei Richard had to use every ounce of his heart to get Preston to take that breath. Preston's thoughts of hate were natural. To do the right thing, he had to be heroic. "That's what you really are," Sensei Richard implored him to listen. "You are a powerful martial artist and you can take control of your rage and focus yourself to not be destroyed as well. Your mother needs you here to be strong and not end up in jail. You have to be her legs now to walk in this world. You need to take care of your family and your Mom's memory." Richard helped Preston to breathe in the light and break through the pain that was gripping his body. Preston knew that Richard had been by his bedside throughout his many hospitalizations. Richard believed in Preston's power to take control of his life and not be pulled downward into the dark cycle of violence that was so natural and yet so overwhelming. Preston wanted to be believed in. He wanted to make a difference, and despite his disease he was doing it. Not despite his illness but even more so because of it, he had a greater ability to teach. Now was his most teachable moment. This pain, greater than any vascular crisis, was his opportunity for greatness, and in that moment he decided to grab it. His light became united with his mother's.

Martez was in Preston's Kids Kicking Sickle Cell class. That program, in particular, brought together a group of disparate kids and made them a family. We are all part of that family. Every time Preston got sick, Martez was on the phone with Richard making sure that Sensei knew Preston needed a visit. Martez had his own share of hospital stays. His disease progressed to the point that he had two brain surgeries. He also had his spleen and his gall bladder removed. In the summer of 2011, Sensei Richard got a call from Martez after the latter surgery. Martez was walking a half-mile to the bus stop, alone. He was going to take one bus and transfer to a second to get home. That was five hours after a major organ had been removed from his body. Nobody asked this young man how he was getting home. He was released from the hospital and that's all that mattered to the busy staff there. Sensei Richard told Martez to find a bench and sit down. He was coming to pick him up.

When a child is diagnosed with cancer, that boy or girl will be treated in a pediatric center and will receive follow-up care well beyond the teen years. Pediatric cancers are different diseases than adult cancers. It is thus not unusual to find a twenty-five-year-old patient in the Kids Kicking Cancer program because he or she is being treated in the oncology section of a children's hospital. However, with sickle cell anemia, once patients are eighteen years old, they graduate to one of the few hospitals that treat this disease. Even when they find the right center, the transition between a warm, caring, supportive jewel like Children's Hospital of Michigan and an adult hospital is shocking and difficult. With Martez and Preston having both "graduated" Children's Hospital, we were their first line of support. That's why Preston called us in the beginning of 2013, worried sick that his friend Martez was going to kill himself because he was in so much pain. Preston reminded Martez that he was a powerful martial artist and that he could breathe through this darkness. Then Preston called Sensei Richard, who brought Martez to a counseling center. That's how Preston saved his friend's life. Martez picked himself up and remembered to breathe through the darkness. Six months later, Martez was standing with a group of our

Kids Kicking Cancer and Kids Kicking Sickle Cell patients at the Charles H. Wright Museum of African American History. Our children were teaching the people of Detroit how to define the darkness in their lives and breathe light and power through that pain. When I asked the children, "What is your darkness?" Martez walked forward and looked at the audience. He looked down and hesitated for one brief second before lifting up his face and stating clearly, "My darkness is the voice inside of my head that wants me to kill myself when my sickle cell crisis is just so bad. Instead, I bring in the light and break through the darkness." Sensei Richard and I just looked at each other. Then we hugged Martez. We could feel that he now understood his real power. Martez and Preston are heroes in a circle that is beginning to encompass the world.

Most of us will never know the pain of sickle cell anemia or the deep, throbbing crisis of bone disease. Many of us are insulated from the dangers of impoverished urban neighborhoods. But we all have pain that creates its own world of stress. Finding the strength to not allow that pain to define us is the key. When we breathe through the center of pain wherever it is attacking our body, we can relax our muscles, calm our pain, and stop our stress. It not only distracts the neurological message of physical or emotional discomfort, but it also attaches us to the power of our soul.

LESSON 9

Robert

PUTTING DESCARTES
BEFORE THE HORSE

> *The first step in stopping the actual stress response is to become observant that you are having stress. Become aware; listen to your voice. If you feel your muscles tightening and you are not exercising, then you are more than likely having a stress response. The nature of that response will usually cascade in a downward flow of more tightness and more stress. If you observe it, you can change it.*

René Descartes framed a philosophy around the maxim "I think, therefore I am." The obverse, "I am what I think," doesn't always follow, however. Defining our reality when we are being mugged by the negative brain chemicals of stress can make who we are a whole lot less than whom we think we are, or want to be.

And yet, that obverse can be very powerful when we understand how to deal with our brain chemistry. We have learned from working with our little martial artists that negative brain chemicals can be grouped into three categories: stress, anger, and pain. Stress includes our hastening heartbeat during fright as well as the anxieties that chronically consume us with the "what ifs?" of life. Anger is not only the roaring tempest of the outward fight but the inner rage that churns within our intestinal tracts. Pain encompasses both physical and emotional discomfort, the depths of despair and

46

depression as well as the searing siren of disease or treatment. Perhaps the best way to remember these three is the acronym SAP. Nothing saps our strength and health more than stress, anger, and pain. But when our children recognize that their brains are under attack and choose to train their focus beyond these destructive chemical bombardments, they are able to change that negative message into something quite different. Using these very same methods, they also teach adults how to take control of their lives. The message of the children of Kids Kicking Cancer is that we can be all that we want to be, if we think that we can. This is what we call the Heroic Response.

The Heroic Response is anything but natural. At the same time that our students are trained to identify this inner strength, we speak openly of the very normal thoughts that accompany our challenges. An important facet of the Kids Kicking Cancer program is that the children are asked to share their experiences with their peers who are going through similar challenges. We speak of our incredible strengths as martial artists, but we also acknowledge the force of the adversity. It is perfectly normal to respond to a world where everything seems to be going wrong with the emotions of stress, anger, and pain. At Kids Kicking Cancer, we never "dis" the natural response. There is nothing more natural for a child who is confused and feeling sick when dealing with adversities that overwhelm even adults to respond with crying, screaming, anger, or withdrawal. We regularly find children who regress years emotionally because their world has become so much less secure than what they had always known. The trauma of a cancer diagnosis does not make sense to children who one day were the same as all their friends and the next day are more different than they ever could have imagined. Their comfortable bedroom down the hall from their mom and dad often gives way to a hospital room where some stranger in uniform may enter at any time of day or night to impose some painful procedure.

The shocks to their lives are multidimensional. Before cancer, medicines made them better, not sicker, and a visit to the doctor was simple and fast. Now, the treatments they are told will help them may make them feel worse, and doctor appointments and treatments can last all day. Also overwhelming for a child is the knowledge that their parents can no longer protect them or make all the bad stuff go away. Closely related is the awareness, even among children of gentle age, that their parents carry their own fears, however close to the vest, tearing up despite their best efforts to hide it. Boys and girls who have reached puberty find themselves in an environment without privacy, in which any part of their bodies is fair game for poking and testing. In a teaching hospital, their lives are open discussion topics among young residents, some not much older than the patients. And what is often the most devastating aspect for a child is the divide created between them and their friends. The scripts they had written about their lives before they became sick are nothing like their new realities. These children have lost their sense of control.

Sixteen-year-old Robert came straight from Juvenile Hall to Children's Hospital of Michigan. He went from selling recreational drugs on the street to taking far more expensive ones to stop the cancer in his blood. He was determined not to be a compliant patient. His attitude was street-tough, and he built a wall around himself that made it difficult for anyone in the hospital to help him get better. But while Robert didn't make many friends, no one wanted to see him die. The social workers called us. Perhaps, they thought, a black belt would garner enough respect so that Robert would engage in dialogue and allow the medical staff to treat him. Sensei Richard responded to the call. Robert indeed acknowledged both Richard's karate *gi* (uniform) and his black belt, but not exactly with respect: "You know I can kick your ---?" "No doubt," Richard responded, not taking the bait. "But what are these people doing to you that you look so mad?" This was a question Robert wanted to answer. "Man, you have no idea," he fumed. "They come in whenever they want without knocking and think that they can do whatever they want." With this, Robert proceeded in his own colorful language to describe the reality of a kid whose highly developed sense of autonomy was being taken from him. Sensei Richard applied all the right levels of empathy. In concert with the medical staff, he suggested a set of rules that Robert could post on his door: "Knock before entering." "Ask me first before you touch me." "Don't wake me unless you really have to." These reasonable requests gave Robert some feeling of control over his world. He was also able to identify the triggers that made him angry, noting a tightness that crossed his chest when he felt confronted. Identifying that "closed in" feeling as the beginning of his stress response allowed Robert the opportunity to begin to take control of his stress and his life. Despite his hard outer shell, Robert felt the love from his new sensei and really wanted to learn the magic of our martial arts. It was not long before he shared with us the realization that getting cancer had actually saved his life. He left the street behind and began a real life, free not only of cancer but also of the dealers and junkies who likely would have eventually killed him.

Don't look for "Robert's Rules of Order" on the hospital doors of other children. Most boys and girls know they have no choice in medical matters and surrender to their new normal. But even if they are blessed with remission and cure, the stress they have experienced is far from healthy, and can impact their lives years down the road. Studies show that even children who respond very stoically to their prognosis and therapy will often act out years later, a by-product of their earlier trauma and distress. This is yet another reason why it is so very important to find a healthy pathway to empower these boys and girls. The Heroic Response—that we can be all that we want to be, if we think that we can—is how our children bring a sense of control to their lives, and teach others to respond as well. No matter who you are or what age you happen to be, the Heroic Response can become a healthy part of growing beyond your stressors and fears. Even Descartes would approve . . . I think.

The Heroic Response begins with an awareness of the natural response. The first part of any battle is to be cognizant of the strength of your adversary. The stress chemicals tighten your body. You are in battle, but neither fight nor flight is going to work here. The children of Kids Kicking Cancer have no choice but to accept their situations. Robert came to understand that he had to agree to be treated or die. The first step in dealing with that stress and diminishing its impact is knowing that we are experiencing it. I often tell busy executives in our corporate seminars, "If you are reaching for your phone and your arm gets tight, that means either your phone is way too heavy or your caller ID has identified the source of your stress." Recognizing that you are under attack can lead to a heroic victory that can have a positive impact on your health, your life, and the people around you. Our kids do it every day.

The practical application of the Heroic Response can be summed up in three other words: Stop, Look, and Listen! When you recognize that your body is getting tight, and you're not at the gym, then you are probably under attack. Take that first breath to relax your muscles. This gives you the ability to feel your power and *stop* the flow of your stress chemicals. Now *look* down at the ground. If there are no major body parts lying there, you're probably OK and need to regain your perspective. Then, as you begin to hear the gentleness of your breath, *listen* for the opportunity to respond with heroic strength and focus. People are watching, and they will learn from the power of your inner peace when you show that you can control the stress, anger, and pain in your head. Every time you do that, you can take a bow and yell out, "Power, Peace, Purpose." Then you will know that you are truly a member of our family.

LESSON 10

Luca

THE "BREATH BRAKE"

As we have learned, breathing is the only part of the autonomic nervous system that you can so easily control. Once you have identified the beginning of your stress response, you can respond appropriately. Stress will always cause tightness in your body. Some people feel it in their stomach, some in their chest or neck, and some in their head. Using your breath to relax your muscles tells your brain that you are leaving fight-or-flight mode and going to a parasympathetic (relaxation) response. You can stop your stress chemicals by creating a breath that relaxes your muscles.

The stress mechanism is a very important biological response that allows our bodies to respond in a heightened way to potentially dangerous stimuli. In jungle terms, "fight or flight" is the response to "eat or be eaten." When pursued by a predator, an animal needs to expend every bit of available energy on flight. No other biological need at that moment is more important than escape. For the predator who may not have eaten in several days, however, catching dinner is its most important function at the moment. Fight is the only relevant focus for survival.

The body, whether of man or beast, is an amazing machine. The stress chemicals of fight or flight always make possible the maximum effort needed to accomplish the most immediate goal of survival. The heart gears up to produce the greatest level of oxygenation through our respiratory system. The muscles tighten. The digestive tract is put on hold. The rationally oriented prefrontal cortex becomes less important than the more primal hypothalamus. Our immunological system ramps up for a few minutes but then cascades downward, set aside for the battle ahead. That's why, when people are stressed, they often get sick. And while the twenty-minute race through the jungle is life saving, twenty hours, days, or months of chronic stress is life threatening. Back when human lifespans were only about forty years, stress was not as much a factor in morbidity and mortality as infection or even childbirth. Today, when we have been blessed with antibiotics and life-prolonging procedures, stress plays a more negative role in diseases and ailments than any other single factor.

With the advent of brain scanning, we are able to see clearly the connection between the chemicals of stress, anger, and pain. People who are afraid and angry have greater pain than those who are not. A look at the posterior cingulate cortex of the brain indicates that people who associate their pain with some purpose have less pain than those who feel victimized by their distress. Stress also multiplies the opportunities for pain because of its role in tightening the muscles. Anger, which obviously can be stress driven, is magnified by the stress chemicals that cause pain and fear. Stress, anger, and pain often loop in a cycle, each making the other worse. In other words, the greater the stress, the more pain. The greater the pain, the more stress. Add anger and fear, which are often fellow travelers, and one has a recipe for a chronic health disaster in the making. These stressors impact all the organs of the body, including the brain. Fear and anger with all their associated stress chemicals thus affect how we respond to that pain, not just physically but emotionally as well. Our world changes when we are under stress. Our response to that world becomes different as well. The Heroic Response begins with our willingness to recognize the importance of this battle and, most importantly, the fact that we can win it.

"Power, Peace, Purpose" is not only a mantra of some amazing little heroes; it is a pathway to a life of empowerment beyond stress. Many of the techniques that we use are shared by other disciplines. Their combination, however, the way we have seen the children put them together, is unique and life changing.

In reviewing the lessons so far, we are able to identify rather easily that we are being attacked by stress just by observing our bodies. Every stress response in the body will create a tightening in our muscles. Recognizing your neck, shoulders, back, stomach, head, or other part of your body giving you that message of tightening is the first step to taking control of your life. Observing that you are in the midst of a stress moment gives you the ability to stop the stress response. It's easy to be alerted to the stress response if you simply stop to feel the tightness in your muscles. If you're not engaged in exercise or some similar physical activity and your muscles are getting tight, then chances are you are in the throes of a stress response.

When you become an observer of yourself, you can recognize the tightness being triggered by fear, pain, anger, or some mixture of all the above. Then you are in position to stop the very chemicals that are causing the stress. It does not matter if the stress is being brought on by your boss, your spouse, your in-laws, or the IRS: the body is responding to stress by tightening your muscles and performing a multitude of other regulatory tasks pumping you up for fight or flight. Most of the time, we are not at a location that is conducive to fight or flight. Breaking into a sprint while being berated by the boss will not look good on the next employee evaluation. Punching him out will probably look worse. So here we are in a situation primed for actual fight or flight, and we can do neither. Those chemicals shooting out of the adrenal gland don't say, "Bad time? Sorry! We'll come back when it's more convenient!" They continue to pour out, priming the body for a battle that cannot be fought in this fashion. If anything, it's your health that's now being set up for defeat.

The good news is that our children defeat stress, anger, and pain on a daily basis. One of our simplest techniques that the children use is the "Breath Brake." It is a tool they have taught to thousands of adults at homes, in hospitals, and in our seminars.

Among the most important elements in growing a not-for-profit organization is marketing. We have a marketing guy in Canada who has stoked the interest of many doctors and hospital leaders. He is good-looking, articulate, and very bright. He is also five years old. Luca Aversa was a Kids Kicking Cancer student from the age of three in Windsor, Ontario. In a short amount of time, he replaced running around the dojo with very effective meditation and breathing techniques. His mother was overjoyed about her son's ability to refocus himself in the clinic. Unfortunately, Luca, who had already undergone multiple surgeries, had to go again for yet another operation in Toronto. At 2:00 am the night after the latest surgery, the nurse on duty came into Luca's room and woke up his mother. "I am going to have to change his bandages and that's going to hurt," she said to her. "Would you mind, please, holding him down so I can do it? Once he is fussing," she continued, "I'll restart the IV." Luca's mom's response startled the nurse: "I don't hold him down." The nurse immediately apologized. "Oh, I'm sorry. I just thought he would be more comfortable if you would be the one holding him. I'll just get one of the other nurses to help me." As she moved toward the door, Luca sat up and protested: "You don't understand. I'm a martial artist. I don't need to be held down. I'm going to teach you how to do our power breathing." There sat Luca, who had just turned five years old, teaching the nurse how we can breathe in the light and blow out the darkness. He was so focused on his breath that he stayed in control of the pain and was able to breathe out the discomfort. Even as the bandages were pulling off part of his skin, little Luca remained totally calm. After the procedure, the nurse turned to his mother and asked, "I have been in nursing for a hundred years. I have never seen anything like this. What is this about?" Luca and his mother were more than happy to tell the hospital about Kids Kicking Cancer, and our new five-year-old marketing director is now helping us to expand up Highway 401 through Ontario.

What Luca was demonstrating was very simple. Your brain controls every muscle in your body. Every time that you have a stress response, something inside is getting tight. Simply using your breath to relax your muscles tells your brain that you are going into a parasympathetic (relaxation) mode and leaving the sympathetic (fight or flight) response. When we first began Kids Kicking Cancer in the late 1990s, many of my medical colleagues suggested that I downplay the breath work element because it seemed beyond the pale of evidence-based medicine. Today, in every hospital in the United States where I have traveled, there isn't one that does not have someone on staff trained in breath work. The evidence has clearly indicated the physiological benefits of focused breathing.

The key to the "Breath Brake" is not simply the breath, but the use of the inhalation to expand and elevate the body from the bottom up. The exhale lowers and thus releases the muscles from the top down. When we exhale and finally relax our muscles, we are telling our brains that we are now in relaxation mode. It regulates the adrenal glands to stop pumping out the chemicals of chronic stress. We are constantly seeing our young and now older patients take control of their stress by simply relaxing their muscles with their breath. Every stress response tenses up muscles. The "Breath Brake" relaxes those same muscles, all through the regulation of the breath. When I teach adults how to do the Breath Brake, at the last exhale I share with them a very simple mantra that has been so meaningful to me. Gently breathe out the words *Baruch Hashem*. In Hebrew those two words mean "Blessed is the Name," a reference to the Supreme Being. No matter what name we use, most of us believe that we all have a Father in Heaven whom we bless and from whom we receive blessing. In Hebrew, however, there is another dimension to the word for "blessing": it shares the same root as that for a reservoir or pool. The implication is that we are accepting everything that comes into our lives as being channeled from a higher power. That which is causing us stress may not seem fun at the moment, but we can also see it as a blessing that allows us to respond with greatness. In other words, a perfect God created this imperfect situation, perfectly. Taking that breath to relax your body and brake the stress chemicals will allow you to find your Heroic Response.

I often mention in our seminars that studies indicate that if you breathe for 120 years, you are going to live a long time. The simple truth is that you are breathing anyway. Why not do it in a way that allows you to stop the onslaught of dangerous, damaging glucocorticoids through your body?

A number of years ago a device was introduced to the market that could register your stress level. It was called the RESPeRATE and was approved as a medical device by the FDA. I don't have to tell you what this machine teaches you to do. I know a number of people who use it and like it. However, if you are not inclined to go out and buy it, don't worry (remember, that's bad for you, too). We all have a built-in biofeedback device already. It's called the human body. Stress chemicals will always make the muscles get tighter. Identifying that tightness is really the first step to taking control of the stress. Lifting your body up with the breath and then relaxing every one of those muscles will stop the stress syndrome. That's why we call it the "Breath Brake." You have all the tools to stop stress and you never travel without them. And they are all free. Even with our registered trademark, we won't charge you for breathing.

After the children have been introduced to feeling their inhaling breath lift up their bodies and the following exhale that relaxes their muscles, we allow them to feel the power of that breath by imagining it as a very bright light. Instead of just breathing in air, these children are able to feel the chi or the light of their breath reaching upward into their body, providing them the same energy that the martial arts masters focus upon. This light fills them and gives them the power to face down their disease as well as their stress, anger, and pain. When we exhale, we don't want to blow out that light. Instead, the children blow out the darkness. Ask any Kids Kicking Cancer child what is his or her darkness, and you are likely to hear, "My cancer" or "My pain" or "My fear and anger" or sometimes "Nausea." Occasionally we hear "My brother." Kids will always be kids, no matter what they are facing.

LESSON 11

Judy

LIAR, LIAR, BRAINS ON FIRE

> *Your brain is capable of lying to you. You can feel impending doom, complete failure, or total rejection when your brain is stress-driven into anxious and often false messages. It is easy to become defined and incarcerated by those perceptions. Using your breathing to quiet the stress chemicals can provide a much healthier and more accurate assessment of the world around you.*

In medical circles, I give a lecture called "The Ontology of Oncology." Ontology is a description of our sense of self. Oncology is cancer. I have found that if you rhyme and serve food, doctors are more likely to show up. (The latter is more important than the former.) In the presentation, I ask pediatricians to not define our children as cancer kids. They are really healthy boys and girls with tumors. That does not undermine the need for drugs or radiation; it just creates a mindset of greater normalcy and hope.

Yitzy Haber loves a sure bet. When he was thirteen and at summer camp, he would challenge the other campers: "I bet you I can keep one foot on the floor and touch the rafters with my other one." Being clearly out of range for such a stretch, he got a lot of takers. He made a fortune. Yitzy would simply take off his prosthetic leg and calmly extend it up to the ceiling. He was indeed touching the floor and the rafters at the same time. He was also making a traumatic amputation into something normal.

Two years earlier, Yitzy had called me to consult on whether he should have his leg amputated. He was confined to a wheelchair with a leg that had been riddled with a rhabdomyosarcoma. He was given a choice: either to keep that unusable leg statically held perpendicular to his body, or have it amputated and replaced with a prosthesis. This young man opted for the prosthesis because it would give him a chance at walking again, even though he would have to lose his leg to do so. He had the surgery, and his rehab was long and strenuous. He worked hard to make his gait natural and his life normal. It turned out, however, that that would never happen. Instead, he quickly trumped normal with an enthusiastic smile and willingness to help every other child he knew. Now married with his own children, he and his lovely wife raise their family with that very same attitude. Similarly, our goal, when we empower children with the tools to "breathe in the light and blow out the darkness," is to make them "normal"—or, as with Yitzy, "supernormal." The more the children can dissociate themselves from a sense of victimization, the more likely they are to experience less pain and discomfort. With many diseases, the ongoing psychological stress of the illness has a profoundly negative effect on all aspects of the body's homeostasis or balance, including our blood pressure and the resilience of our immunological system. Being a victor is a lot healthier than being a victim.

All of us carry around the baggage of stress, anger, and pain from time to time. As on any airport conveyer belt, it can come in all colors and shapes. The problem is that when luggage gets too heavy, it can hinder our ability to get where we need to go. The emotional burden can make us feel scattered and lost. For that we can employ the Heroic Response. It does not ignore our stress, anger, and pain, but it allows us to recognize how to overcome the natural responses that would toss our luggage all over the place. As a result, we can arrive home with our luggage (and ourselves) intact. So rather than being forced to carry the baggage of victimization, we can learn from our children how to overhaul the loads we carry into much more effective packaging. We all have the ability to get rid of the bad stuff and effectively store and use the good. Sometimes we just have to be told that we can. And by the way, carrying heavy loads can make a person very strong. Just ask our kids.

The ontology of oncology can be translated to fit any trial of the human condition. Stress, anger, and pain can easily overwhelm us and define our very being when we are confronted with physical illness or emotional challenge. But there is a significant therapeutic distinction between someone who is depressed and someone who is challenged by depression. A person who is depressed is defined by the disease. Just as a person becomes their injured body part when it is throbbing with pain, darkness and melancholy can define the very essence of a person who is depressed. A patient who looks at herself as not depressed, however, but as challenged by depression still has herself intact. We have a greater capacity for fighting through the painful waves of brain chemicals when the essence of our light or life can be summoned into battle. When we become the baggage, it is much more difficult to reshuffle the load and continue forward. The children of Kids Kicking Cancer have created a Heroic Response that allows them to reach into their essence, the incredible power of their souls. They are able to get to an inner place of peace by quieting the stress chemicals that accompany the fear, pain, and anger of their lives, and they are now finding purpose in their struggles because they are teaching the world.

As little martial artists, the children are trained to identify the nature of their adversity and use their inner light to face down all darkness. When we perceive the world through the disturbing colors of stress, the resulting anger and pain make for a very different world.

Our children succeed as teachers because adults are so moved by the tragedy of young lives touched by disease. The natural barriers of skepticism and denial fall away quickly when listening to these kids, allowing audiences to observe how their own lives are colored by stress, and usually of a far less serious nature. Adults come to realize that a brain on stress is going to perceive a very different reality from someone with a calm and focused outlook. Our perceptions can be easily manipulated into unhealthy distortions by those very same chemicals that wrack our bodies with stress. We may have every right to be upset because "my friend treats me terribly" or "my job is awful" or "my kids are impossible" or "my spouse does not appreciate me." And it is totally natural to accept what we see, hear, and feel as the truth. But being skeptical of how we perceive the realities we face is essential to reaching the height of our potential.

Years ago, I served as a high school guidance counselor. It was there I met Judy, a seventeen-year-old girl from an affluent family who was starving herself to death. When I first visited her in the hospital I found her hooked up to an IV and very angry. "Look at me," she cried. "They are forcing me to eat and get fat." It was hard for me to believe that she could look at her shrunken face and figure and see fat. I held my arm near hers. It was three times wider than her emaciated limb. "Whose arm is thicker?" I asked her. "Yours," she admitted, "but on you it doesn't look fat." I couldn't help but think: Why is she saying that? Who is she punishing? Years later, after we learned more about anorexia, studies would indicate that Judy was indeed telling "the truth," but it was her truth. Her brain was lying to her. Unfortunately, she really believed it. In one investigation, anorexic youngsters were shown several photos of themselves. One was their actual untouched picture. The others were morphed to make the subject look 150-200 pounds heavier. Invariably, the anorexic youngsters chose the most bloated pictures of themselves as the actual photo. A polygraph indicated that they were telling the truth as they saw it. They just saw it wrong. Their brain was reshaping their image in a gruesome and sometimes deadly lie.

Brains that rob us of food because they project our self-image in perverse illusion are clearly pathological. But those are other people's brains, not ours, or so we tell ourselves. For most of us, we know what is really real. At least that's what we think, and we are what we think, aren't we?

Although there are some who wish they could "catch" anorexia for a week or two, it is a very serious and sometimes deadly disease. It is also a great example of a reality that we all share. Our brains tend to lie to us—all of us—from time to time. Stress, anger, and pain are part of a primal syndrome that can color every aspect of our perceptions and our reactions to life. Under normal conditions, the human brain has a neurological executive center that communicates through an extensive network of triangular-shaped neurons called pyramidal cells. These neurons extend into the far reaches of the brain where emotions, desires, and habits are controlled. The network assures the amygdala (which controls fear reactions) that all is well and keeps our emotions focused. Even small stressors, however, can significantly change the neurochemical environment and instantly weaken the synaptic connections of our reasoning center. Dopamine and norepinephrine can quickly spread through the brain, diminishing network activity and our ability to both perceive reality and respond appropriately. This situation deteriorates further when adrenal glands located near the kidneys join in the fray by spraying the stress hormone cortisol into the bloodstream. As these stress chemicals begin to switch off the neurons in the prefrontal cortex, our center of reason and restraint, the more primal parts of the brain such as the basal ganglia that regulate habitual emotional responses and cravings get ramped up. (It's no wonder that people under stress often calm themselves with the emergency gallon of ice cream they have stored in the back of the freezer.) The amygdala alerts the rest of the brain to prepare for fight or flight and at the same time strengthens memories that are related to stress, anger, and pain. When stressed, we are more likely to misperceive those around us and inevitably respond in counterproductive ways.

As we saw in Lesson 9, the more observant you are to the tightness of stress in your body, the greater chance you have to breathe in the light and blow out the darkness of that stress. When you use your breath to relax your body, you are telling your brain that you are taking control and moving yourself into a state of relaxation. Your breath will stop your body from squirting out the chemicals that turn your brain into a forty-six ounce liar that can easily control your life and make you and those around you miserable. That's why we all need the "Breath Brake." It allows you to reach your essence, your place of power and truth. It also makes you feel a whole lot better.

Tali, Zoe, and Desi

NEEDLES OF LIGHT,
GETTING THE POINT

Imagery is an important component of the martial arts. You have already read how our children imagine light coming into their bodies as they do their martial arts therapy. As you relax and allow yourself to bring this light into your being, imagine this energy as part of the fabric of your soul. Focusing on your true power will allow you to face down whatever comes your way. The breath not only relaxes the body by releasing the muscles, but also brings a powerful light into our being that you can see and feel.

We never have our children break boards or spar with each other in Kids Kicking Cancer. Children undergoing chemotherapy tend to have very brittle bones that can easily fracture. We therefore supply soft targets on which the children demonstrate their power. Before we strike anything, however, we visualize the target being destroyed. Imagery is a vital part of the process. Before the children hit their target, we ask them to focus on the pad and to see within it their greatest darkness. The other children in the class stand around the one in the center, focusing their karate energy toward their classmate. The child in the middle gets very quiet and, in true martial arts form, sees only the target. As we have seen, some of our students will describe this symbolic enemy as their tumor. Others view it as their nausea, their pain, or their anger. One nine-year-old boy looked straight at the pad and proclaimed, "The target is my fear of death and I can break through it." All of us who heard him were blown away. According to the medical staff, he had never before verbalized his fear of death. No one had ever allowed him to externalize that fear onto a pad.

The first time we used the technique of projecting the disease onto the pad was at a class at Children's Hospital of Michigan. I was surprised to see one of our teenage girls, who was being treated for a very aggressive tumor, banging away at the target that she was calling "my cancer." Within seconds she began to cry and even more energetically attack the pad. At first, I was concerned that she had hurt herself. After another moment it was clear that that was not the case. When she finished, almost out of breath, I asked her, "What happened?" "It's my tumor," she said. "I hate it. No one had ever given me permission to destroy it." By externalizing her cancer, she felt a sense of liberation and empowerment to play a role in affecting her outcome and life. While we have had significant studies indicating our positive impact in decreasing children's pain, we have never had the resources to fully study what affect this has on survivability. No one, however, would doubt the psychological benefits of being empowered to "kick that cancer." What has been well studied is the devastating relationship between chronic stress and morbidity in general. The more we can control the factors of stress, anger, and pain in all of our lives, the greater our ability to not fall prey to the stressors of life, no matter our baggage.

Tali was a beautiful girl who had just learned that her latest drug therapy was not slowing the rare but deadly tumor in her retina. The memory of sitting with her sixteen years ago on a bench at Camp Simcha, shaded by an old oak tree, is still very vivid. Despite the cloudless sky, that day had become dark, and the verdant colors of summer's life had transformed into a lifeless gray. Together we began to talk about the light that was above all the clouds of fear and disappointments that Tali had known in her very young life. The light was her soul, I told her, and that light is forever. By then I already had years of experience with children facing the challenges of death, but I was surprised by her next question. "Rabbi G., does that mean that your soul can't get cancer?" "No, Tali," I told her, "Your soul can't get cancer." "Then I'm okay," she said, and ran off to play with her friends.

When we meet new Kids Kicking Cancer students and get down to the serious business of creating young martial arts heroes, one of the first questions our therapists ask is "What do you think is the most powerful part of your body?" Many children will suggest the hand or the foot. Some of the more advanced students may point to the elbow, a very forceful conveyor of blows. However, once in a while, a child will instinctively zero in on the right answers: the soul, the heart, or the mind.

As I have mentioned, the Hebrew words for "breath" and "soul" are from the same root, suggesting that as concepts they are one and the same. The opportunity for victory in the constant struggle that we all have in life is predicated upon our decision to respond to the challenge with the powerful energy of our soul rather than the primitive stress reactions of our body. We have seen how using the breath to relax the muscles of our body informs the neurological system of the human being to go from the sympathetic fight-or-flight response to the parasympathetic relaxation response. What we are really doing is making that life choice to respond with our soul rather than our bodies.

Responding to life with the focus of our soul makes us very powerful. This is the lesson our children teach every day. Separating our souls from cancer and the attendant stress, anger, and pain of our lives liberates us. It gives us Power, Peace, Purpose.

Professor Harvey Sober is a mentor of mine. He has survived very serious health issues that would surely have robbed him of his life had he not been directed to practice the Chinese martial arts that he learned as a young man as a healing therapy. As his life was being sapped away, he drew himself from his hospital bed, spent hours meditating, changed his diet, and defied death. I have never seen a martial artist able to manipulate the inner energy of chi as powerfully as Sifu Sober ("sifu" is Chinese for "master"). When I directed Camp Simcha, Sifu would demonstrate to our children the power that dwells within us. We would give him a large stone or brick that he would hold in his hands. Many martial artists have mastered the dynamics of breaking substantial materials. However, without striking or kicking the stone, Sifu could break it in his hands as he exhaled, focusing his chi onto it. He would also take an empty soda can and poke a hole through it from one side to the other with his bare finger. (This was before there were deposit cans.) Having dabbled in a number of different martial arts styles, I once asked him his thoughts on a particular Indonesian martial arts that I was practicing. "It's like going to a wedding celebration," he responded. "There are two hundred different ways to serve chicken, rice, and string beans. But it's still chicken, rice, and string beans." Though there are many differences between various martial arts, there are many more similarities. The key to all of them, according to Sifu Sober, is to reach the essence of ourselves, our very soul. When we define ourselves by this inner power, we can take on whatever comes our way. It starts with imagining the power to create peace within ourselves and fulfill our purpose.

Kids Kicking Cancer martial arts therapists are culled from dozens of different fighting styles. Together, we design the kata, or moves, that will most empower sick children. As Sifu Sober described it, the common denominator between all the different disciplines is the harnessing of our inner energy, the power of the soul, heart, and mind. It does not matter if one calls it ki, chi, prana, tenaga dalam, neshama, or spirit. When we allow ourselves to feel this energy, we become very powerful. To borrow loosely from Descartes, "I think I am powerful; therefore, I am." As much as stress, anger, and pain cause us to feel out of control, the techniques of martial arts breathing accomplish exactly the opposite.

Zoe Bergen was diagnosed with a neuroblastoma when she was fourteen months old. By the time she was four she had to make regular visits to a clinic that required vein sticks. These visits became the subject of an ongoing contest between Zoe's mom and dad. The loser had to take Zoe. Each visit seemed to be worse than the one before: their feisty little girl was not about to be held down and stuck without a fight. On one particular trip, David, Zoe's dad, was to have the unenviable role as enforcer. But before they arrived at the clinic that day, Zoe reported that it was going to be different this time. "It's not going to hurt me today," Zoe told her father. "I am a martial artist now." "Sure, sweetheart," David replied, convinced that nothing was going to change and they would have to replay the same traumatic scene as always. But when it was time for the vein stick, Zoe looked at her father matter-of-factly. "Here's what we do, Dad," she continued, and then demonstrated what she had learned. David couldn't believe it. His daughter was lifting up her little body with her breath and, instead of tensing up and trying to scurry away, remained focused on relaxing her body. As the needle penetrated her skin and continued into her vein she took an even deeper breath and then turned her little head to the other side and blew out her discomfort.

We don't tell the children that the needle is not going to hurt. Some of them have already heard that and it's not true. While it is perfectly natural to get all tight and try to push back against the pain, we remind them to relax their muscles with their breath and pull in the discomfort. When the needle comes into their bodies, they use their breath to inhale that "ouch" and then turn to the other side and blow it out. David Bergen could not believe that his four-year-old girl was not screaming or crying as she had done many times before. Zoe was focused on blowing out the pain and teaching her dad what martial artists can do. With all that on her plate, she was too busy to remember that four-year-olds aren't supposed to stay in control during painful vein sticks. Throwing a fit was for other kids, not for this martial artist. David called our office in tears as soon as they walked out of the clinic. He was returning home not with Zoe the victim, but with Zoe the victor.

Not everyone gets vein sticks, but everyone gets stuck. In October 2013 I was invited to give an online lecture for the Graduate School of Psychology at Pepperdine University. The video conference was to be accompanied by a running blog of students' comments on the lower part of the screen. In the middle of my presentation about the lessons we have learned from our children on pain management, a student named Nicole wrote, "Wow, I could use this to deal with my fear of needles. I have to get a vaccination on Thursday and I literally faint when I see the needle. It makes my life miserable." I stopped my lecture and decided to address Nicole directly. Just two days before, I told her, I had been on call when I fielded a request from the mother of one of our patients, Desi Smith. Desi was a superstar in our program who had used her breath work to help her deal with her infusions to stabilize her sickle cell disease. Unfortunately, the first IV team had infiltrated her site. The second one had an equal lack of success and she was now in significant pain. Furthermore, she had come to rely on her martial arts power, which now wasn't working. When I spoke to her mother, Pam, I could hear Desi sobbing in the background. Unfortunately, I was too far away to get to Desi before she would meet the next assault on her body. "Give Desi the phone," I asked Pam. "Desi, this is Rabbi G. I am sorry that you are having a rough time today, but you are a very powerful martial artist. The greater the adversity, the greater power we have to face it down. Let's do this together." Desi took a few deep breaths and settled into a focused meditation. She did great. By the time we had finished, the nurses had already hung her second bag.

"Nicole," I continued, "I am going to teach you Desi's meditation. I want you to try it. If it works for you, please send me an email and address it to Desi and let her know that you did it."

Three days later, I received an email from Nicole. "Dear Desi: You don't know me," she wrote. "I was sitting in a lecture with Rabbi G. and I admitted how very afraid I was of needles. Not just scared. Every time I would go for a shot or vaccine and I would see the needle, I would faint. It was really creating havoc in my life as we all need to get shots or blood tests from time to time. Rabbi G. told me all about you and the power of your meditation. I had to get a vaccine today. The whole time I was sitting there, I did your meditation. I didn't faint. I did cry, but those were tears of joy because I no longer had this fear in my life. The whole time I was thinking of you and how brave you are. Desi, you changed my life." We sent this off to Desi's mom. Pam wrote us back: "Desi is walking around the house this morning saying, 'I can't believe it; I really am powerful.'"

The ontological message is not reserved for four-year-olds, nor for cancer therapy. There are all different types of pain and all variations of negative messages that accompany them. Zoe and Desi had a tool. It was a lens that reframed their self-image and what they were going through. They also had a pathway: their breath could stop the onslaught of stress and fear in their young bodies. On top of that, they had a purpose: to teach the world. Sometimes, it takes a child to raise a village.

If you are a member of the village, then your life is filled with good and bad, ups and downs, and all the normal things that villagers share: the stressors of pain, fear, and anger. But you have the ability to use your breath to calm your muscles and thus quiet your stress chemicals. Simply allow your mind to imagine the light that enters with each breath. Feel that power. When we begin to feel that light, all our darkness can be conquered.

LESSON 13

Miles

A MEASURE OF GREATNESS

Pain is one of the most powerful messages in the brain. As we have seen, it is associated with dying tissue and produces a primal alert. It's easy to become defined by it. Refusing to allow that pain to diminish our inner being is the Heroic Response. When it comes from children, everyone notices. You, too, can turn your pain into something else that can define you: your personal Heroic Response.

We often give an example of pain when we begin our classes. "Imagine you are standing in a bank," I tell the children. "And all of a sudden you stub your toe really hard against the leg of a table. You start hopping up and down; you might cry out. It could get so bad that you have to call a toe truck." (Very young children think I am funny.) "However, if your were in the same bank and a robber came in and started shooting an AK-47 and you dove for cover under a table and you stubbed your toe, just as hard, you wouldn't even know that your toe hurts."

Why is that? Because the fear of getting shot is an even stronger message than the "ouch" from your toe. What is the lesson here? That pain is a message you don't have to listen to. It is not, however, a natural or easy thing to control. It is, after all, a very loud message.

All pain is processed in the brain. Even though a child with a tumor in his leg has a leg that hurts, that sensation must go from the leg to the brain before the actual pain can be perceived. The old model before the advent of brain scans was that there was a pain center in the brain. Our friend Mr. Descartes has a picture in his *Treatise of Man* of a rope-like element that ascends from the body until it reaches just such a pain center. That fixture in the mind would receive a message from the part of the body under assault and then assign pain to that area. With the use of fMRI's and other brain scanning tools, however, we are able today to clearly describe that there is no single pain center in the brain. As I have mentioned, there is an entire neural network of pain messages. We can see, for example, in the posterior cingulated cortex of the brain that if a person has great frustration, fears, and angers, the level of perceived pain increases. Those people who have a purpose associated with their pain, however, actually experience less pain over all.

Because pain is associated with the most primal human message—"Survive!"—it is usually ranked number 1 as far as getting our attention. It does not matter if that pain is based on a raging wound or tumor or if the neurological system is creating false pain messages. Pain is supposed to hurt. It warns us of danger. It tells us to take our hand off that hot cast-iron skillet before we burn ourselves even more. But we would be very happy to do without most of the pain we suffer, and we spend billions of dollars in drugs just to quiet its disturbing message.

Pain is also associated with memory via our neurology. Unless a person has had a closed head injury, every memory that gets wired into our synaptic system remains in our brain. It may be hard to recall them consciously, but they are there nonetheless. Memories are organized in our brain in similar categories. So if a person had terrible back pain five years ago and then gets even minor pain in the same area, the brain will often magnify that minor pain in line with memories of greater suffering.

Also, because pain is so intimately tied to the emotional system, it triggers feelings of fear and anger. The more fear and anger, the greater the pain. As the pain becomes more invasive, even more stress chemicals are secreted and an unenviable circle is created that is anything but heroic.

Miles Levin was one of the most brilliant young men I have ever met. When I was first introduced to him, he was also very sick. The intensity of the negative reaction to his chemotherapy was overwhelming and he had bouts of illness that were long and hard. When he found himself feeling strong enough to sit up, he would spend time talking to his friends—all thirty thousand of them. Miles, still in high school, began a blog that attracted readers from all over the world, and then received more attention when he was profiled on CNN. His writing style was a mix of Kierkegaard and Ionesco. People looked forward to reading the insights of a seventeen-year-old who was staring down death with both wisdom and wit. As his capacity to teach grew, bolstered by the connectivity of the digital world, he became more in control of his life and his disease. When he realized that his death was imminent, he wrote about hitting golf balls on a driving range. He described how you start out with a big bucket of balls and you find yourself hitting them without much thought or focus ... until you realize that the pail is not as full as it once was; it is getting emptied. At that point your swing becomes more deliberate, slower, steadied, perhaps more important to you. And then finally you are facing your last ball. Being seventeen years old and looking directly at the prospect of having fewer and fewer days is a feat in itself. But taking control over pain and indignity while creating purpose became Miles's everlasting legacy. Miles became a teacher extraordinaire.

On one hospital visit, Miles shared with me an incredible correspondence with one of his readers in St. Louis. "Miles," she began, "you don't know me but I have been following your blog for a while. I want to tell you my story. Recently my husband of forty years committed suicide. I was devastated, alone, angry, and afraid. I was also very depressed. The more I contemplated life in this new situation, the more I came to the conclusion that I had no more reason to live myself. I was so afraid that I would become a burden to my daughter and her family that I came to the conclusion that I had no choice but to follow my husband's path. I sat down at my computer to write a farewell email to my daughter explaining that I loved her and was so sorry but that I could not go on any longer. As I was beginning to compose my suicide note, the notice of your blog came on. You had not written for almost two weeks. You had been so very sick, you explained, that you could not even lift your head off the pillows—until that morning. That very morning you woke up and did not feel so bad. You wrote how you looked out of the window from your hospital bed at Sloan Kettering and noticed that the sky was bluer than you had ever noticed it and the tree that normally sat passively outside your window seemed to become alive with the deepest greens that danced upon the leaves. 'It is not that I am afraid to die,' you wrote. 'It is just that I don't want to miss any days. They are too beautiful.' I immediately got your message. Thank you, Miles, for saving my life."

Miles touched so many people. Among his legacies is that his mother, Dr. Nancy Levin, a wonderful psychologist, volunteers her time to teach our therapists about the indescribable challenges that parents face watching their children die. More directly, Miles took people beyond their fears and angst about living by helping them to see a truth that their brain was concealing. Every day can be beautiful when we stop being afraid of being overwhelmed by our fears—yes, of fear itself. Our own brains can create a false reality. Our greatest challenge is more about living than it is about dying. In his short life, Miles Levin conquered his stress, anger, and pain by merging them into a blog of life, inspiration, and a connection to the infinite.

Brittany

OUR MOST TEACHABLE MOMENTS

> *The grief that you feel when you have lost something precious is a great source of stress. It can easily defeat you. Many people focus so much on their loss that they end up losing themselves in the process. Stress and anger often follow those pathways of pain. Finding the purpose to continue going forward will allow you to turn pain into strength and defeat your stress.*

The greatest adversary of martial artists dwells within our brains. Going into a sparring match with thoughts of stress, anger, and pain is an almost certain guarantee for defeat. The wrong kinds of thoughts make it very easy to become overwhelmed, especially when facing down an opponent. We have seen that the universal approach of all martial arts is to use one's breath to reach our inner power. This philosophy translates well into other sports, too. In 2011, we brought a group of our Kids Kicking Cancer children to the Crisler Center, home of the University of Michigan basketball team, to teach these really tall people how to use their breath to focus in their lives and in their games. If you watch players at the foul line, it's clear that they have been taught to take a breath and clear their mind before they shoot. In life, we all get fouled. We should just look at it as an opportunity to score points. If you continue to focus on how unfair it was and all the whys that accompany our memories of pain, you'll miss the free throw. As Miles taught us, if you realize how precious every day of life is, you will make every shot (or swing) count.

Each slight that offends us, every fear that withdraws us, the angers that enrage us, all are based upon a foundation of reality—or so we think. One of the miracles of vision is that we see a different picture with each of our two eyes. The brain puts those two pictures together into one flowing vision. Similarly, our perception of anything around us is a formulation of many biological factors that contribute desire or toxicity into how we see things. Smell, touch, and hue affect how we value the food in front of us. Memories, good or bad, will also color the picture of how that meal tastes. This is not only a description of dinner, it is also how we view the people and relationships in our lives. When we do our meditations with children from the inner cities, it takes them a much longer time to be able to close their eyes than it does with other children. They have often learned the hard way not to trust their safety to anyone else. Memories colored by fear often determine who we can become and who we can't. We spend a great deal of time mourning over our lost opportunities or possessions. We grieve over what we have not become or what we are now becoming. Darkness flows naturally into the crevices of grief.

Cancer is a family illness. For that reason, Kids Kicking Cancer welcomes siblings into our programs. It is not unusual for the siblings who are well to begin to resent the inordinate amount of time that their brother or sister is receiving from their parents. These natural jealousies can become laden with guilt if the sick child's condition dramatically worsens. It is thus important for us to create an atmosphere of purpose for everyone in our extended family.

We met Bernard Johnson in Lesson 1. It was Bernard who said, "You can breathe in the light which is your essence and blow out the darkness." Brittany Johnson, Bernard's twin sister, never felt an ounce of resentment toward her brother as his tumor consumed everyone's attention. The two were so close that Brittany would climb next to Bernard and literally breathe for him. When Bernard was mostly comatose, she would walk in from school and start yelling at him, "You open up your eyes—I have to tell you what happened in school today." Open them he did, and somehow those two locked into conversation that only those who shared a womb could understand.

It was an unenviable task that fell to her grandmother and me to let Brittany know why Bernard was no longer in his bedroom on a Thursday afternoon on the last day of March in 2011. Her screams when I sat and explained that Bernard had passed away tore at my heart. I let Brittany cry herself out for a full half-hour. It was then when I leaned over and grabbed her eyes with mine. "Brittany, take a Breath Brake." My voice was emphatic and her eyes, bloodshot with grief, acknowledged this plea. She slowly exhaled a breath that was heavy with the aftermath of her sobs. "Very good. Now take one for Bernard." This time her body responded with her martial arts training and she began to physically relax. "What did your brother teach more than anything else in his life?" I asked. Her response was immediate: "No matter what we are facing in our lives, you can bring in the light and blow out the darkness." "That's right," I continued. "That message is so very important. We can't drop it. We need you to be his mouth in this world to continue that message while Bernard helps direct us from Heaven. Can we do this together?" Brittany, who for the previous forty-five minutes had looked as if she had just drowned, suddenly sat up straighter. A hint of awareness crossed her face. There was a purpose for her to continue.

The next Sunday, accompanied by an honor guard from the U.S. Army, Brittany accepted Bernard's black belt in the beautiful Compuware Auditorium in downtown Detroit in front of hundreds of the Kids Kicking Cancer and Johnson families. One week later, she was standing among our students in front of seventy-five employees from the PVS Chemical Company, teaching them how to use breathing to eliminate the stressors that break down communication and compromise safety. I called her forward. "I'm Brittany," she said in a voice that sounded like her twin's. "My brother Bernard taught us no matter what we face in our life, we can breathe in the light and blow out the darkness." With that, Brittany demonstrated how Bernard would teach the world the Breath Brake. By becoming his voice, she found purpose for her own. This is a theme we continue to use to help Brittany deal with the stress and overwhelming sadness of her loss. She has found her power and she is using it in the role of the beautiful teacher that she is.

People spend a great deal of time and emotional energy trying to push away their stress, anger, and pain. This tends to be a cyclical process. The more we worry about our stress, the more stress we have. Issues that should seem relatively small can send us into a tailspin of anxiety that only gets worse and worse. Our Kids Kicking Cancer children have so many overwhelming things to balance in their young lives. If they can learn how to take control of that downward vortex, then adults should be able to do so as well. Just as our children continue to demonstrate their power, the impact that we have on the world when we are able "to bring in the light and blow out the darkness" is profound. No matter who you are, others are watching. You become a teacher.

One of my dearest friends, Bunny Kelman, developed a serious internal leg infection from her diabetic neuropathy that required amputation in order for her to survive. On the day of the surgery, her son Robert called me in a panic. "Mom changed her mind; she is refusing to sign for the surgery. Can you come back to talk to her?" I was on my way to catch a flight but quickly turned around to join Bunny at her hospital bedside. She was afraid. The thought of not being able to walk again, coupled with the fear of losing her independence, prompted a decision that would spare the infection but take her life. Knowing my friend and the many good years that she could have with her adoring family convinced me that Mrs. Kelman had to change her mind. "Bunny," I told her when I reached her bedside, "you have spent your life planting values and faith into your children. You taught them very well. But right now is the most teachable moment in your life. They are sitting down the hall in the waiting room. They are watching how you respond. You have an opportunity to breathe in the light and blow out those fears and put an amazing smile on your face and continue forward with the real inner strength and faith that defines who you are no matter what else is going on. This is your most teachable moment. It is the one that they will talk about to your grandchildren and to theirs." Bunny did not hesitate. The old twinkle returned to her eyes as she looked up at me, a smile beginning to form on her worried face. "Rabbi, I got it. Thank you." I didn't even have time to speak with the family in the waiting room as I raced to the airport. About fifteen minutes later, my cell phone went off. It was Robert. "What in the world happened with my mother? What did you say to her?" he asked. "She just did a 180 and signed the papers—with a smile!" I hadn't done anything. I just allowed this beautiful woman to look beyond the grief she was experiencing for her leg and her life of independence and see instead the opportunity she had to teach. It is the last "p" in our mantra, "Purpose."

I have been privileged to have been given an appointment at the Wayne State University School of Medicine, mostly because of the great partnership that I enjoyed with Dr. Alan Gruskin of blessed memory of Children's Hospital of Michigan, where we started our first program. This has allowed me access to address the medical issues of stress and pain as well as our focus on end-of-life issues for children. When I speak to hospice professionals who work primarily with geriatric populations, I continually emphasize to them the power of purpose. One of the greatest challenges that the declining elderly feel is the fear of being a burden on others. As long as we are able to go out and support the family, cook the meals, and tend to the scraped knees, we have purpose. But when it is parents who are now sporting the diapers and aging has left them dependent for nearly everything, despondency is often a close companion. Allowing these individuals to know that this truly can be the most important teaching time of their lives is transformational. The beauty of the message is that it is so true and so simple. Power, Peace, Purpose is for every age and every life. It is all the more effective when young people like Brittany teach it. They are uniquely capable of opening the hearts and minds of so many others who see the heroic response of a young person rising above her stress, anger, and pain so that she can teach the world.

The applicability of Power, Peace, Purpose to anyone at any time in their life was brought home to me after an "Oh my gosh" moment in 2010. I was invited by Joel Jacob, a dear friend and long-time board member of Kids Kicking Cancer, to participate in a special presentation that he was making to the young people of an inner-city organization called STEP (Services To Enhance Potential). Even though I have long left the active rabbinate, I confess that one of my greatest joys in life remains hearing myself speak. So I try to do that a lot. Joel, who is chairman and founder of a company that makes bottles, closures, and trigger sprays, was involved in so many good deeds of philanthropy across the globe that I should have done my homework and not assumed what this was all about. I only knew that Joel was involved in groups that mentored young entrepreneurs who were learning how to become successful in the world of business, so I prepared my remarks accordingly. As I was standing behind the curtain with Joel, I heard myself being called out to say a few words. But when I greeted the audience I was more than a little startled to see three hundred young people who were not anything at all like the bright entrepreneurs I was expecting. In front of me sat a large group of cognitively challenged young adults. Many of them had such severe difficulties that their affect and posture were immediately noticeable. They were a group of young men and women who were being trained to put different bottle components together for Joel's company. Joel was making it possible for them to know success in their lives. It was a beautiful group, but not the one I was expecting.

It did not take long to realize that my opening joke was not going to work. Not only that, the closing line would have to go too, and I had nothing in the middle that would relate to this audience. So I took a quick Breath Brake and shouted, "Hi, my name is Rabbi G. Do you know what I do?" That question posed to an average audience would have elicited at least a little response. In contrast, this particular group looked as if they could not care less. Another Breath Brake. Then: "I teach karate to kids with cancer, and do you know why? Because some of these kids look different and people stare at them when they get on a bus." Now we were connecting, and I saw a few heads firmly nodding in empathy. "These kids are really smart," I continued. "You can tell them that other people are not looking at them, but they know better." A lot of heads were now joining the chorus of silent affirmation. "So we tell our kids that they can respond as powerful martial artists. Not with karate chops. We teach them how to take in a really big breath and pull in the powerful karate power. It looks like this," and I demonstrated. "Then we can blow out all the darkness, the feelings of it not being fair. Why are they staring? Why am I different? We just blow that out. And then, you can put a powerful karate face on." At this point I painted the biggest smile I could muster onto my face. "When the man who is looking at you sees this," I said pointing to the smile, and now addressing the audience as "you," he is saying to himself, 'Wow, if I had that challenge in my life I couldn't respond like that. Look at that kid's power.' And you know what? You just made that man into a better dad. The woman who is watching you and saying to herself, 'Look how powerful that young person is!' just became a better mom. You guys," I said to this group, "can do that every day. You can change the world with your power."

I have been in front of many gracious audiences, but the ovation from these young adults is one I will always remember. It did not matter that they were not going through cancer treatment. They were grieving for the normal that they would never know. This was made even clearer to me by a young man named Steven. His walk toward me when I came down from the stage was deliberate, impaired, and an obvious challenge. He slowly grabbed my hand. "Thank you," he said with the same deliberate delivery that mirrored his walk and, I would imagine, his whole life. A big "thumbs up" from Steven was the end of an amazing reception. His smile lit up his face. It was clear that Steven was a teacher. The course he taught was slow but powerful. All these young men and women "walk a walk" and "talk a talk" that looks and sounds strange and makes them the object of stares. But they understood that, given the opportunity, they can turn their challenge into an enormous opportunity. This is the theme of Power, Peace, Purpose. These folks can make up their minds to let go of "unfair" and become teachers. Brittany learned that despite her pain, she had to continue to spread Bernard's message. Bunny was willing to let go of her fear of living as an amputee because she saw that her life still had purpose, to be a teacher to her grandchildren.

Power, Peace, Purpose is not only for those of us whose genetic makeup makes them objects of public curiosity. We all have challenges, and a lot of them. Our mantra is also not about dying. You don't need a book for that. Since the beginning of time, everyone has eventually figured out how to expire one way or another. And it is not about getting angry, afraid, or down on yourself. Those emotions come naturally enough in response to all the unfair turns in life. Instead, Power, Peace, Purpose is about a much more difficult task: living heroically. Our children have produced a guide to living inspired, informed by an awareness that we can take control of our body and our lives. We can recognize the grief that causes stress, anger, and pain as the chemicals that challenge us. We can identify the tightness that lets us know that the stressors are threatening our lives and we can breathe in the light and blow out the darkness in a way that allows us to respond beyond the messages of those chemicals. When we do so, we can impact this world with a greater purpose.

LESSON 15

Bruce

MARTIAL-MARITAL: THE ONLY DIFFERENCE IS WHERE YOU PUT THE "I"

> *The natural stress response to something in our way is to push. In the martial arts, one learns that pulling an opponent is a lot more powerful than pushing. In life, if we're in a relationship in which we're pushing the other person, that's a relationship that's not working. Power, Peace, Purpose can be integrated into every relationship in your life—even the ones that cause you the most stress. Here is a quick guide to integrating all the lessons you have learned so far into a very important relationship—one that's been known to generate a little stress from time to time.*

A great example of integrating Power, Peace, Purpose into our lives is in the institution of marriage. There is a very famous book whose title is something like *Women Are from Venus and Men Are Wrong.* I may be a little off in the exact wording, but the theme suggests that there is some sort of galactic divide between the sexes. If that's the case, then bridging the gap will always be a challenge, but remember: a perfect God created an imperfect marriage, perfectly. In that challenge lies the greatest opportunity to create the most powerful bonds of love. As the rabbi of a synagogue in Southfield, Michigan, I became actively involved in marriage counseling in the greater Detroit community. In my training as a pastoral counselor I studied the works of existential therapists and behavioral psychologists. After many years of working with couples, however, I discovered that a great deal of my worldview was informed by what I was learning from the children. Power, Peace, Purpose is an extraordinary tool for all human relationships. Marriage, in particular, can draw great benefit from it.

I have a friend who once related, in front of his wife, "I have been blessed with twenty-five years of happy marriage." His wife, ever the stickler, interrupted: "What do you mean twenty-five? We're going on thirty-six years together." The husband, unrepentant, responded, "True, but I was just thinking about the happy times. If you add those all up, it's closer to twenty-five years." Ouch!

As a martial artist, I have always found the theme of fighting to be a colorful backdrop to marriage counseling sessions. Perhaps there is some connection between martial and marital arts. Teaching people how to fight is essential because, as much as we are in love and adore being loved, it is normal that two people in close contact will inevitably hurt and frustrate each other. We are going to get fouled by those around us, and that means we often have to go to the line. How should we respond? Learning how to deal with conflict while armed with the mantra of Power, Peace, Purpose is a totally different experience from a foul-shooting contest. It is essential to teach young people before marriage that struggle is an inherent and important part of a married relationship. Too often, people are so surprised and hurt by the early bumps of a young marriage that they lose the vision and the staying power that could transform those challenges into a strong and beautiful relationship.

We are all born with gross insecurities. As babies, we are dependent upon our parents to put food in our mouths, clean up our messes, and deal with our tantrums. Not much changes with our teenage years. There is nothing more validating to our sense of self than the knowledge that some woman or man is eager to spend the rest of his or her life with you. There is a thrill of being attracted to someone who is attracted to you. There is even greater affirmation when the commitment of marriage is introduced and an informal relationship morphs into a statement of a life-long vow. But somewhere along the way, doubts can easily creep in. "Does he really still love me? How much?" "Is she sorry that she made this choice? Why does she not seem happy?" It often doesn't take long in a marriage before the stress of daily life begins to reach deeply into the recesses of our pain memories, exacerbating the basic insecurities that we all have. Often tensions are created in snowball-like fashion. Sometimes these tensions derive from the cultural differences between one family and another. No matter where people come from, every family speaks a different emotional language.

Take Jack and Susan as an example. Jack comes from a family in which, if he were to win the Nobel Peace Prize and the Heisman Trophy, find a cure for cancer, and be appointed to the U.S. Supreme Court all on the same day, his father would look at him matter-of-factly and say, "Not bad, son." Susan, on the other hand, grew up surrounded by parents who responded to her every cough or sneeze with sympathy and support: "Here's a tissue for my beautiful brilliant daughter." Somehow these two end up getting married. With every intention of doing something awesome for her new husband, our young bride wakes up in the middle of the night. She spends hours preparing a scrumptious meal and quickly puts it into the freezer before sneaking back to bed to get an hour's sleep. The next day, she rushes home to put it in the oven, sets the table, lights candles, and sets out her lavish feast. Hubby comes home elated and overwhelmed. Biting into the miracle meal, Jack is so overwhelmed with love and appreciation that he looks over at his bride and proclaims, "Not bad." Ouch! "Not bad?" Susan thinks. "Does he have any clue how hard I worked to pull this together? How can he not show some appreciation for what I have done?" She is devastated, and before long she expresses her frustration and disappointment by complaining about something his father said to her uncle at the wedding. Not understanding why she dug that up, Jack responds with equal indignation over what her brother did to his mother the day after their engagement. What should have been a beautiful evening descends into a mess.

Another common example where marital and martial converge involves Barbara, who comes from a family where anything after five minutes early is considered late. Stan, on the other had, is from a world in which being on time is indicated by a calendar rather than a watch. Barbara wants to eat dinner by six, and her new husband is more than happy to say that he will be "on time." By seven Stan strolls in, more or less "on time." After several days of being upset and urging him to please just call in case he is going to be late, our young wife is fit to be tied. With the meatloaf shrunken in the oven because of another late arrival, Barbara lets loose at Stan with both barrels as he walks through the door. "You don't care about me and what I do for you," she yells. "I work and prepare a dinner and you don't even have the decency to let me know you're going to be late again. Every night!" Of course, Stan, feeling attacked after a hard day on the job, is more than righteous in his response: "If you didn't spend so much money on the Visa card, I wouldn't have to stay late at work." Sound familiar? This is a marriage adorned with the fight-or-flight chemicals we know all too well.

These stressors often put two people who really do care for each other into opposite corners. Those locations are just dripping with the chemicals that enhance our anger and fear while amplifying our pain. Sometimes we try to circumvent the conflict by telling ourselves, "It's not worth the fight. I'll just swallow this one." But while that may sound like a better choice than going into battle, all that swallowing can cause indigestion, big time.

Power, Peace, Purpose has at its core the concept of teaching. The contours of a marriage relationship require each spouse to teach the other what gives them pleasure and joy, and, conversely, what causes them pain. The yin-yang of marriage is an opportunity to grow. The greatest growth, as in most of life, takes place very often in the context of dissonance and challenge.

As we have learned from the children, Power, Peace, Purpose begins with an acceptance of pain. We can't effectively run away or overpower the source of pain at every given circumstance. In fact, the more we pull that pain into ourselves, the more effectively we can blow it out in the other direction. This means that the first step in any relationship begins with each individual. Success is inversely proportional to stress levels. Stress kills and makes us ineffective teachers. When you are confronted by the inconsideration or weakness of a spouse, understand that a successful relationship demands that you step up to the line not as an irate husband or wife, but as a willing and patient teacher. When you can identify your stress, anger, and pain, then you can take control.

When I first worked with Bruce, in the hematology/oncology clinic at Children's Hospital of Michigan, he was seven years old. Bruce was curled up in a ball on the table while having his port accessed for his chemotherapy. His traumatized mother was doing all she could to calm her son, but nothing was working. Bruce was already screaming when a nurse motioned me in. Timing is everything and in this particular case, it could not have been worse. Bruce was not at all receptive to hearing about martial arts therapy, or anything else, for that matter. I remained in the room, however, and waited until Bruce's sobs elapsed long enough for him to breathe. "Take that powerful breath," I told him. "You are very powerful." He continued crying but I now had just enough of his attention. "I see you took a big breath during your procedure," I told him. "That's very powerful and that's what we do in the martial arts to take control. And you know, a lot of kids we work with tell us that it helps them get through their stuff without feeling so bad."

We never tell a child not to cry or not to ask for pain medication. We do tell them, however, how powerful they are and how they can use that power when they want to. It starts by facing down the things that make us cry, that cause our fear and make our whole body tight. When the needle is poised to hurt us, we naturally get tight and end up coiling our muscles to try to lash out against the needle and the pain. But as martial artists we know that pushing is weak and pulling is powerful. By the time of Bruce's next appointment at the clinic, he had learned how to use his breath to calm his body and breathe in any feeling of discomfort. He was then able to turn his head and blow out the pain in the opposite direction. We walked through the whole procedure, even opening the alcohol pad so that he could practice his power breathing as the smell of that pad was reminding him of the procedure to come. This time Bruce was totally in control. There were moments here and there that he needed my voice to focus him away from the anxiety and pain that he was all too familiar with. But he was going to do this. He was going to pull in the discomfort and totally take control of it. Bruce was a martial artist.

A marriage is an ongoing life clinic. The first step in attaining inner power is to identify the triggers that cause us the pain, fear, and anger that in turn make us push out against each other. The advantage that we have is the built-in biofeedback our body supplies us when we are experiencing stress. If your muscles are getting tight, especially your neck, chest, shoulders, or head, and you are not in the midst of physical exercise, you are having a stress reaction. Inhale to lift up your muscles with the air, hold it, and then after three seconds slowly exhale while letting each and every muscle in your body fall and relax. This will stop your stress response. If you simply focus your breath to relax your body you will, in short order, stop the brain from shooting out the stress chemicals that rob you of your real power, that leave you no peace and emasculate your ability to achieve any real purpose.

Bruce taught us to identify the sources of his stress. In his case, it was the sound of the examination room door opening up, the smell of the alcohol swab, the spike of the needle beginning to penetrate his skin. Facing that reality and controlling his body to respond with Power, Peace, Purpose made him a very formidable little boy. He first used his breath to relax his muscles in the place of the shot. By blowing out his discomfort in the other direction, he joined the rest of our little heroes who are totally calm while getting an injection. The most important thing is that all this meant that it hurt a whole lot less.

"I am a little guy," I tell the children. "If someone is pushing me and I push them back, I am not going to accomplish much. However, if I pull them toward me, I can throw them wherever I want." Push is weak and pull is powerful. Therefore, when the needle begins to penetrate their skin, we never tell the children that it is not going to hurt. Instead we train them to take in a sharp inhale when they begin to feel discomfort. That breath pulls in the discomfort which they can now control by bringing it into themselves. They then turn their head in the opposite direction from the site and, moving their free hand in the same direction as the breath, they blow out the pain in the other direction. With that exhale, the opposite hand is also involved in gently but strongly pushing away the pain.

What our kids demonstrate is a principle of life. Push is weak. Pull is powerful. Learning how to pull your spouse is much more effective than the natural process of pushing away. We may feel better for the first minute of fight or flight. But the yelling and emotional pushing leaves us in a deeper emotional hole than before.

In marriage as in all of life, we naturally respond to the stressors of confrontation with stress, anger, and pain. Identifying that we are under attack from our own chemical makeup allows us to face down those stressors, take control, and eventually to teach. No one is more capable of hitting our triggers than the very person who promised to be with you forever. Intimacy, by its very nature, creates vulnerability. The more you love a person, the more capable you are of hurting him or her, and the reverse is equally true. Besides the obvious hurts that assault us, human beings also retain the memory of earlier pains. These remain in our heads even when we don't think about them or can't easily identify them. I like to call them our "UFOs": "unidentified fears and obstacles." They play a prominent role in our experiencing pain even when we can't identify exactly where that pain is coming from.

Every time we respond to our spouse, or for that matter to anyone, the sum total of memories from similar confrontations is dragged out by those stress chemicals, creating even greater levels of pain and challenge. Every time we have been disappointed still resides in one place in our brain. All the memories of being put down or not respected are stored at another place in that familiar cranial cafe. Each experience of being unloved or rejected has its own corner. It only takes a small, similar experience to get all those memories up and running, streaming out like lava in reproducing an experience that is not simply a response to the moment, but a reaction of the cumulative past of pain. The memories of these stressors jump quickly from the past to the present, reframing a level 3 slight into a level 8 or 9 insult.

We have children who have pain in their leg even after it has been amputated. "Phantom pain" is not only very real, it can be very painful. One of the treatments for phantom pain is using mirrors to "re-create" the leg. Once there, the patient can be taught to allow the pain to leave. It does not matter that the pain is in our brain. All pain is. Taking control of that pain is the key to responding with power. Knowing that the pain is in your brain and that you can control it is the most important piece of information that you can have to master that pain. Physically blowing out the feeling of pain while relaxing your muscles will have a profound impact on your life, regardless of whether it is the pain of a needle or the discomfort of being needled.

The marriage relationship is as much about pain as it is about joy and pleasure. In the Bible its very design is described as "one who helps" and "one who is against." The classical "yin/yang" of life is part of the marriage equation because we can become greater through confrontation. Every marriage has periods of pain and confrontation. Using those periods as a teaching opportunity creates a platform for greatness. As Jack LaLanne used to say, "No pain, no gain!" So, too, in all of life, the moments of challenge create the greatest opportunities for growth. This is true of individuals and it is also very apt for couples. The first step in taking control of your marriage is to take control of yourself. Going back to our model of Power, Peace, Purpose, being aware that you are upset, uptight, hurt, or just feeling down gives you the ability to re-channel the negative into a positive. Stress will always create tightness somewhere. Feeling that restriction in your neck, arms, chest, stomach, or head allows you to release those tensions with your breathing. As already mentioned, breathing is the only part of the nervous system that you can so easily control. Every stress reaction creates tightness. Using your breath to first lift up your body, hold in that air to a slow count of three, and then relax your muscles with the exhale will allow you to approach the reality of your issue from a place of power. Take several of these breaths until you feel your body begin to relax. When you are relaxing that tightness you are telling your brain that you are engaging in a parasympathetic relaxation response rather than the sympathetic fight-or-flight mode. You create a place of peace when you can bring in that breath of light and feel that power. Ultimately, understand that a perfect God created an imperfect world perfectly. You have been given this challenge from your spouse because it is an opportunity. This knowledge, and the ability to bring in that light, is your power.

Here is the Power, Peace, Purpose guide to marriage. Allow yourself to get to that place of peace. Before discussing whatever issue needs to be spoken about, give your partner the opportunity to calm him/herself down, to take a Breath Brake, or to walk around the block. Allow yourself or your partner space, but not more than two hours. Issues need to be handled and timing is important.

Often your spouse may not even be aware that he or she did something wrong. (Imagine that.) As a spouse you have the obligation to teach him or her. However, teaching requires you to be in a place of peace so that you can be a good presenter. It is also essential that the time and place correspond well to the lesson that needs to be learned. When the hubby who uses a calendar rather than a watch for promptness comes home, allow him the opportunity to remove his coat, eat his meal, and then be in the best position where he can learn what you need to teach.

If one approaches the purpose of this challenge as a teaching moment, then the chances of quick and painless success multiply significantly. Remember, your most effective teaching posture is to pull rather than push. Begin with something positive. It has to be true but make sure it is positive. For example, "I know that you love me and do generally show appreciation." Don't say anything disingenuous, but there is always something positive to articulate that can help in the pulling process. Next, speak about your perceptions, not about what he or she did or did not do. The "he said, she said" thing is nothing but pushing and will create an opposite pushback. No one, however, can debate that your perceptions are real to you. "That's why I need to tell you that tonight I felt very unimportant to you, as if you did not care how hard I worked to have dinner ready for you at six o'clock. I really felt so small. If you would have just called to let me know, it would have made a big difference. I need to feel important to you, always."

No one will respond to the above by complaining about the Visa bill. These were not fighting words but a gentle pull from someone who loves you. In our first example, Susan, the young bride, could simply have expressed, "I know that you love me but I feel very hurt that you did not appreciate how hard I worked to get this special meal together." That message would have allowed the clueless Jack to respond that he was, in fact, overwhelmed by the most amazing, delicious dinner that he had ever had and that he thought he had expressed it with "Not bad." Jack will learn that he has to be more articulate in how he expresses his love and appreciation, and Susan will learn that "Not bad" is synonymous with "Unbelievably great." When we stop being victims of our situation and its accompanying stress, we become victors in our lives. Most importantly, we become teachers. I have found that this philosophy of Power, Peace, Purpose has made a profound difference in many marriages. It does not hurt that the stories of our little warriors make it so easy for those we teach to hear and integrate them into their lives.

Just as the martial arts has a place in the marital arts, the lessons about how to fight is replicable in any human relationship. You are constantly given the opportunity to respond naturally or heroically. There is nothing natural in what our Kids Kicking Cancer children do, nor in this process they teach. The natural response to stress is fight or flight. However, natural does not mean better. The stressors of anger and pain waste a lot of time and energy. The primitive response stops you from being who you can be. Facing down the pain allows you to not be victimized by it. In your relationships as in your life, you have a choice whether to respond as a victim or victor.

LESSON 16

Rose

OVERCOMING THE THORNS

> *Can we actually change our brains? Before the advent of scans, the assumption was that the brain's ability to change does not go beyond adolescence. Today, science indicates that when we face down the challenges from a place of focused peace, we can change our brains. Power, Peace, Purpose not only can stop your stress but change the platforms from which you are attacked. You can fundamentally reshape your life from inside your cranial cavity.*

It's amazing how quickly the brain can produce stress chemicals that can take control of our essence and overshadow our lives; one of the best examples of such a psychological onslaught of stress chemicals is Obsessive Compulsive Disorder (OCD). However, even that challenge can be conquered with Power, Peace, Purpose.

Today, with brain scans, we are able to understand how OCD works. People with this disorder have specific fears that remain in the brain and signal a stress response long after rationality should allow it. But even people without OCD go through some of the same neurological paces—up to a point. It is not uncommon for someone to lock the front door upon leaving home in the morning and then think, "Maybe I'm forgetting something?" One of the classic scenarios people consider at such a moment is if the iron was turned off after a shirt was pressed. The fear of a hot iron causing a fire is real, leading our brain to produce the stress chemicals of anxiety that then force us to reopen the door and check on the iron. The moment we see that it's off, a chemical called serotonin is secreted in the brain, giving us that "ahh" feeling. This positive sensation replaces the stress chemicals so that the non-OCD person can be on his merry way, enjoying a productive day of work and maybe a few rounds of solitaire when no is watching.

The classic sufferers of OCD lock their door as they are leaving for work in the morning and also experience that "Did I leave the iron on?" feeling. As with everyone else, their caudate nucleus gets hot with the stressors of anxiety, and they unlock the door to see for sure that not only is the iron off, it is disconnected from the wall. At this point, the serotonin kicks in, all is well, and our OCDers make their way out the door, content with the knowledge that their home will not erupt in flames from a felled iron while they are gone. The "ahh" feeling doesn't last very long, however, because the person afflicted with OCD uses up that serotonin very quickly. When locking the door for the second time, the person feels that gnawing uncertainty and anxiety resurfacing. It's not because these folks are stupid. They remember what they saw and they don't believe in space aliens or little blue men who may have turned the iron back on. Yet their anxiety stressors become so overwhelming that the only way to quiet them down is to open the door again and check the status of the iron. Again, there is the rush of serotonin, but just as quickly the caudate nucleus burns it up and the OCDer is back on the other side of the front door, wondering about that iron. Some people spend hours trying to make it out of the house; others end up just taking their iron to work with them. Psychiatrists prescribe large dosages of SSRIs (selective serotonin reuptake inhibitors) to allow that chemical to remain in the brain longer. The problem tends to return if they stop taking the drug. The reason? Their brains "lie" and enslave them with the stress chemicals of fear.

A number of years ago, I was asked to see a young woman whose OCD focused on her vehicle. Rose drove an old car. Despite having no interest in its style or horsepower, this car controlled her life. She had a constant fear that she might accidentally leave a door unlocked and her car would be stolen. That was not such an irrational concern; car thefts do happen. But it so occupied her thoughts that she would wake up several times a night and run outside to check the doors of her car. It didn't matter if it was subzero weather or even if the car was partially buried in snow, she would be awakened in the middle of every night with the fear of an unlocked door, and she could not go back to sleep without her ritual of pulling every car door handle at least twice—and this went on every few hours of her life.

The first time Rose pulled up to my office, I was able to see her through the window. She circled around her car several times, checking each door handle until she felt secure enough to approach my entrance. The chairs in my office faced the open window, and she frequently glanced outside to her car parked right outside. Rose understood that her behavior was upsetting both to herself and her family and that it did not make sense. Taking a rational perspective, I noted that the amount her father was paying me per hour was more than her insurance deductible. There was no reason not to take on the battle that was raging inside her head and controlling her life, and so we focused on the importance of that battle. Existentially, I told her, we are given these challenges to give us the opportunity to fight back. That very fight defines the greatness that lies within us. In other words, a perfect God created an imperfect brain, perfectly. As she would gain the skills to succeed in this battle, she would make a wonderful teacher of this power to others. And she learned our mantra, "Power, Peace. Purpose."

Our first session allowed me to introduce to her several stories of our amazing little teachers. I then began to train her in the same techniques that these kids use to face down their pain, fear, and anger in their disease and treatment. Power, Peace, Purpose became our approach to understanding that this misappropriation of brain chemicals was not her doing. It was not who she was. Her mental actions, aggravated by the precipitous drop in serotonin, caused thoughts and fears that were not her essence. She was not her brain. Moreover, we discussed how brain scans indicate that we can take on this battle and change our brains. Unlike pharmacological interventions, we can make these into lasting changes.

Rose understood that we don't write the scripts of our lives; rather, our purpose is defined by how we respond to that script. She was a spiritual young woman, and the thought that she could engage her soul with her breath and that her victory could have an impact on our world resonated with her. We decided by the third session that she was now equipped with enough power that the next week she would park her car outside my office and not lock the doors. My office was in a low-crime neighborhood, and her vehicle would still be right in front of my window in broad daylight. This would be an opportunity for a real victory.

The next week I watched as Rose exited her car, determined to follow our plan. But it was as if a chain were pulling her back. She vacillated between focused determination and pitiful surrender until she finally made it up the fifteen yards to my door. At that point, she could do no more than blurt out, "I can't do this." It took much cajoling on my part and a promise that she would be out in five minutes to get her to sit down and focus on her breath. Together we allowed her to ride the waves of anxiety, relax her muscles, and breathe in the light. It took three weeks of sessions for her to be able to sit with me for a full session with her car door unlocked. Two weeks after that, Rose went into a drugstore for ten minutes, consciously leaving her car door unlocked. She had rewritten the brain messages that had kept her incarcerated. From that point on she could lock her door with confidence and never have to go back and check it. I asked her how she felt. Rose responded, "I feel very powerful. There are a lot of people I know who can use these techniques."

While there are many OCD sufferers, that population is relatively small compared to those who suffer from general anxiety disorders. The ongoing stress of "what if?" is enough of a challenge to millions of people that they will not reach the success that should be theirs. They live lives plagued by enormous self-doubt. Among the many available counseling and behavioral therapies, Power, Peace, Purpose is an accessible and important model. If you accept the battle to take on your fears, then you can rewire your brain. The Breath Brake is a great mechanism to allow you to get to that point. When you allow your body to turn off the stress mechanism and replace the anxiety messages in your mind with something more powerful—the light of your soul—you are changing your brain.

LESSON 17

Fred

WALKING THE WALK

> *It is important to have a quick escape route from the world of stress. Underlying chronic anxiety can make you feel that something terrible is happening. That's the time to "stop, look, and listen." Use your breath at that moment to stop the stress chemicals. A reality check to keep you from falling victim to the chemicals of stress, anger, and pain can consist of a simple glance downward. If upon observing the floor you don't see any major body parts lying there, chances are you are fine. Listen to your breath while you think of this challenge as an opportunity to teach others.*

David was a young man in his early twenties who had been on multiple anti-anxiety and anti-depression medications. As the stresses of anxiety and pain share many neurological connections, they often partner with depression. Despite the meds, David has gone from failure to failure. He was continually clutching defeat out of the jaws of victory because of debilitating self-doubt. His parents are long-time friends of mine and they asked if I could help him. I met with David's psychologist and shared with him the principles of Power, Peace, Purpose and the mechanism of empowerment through our Breath Brake. His therapist was very open-minded, and we began a process of redirecting David's thoughts and rewiring his standard responses. The therapist worked on this twice a week, and I was available for infrequent phone calls from David. Eighteen months later, David was still going to school, completing his degree, holding down a job, and actively dating—a "normal" he had never been able to experience before. The task of checking for any fallen body parts was a simple technique very similar to the tools of logotherapy employed by Victor Frankl, the Viennese psychiatrist and author of *Man's Search for Meaning.* It works well for anyone who is not in the habit of dropping their major limbs and organs on the floor. With this exercise, we can reframe our brains and limit our stress response.

Recently, David called me because, having moved and started a new job in sales, he found his stressors to be quite exacting. David is extremely good looking, articulate, bright, and personable. He has all the tools of a great salesman. However, he now found himself in a position where the competition would resort to bribery to make their sales, a tactic David's company frowned upon and his personal scruples would not tolerate. Every new meeting was therefore doubly fraught with anxiety. David is a very religious young man who viewed his access to the light as a conduit to a Heavenly force. We focused on bringing in that power with a short prayer for success before he walked through the doors of potential buyers. At that point he was to do a Breath Brake, using the light to relax his muscles, and then breathe out and say, *"Baruch Hashem."* Then he was to use that light to connect to buyers with the warmth and friendship of his soul. It came naturally to David as long as he was not afraid. Lastly, making the pitch with what he believed to be the truth and walking out the door afterward was the definition of success. If God wanted him to make the sale, he nailed it. If he wasn't supposed to make that particular sale now, maybe he would do it later. If no major body parts ended up on the floor, then it was a pretty good meeting. But what really brought David peace was the acceptance of doing his best and being satisfied with that. Connecting to the light above and the world around us with power is all that we can do. And that's a lot. A perfect God created an imperfect world perfectly. When we are not afraid, we can reach our purpose.

The children of Kids Kicking Cancer have taught me that when we feel that we are powerful, that's exactly what we become. But we must battle the stuff in our brains to reach a place of peace. The best way to do that is also the simplest. Stop the adrenal gland from shooting out the glucocorticoids of stress. Using our breath to relax those muscles puts us in charge.

Breathing in the light gives us the strength to continue. Knowing that we are being watched and that we are teaching those around us gives us the motivation we need to keep going. On this path we can reach our goals and our essence at the same time.

I told David about a young man I knew named Fred Stringer. A few days after giving a lecture to the medical staff at Children's Hospital of Michigan, I received a phone call from the interim head of the bone marrow transplant unit at the Karmanos Cancer Center in Detroit. They had a thirteen-year-old patient who was so noncompliant that he was putting himself in great danger. Fred was three weeks post-transplant. He was so depressed and angry that he refused to respond to any of the medical staff's requests. And he was so weak that he was convinced he was dying. Fred's method of taking control over his life was closing his eyes when any adult walked into his room. At this point, it was imperative to get Fred up and walking, but he would hear none of it. Although he was quickly developing pulmonary edema, threatening his very fragile recovery, he still refused to move. The medical team had sent in psychologists, psychiatrists, social workers, physical therapists, and occupational therapists—anyone willing to try to get Fred out of bed and walking. Nothing worked. He was going to die. I didn't know if I could do any better, but I readily agreed to visit him. His room at Karmanos had a large pane of glass in the door. Through it I was able to see Fred sitting up in bed watching TV. It was a good time to come in. As soon as I opened the door, however, Fred closed his eyes and slumped back into the large pillow that had been propping up his head. Undeterred, I walked over to him and said, "Fred, my name's Rabbi G. and I am a black belt. Your doctors are great, but I am going to teach you some karate to get you out of here faster. You have some amazing power inside and I want to show you how to use it."

I must have piqued his curiosity a bit because he opened his eyes. But when he saw a short, balding, funny-looking guy standing there, he instantly shut them again. He probably thought he was having a nightmare. "Fred," I continued, "I want you to learn how to find this karate power and use it to get yourself out of here. I am just going to hold my hands in front of you. Tell me what you are feeling." I closed my eyes and held my hands spread out near his face. Fred was lying there doing a great job of not responding. I, on the other hand, had nineteen years of pulpit experience, so I was used to talking to people with their eyes closed. After a minute Fred's voice startled my concentration. "Warm," he said. Then, "Hot, hotter." "Fred," I told him, "this is your power. We are going to push this Chi through your body. Right now you are really tired, but you are going to feel this power very soon." With that I left the room. The next morning I got a call from the nurse's station. "Could you come back? Fred walked yesterday."

To this day, Irene Stringer, Fred's mom, tells people that her son got out of the hospital earlier than expected because of Kids Kicking Cancer, and that Kids Kicking Cancer saved Fred's life. The truth is, we didn't do anything for Fred other than letting him know that he had that power. His disease and treatment had created a paralyzing depression and a feeling of despair. The only power he knew was tuning everyone out of his life. In doing so he almost tuned out life itself. Today, after two hip transplants that he needed because the chemotherapy broke down his joints, Fred does Michael Jackson dance moves better than anyone else around. This was only a few months after physical therapy so painful that he had to constantly focus on his breath work simply to get through it. Fred showed that even though we can feel incarcerated by the stressors in our lives, we can also find the inner light to respond. No body parts on the floor? Then we are just fine.

He inspired David. He inspired me, too, and Fred continues to inspire the world.

LESSON 18

Randy

CLEARING THE AISLES

> *It's not about me.*
>
> *It is natural for us to internalize the challenges that others present to us as being about ourselves. When you find your child, spouse, employee, or client is not listening to you, and you obsess on this as a sign that you are not being respected, then your response is more likely to be filled with stress than strength. Your chemicals are responding to the memories of pain, because you think this is really about you. Take a deep breather and tell your brain what's really going on. This is just another opportunity for living greater.*

Whether you are at work or at home, interacting with your family or with your community, you are naturally responding with your built-in set of UFOs (unidentified fears and obstacles) and running for cover. It is the exceptional person who does not let him- or herself be defined by the sources of stress. In our relationships, these chemicals so personally intertwine us with our issues that we lose perspective and don't focus on the real purpose of our lives. I remember the telling response of a major rabbinical figure who was approached by a man who complained, "Rabbi, I have a problem with my daughter." The rabbi gently stopped him before he could continue and looked him straight in the eye. "You really mean that your daughter has a problem and you would like to help her." We all can become chemically drawn into pushing matches with everyone around us and frequently respond as we are programmed to react to stressors: fight or flight. Rather than teaching, we end up defending or defeating. Either way, we lose.

Using the Breath Brake in marriage works wonders. It is also a great tool in raising our children. Even on the job it can be very effective, protecting us from significant grief and saving companies a great deal of money. Patrick Shanks was a district manager for Wal-Mart in the Midwest. He invited me to present the Breath Brake to a group of his store managers. These are not people without stress. They have to reach demanding sales numbers. They must also manage a team to run a store efficiently. And inevitably, there are team members who don't understand, who want to do it their own way, or who are just not right for the position. For store managers, there are so many triggers that can set them off that it is hard to transcend the fight-or-flight buttons. Responding to those triggers with fight or flight may be natural, but that's clearly not an effective route to go. Most of us have been around the boss who loses his cool or, conversely, runs from confrontation and allows an issue to fester. Either way, it's more often true that we have a problem with that employee rather than the employee has a problem and we want to help. The latter response is pulling, but the first one is all about pushing. Pushing is weak; pulling is powerful.

Step number 1 for the Wal-Mart managers was to learn how to identify the tightness in their bodies as a flag of stress and thus a signal that it's time for a Breath Brake. Just as the Starship Enterprise required Captain Kirk to be cool and collected, so too store managers have to be in command while not getting frazzled. If you think about it, Superstores are a lot like Starships. There are the many different divisions and specialists on board, the exacting directives from Starfleet Command, and the Klingon competitors that would like to photon-torpedo you into the next galaxy. There's some real anxiety. Exhaling all the negative feelings associated with stress and bringing in the light with each inhale allows us to focus ourselves. That light shows up as a smile on our face and as strength in our demeanor for when we direct others. The voice is soft, the face is welcoming, and the leadership is potent. If, on the other hand, we are responding to our own fears rather than the needs of the moment, we will not be fulfilling our purpose. When we can separate ourselves from the issue, then we don't become part of the problem. It is not about you!

The second step for the store managers was meeting Randy, a transplant patient who has been challenged with chronic pain. Randy joined our group only two weeks before the presentation, but he was already taking control of his pain by using his breath. This nine-year-old boy was now very focused on being a teacher. It made sense to him that there had to be a reason why he was given his painful script. Taking control of that pain was a special skill that he was now uniquely positioned to promote.

The first thing Randy gave these adult students was perspective. Perspective allows all of us to take a step backward and reevaluate the depth of the challenge at hand without the negative amplification of our stress chemicals. Effective management requires an inner calmness with which we can build up the people around us rather than tear them down just because our chemistry has been triggered into fight-or-flight mode. The key is to pull rather than push.

Inspired by our amazing little teachers, 97% of the adults we teach describe our seminars as having had a "profound influence" on their lives. This group of managers was no exception. Less than a week after the seminar, Patrick called me just as one of the stores in his region was nearly in crisis with a change of management. He couldn't believe that when he came into the store, the associates in the aisles were doing the Breath Brake. Apparently the manager had taught the assistant manager and the assistant manager had then taught the associates. According to Patrick, it changed everything. A crisis had been averted because children with cancer were teaching the world how to breathe in the light and blow out the darkness. In place of stress, they created light.

What works in marriage and in the aisles of America's superstores can work in every corridor of our lives. When we do seminars for teachers, we ask them to listen to the sound of their voices. The most effective teachers can communicate discipline and direction without having to say one word. I still remember the eyes of my sixth grade teacher, Mrs. Heller, whose eyes could burn a hole in the head of an errant child. She never needed to raise her voice. The more a teacher has to yell, the less control he or she has over the pupils. Certainly the lesson of real power to the students becomes compromised by the teacher's level of anger. More often than not, the response of the angry teacher is an amalgam of stress, anger, and pain shaped by the "What if?" fear that the pupils are not listening. Power struggles in the classroom are an indication that there is way too much pushing going on. The successful instructor teaches from a place of inner peace. We instruct teachers to identify their own UFOs and remove themselves from the equation. Then they are able to identify that their body is getting tight, the first step in the biofeedback process of the Breath Brake. The second step comes with that slow breath that lifts up the body and holds in the air for three seconds. Slowly blowing out that breath and relaxing the muscles can be done while listening to the question that irks you or observing the behavior in the classroom that is getting you upset. It can be done in the sanctum of one's mind so that no one can see what is going on inside you. But what will be seen is that the teacher's response is one of power and not weakness. Kids know the difference, and the teacher has the opportunity to impart a valuable lesson that will have a profound impact on students' lives.

Ultimately, we are all teaching. Our children, friends, coworkers, neighbors, and strangers are watching how we respond to life. It makes a difference. Whether you are a special-needs child getting on a public bus, a hurt spouse, an anxious salesman, or a stressed-out store manager, people are watching. When you bring in that light to relax your muscles and blow out the darkness, the smile that you wear will light up the world. Our children do it every day. They call it Power, Peace, Purpose.

Viewing life as an opportunity for greatness rather than an amalgam of frustrating problems is essential for connecting with our true power. The understanding that a perfect God created an imperfect world perfectly makes it all easier when we realize that there is a purpose behind our problems. In some of the most difficult relationship issues that I counsel, I often offer the following analogy. Imagine before walking into your house one day after a hard day's work that you hear a voice coming from behind the bushes by the door. "Psst, over here! But don't look down—they're watching you." Curious and a little frightened, you peek behind the shrubs and barely make out someone hiding there. "Listen," the voice continues, "you are being set up by *Candid Camera*. We have placed hidden cameras throughout your home and have challenged your spouse and kids to drive you crazy. Now here's the deal: if you can respond to them without getting angry for a whole week, you win a million dollars." (Remember, *Candid Camera* was from the days when a million dollars was real money.) "I'm just giving you a warning," the voice continues, "so you'll have a fighting chance." Who would not be able to keep their eyes on the prize and transform into the calmest, gentlest respondent under that scenario? Every irrational rant of the Mister or Missus, or the whines of your beautiful little angels, becomes part of a greater opportunity to prove to the watchful eyes of the camera that you are worthy of the big prize. Could you do it for a week? How about a month? The answer is probably yes, because you now know It Is Not About You. You are not bad or mean or at fault. Minus the stress chemicals with their accompanying UFOs, you will amaze yourself, pulling your spouse or your children toward you with kindness, patience, and forethought because the brain is not being triggered by the negative pushers that sap your focus. If in fact you do something wrong, you can now find the wherewithal to apologize and learn from the experience. If there's a miscommunication or misperception, you can explain. We get it now. It's all about the prize.

But this is not just some alternate-universe scenario. After sharing the *Candid Camera* analogy with the people in my office, I point out that we all have lenses around us. They are in the eyes of your children who are watching how you respond to stress, anger, and pain. They are within your husband or wife who is learning to respond in kind to your responses. The lenses are on the spectacles of your colleagues, neighbors, and peers who are impacted both by your strengths and your weaknesses. Sum it all up and the value of the lesson that you can impart to the people whom you care about is worth a lot more than a million dollars. When you breathe out the stress, then and only then is it really about you, but in a good way. You have become, like our kids, an amazing teacher.

LESSON 19

Igor

DELIVERING THE UPS MESSAGE

> *You may not always realize the effect of your anger and fears. You are being watched, however, and not just by the NSA. There's also our friends and family and, for most of us, there is Heaven above. Know that your response to the world through the prism of peace will allow you to demonstrate a power that will positively influence the world.*

The "watchful eye" is a theme in many theosophies and cultures. What we do matters. Ultimately, it is all seen. When I was a young man, it came in the person of Sergeant Murphy. Before directing Camp Simcha for children with cancer, I had a stint as a division head and then a head counselor in a boy's summer camp located in Barryville, New York. This camp had a number of children from troubled backgrounds, and the issue of theft on the campgrounds was not uncommon. To help a child repair this negative behavior, he has to admit to his crime. Rehabilitation is much harder otherwise. When we were absolutely certain that a particular camper had stolen, I employed the proficient detective work of Sergeant Murphy, senior officer of the world-renowned Barryville Police Department. The best thing was that there really was no Sergeant Murphy. But this mythical figure was able to extract the truth from many a young criminal.

The process was simple. The errant camper was called to wait for me in my office. A police file with that child's name was already in sight, poorly concealed by other papers. As I came into my office to sit with the child, I would inquire if the young man had noticed Sergeant Murphy and his officers planting hidden cameras throughout the camp. Of course he hadn't, to which I responded with pride: "They were undercover, of course." After another minute or two, I would receive an important phone call from none other than Sergeant Murphy himself. It wasn't every day that I received a call from such a legendary arm of the law, and I would rise with the greatest respect to take his call. After directing the camper to the opposite side of the office—but well within earshot—I would relate to the good sergeant that the perpetrator was in custody and was neither armed nor dangerous. A quick glance over at the now anxious young man was all I ever needed to be assured of this fact. I would then casually drop a hint that Sergeant Murphy would soon be on his way over to take away the perpetrator. Calling the child back to my desk, I would then ask, "Let's see, what will you need to take with you if you'll be going away for a while? I assume you will need your toothbrush, soap, a few pair of shorts. . . ." This charade would take anywhere from thirty seconds to two minutes before the young man would confess his crime, express his regret, and look to me to keep him out of the cold clutches of the law.

It always went like clockwork—except one time. This child wouldn't budge. We must have made a mistake, I thought. Maybe he didn't really do it? Sergeant Murphy's subject in this case was Igor, a ten-year-old from the former Soviet Union. He was not budging from his protestations of innocence. He was cool, calm, and totally innocent in appearance. I was just about ready to bend and admit to a probable case of mistaken identity when just then a UPS truck showed up outside. When Igor saw the brown-uniformed delivery man march out of the dark, windowless, rather scary-looking van, he broke down completely and jumped onto my lap. "Don't let them take me!" he pleaded. "I'll tell you everything." Igor then supplied quite a list of goods that he had pilfered and hidden away in the camp. It was only then that I could share with him that there was no Sergeant Murphy. There were no video cameras, either, of course, but that didn't mean that what he did was not seen.

Ultimately, Igor learned that we are so important that our actions are indeed watched and observed. We are challenged, and sometimes we fall down. But when we struggle against the feelings of our jealousies, angers, and fears, we can make a big difference in the world. There is an "eye" that sees because we are put into this imperfect world to make a difference. Every one of the children "captured" by Sergeant Murphy was made to understand the challenge that we all have, as well as the opportunity. They all became very important because they all rose to the challenge. At that time, I had not yet made a serious study of the martial arts, nor did I know well any really sick children. The concept of Power, Peace, Purpose was already beginning to form, however. It was being shaped by Sergeant Murphy and the brave men of UPS.

LESSON 20

Jack

FORGETTING MEMORY

> *We all have memories. Some of them you don't actively recall but they dwell within your subconscious. The bad ones cause you stress even when you don't know they are being triggered. They are the UFOs that cause us to react totally out of our character. Most often they trigger stressors that negatively impact how we respond to our situation and the people around us.*

When we're under attack from stress, anger, and pain, we can't recognize where to properly direct our energies until we identify that there is a battle taking place. That's what gives us the ability to mount our defense against our internal adversaries rather than lash out at those around us. Frequently, however, we are not even aware of what those stressors are, and we have no clue where they come from.

Jeffrey was a middle-aged friend embroiled in family issues that were, at least in part, due to his own behaviors. It was clear that he had developed a trust issue when he was young but he could not understand why. His family was caring, supportive, and pretty normal. Why was he so afraid of relying on others? Jeffrey also saw me for counseling. In a session together, we went through a meditation that both relaxed and regressed him back to his childhood. It did not take more than a few minutes for this prominent attorney to turn into a nine-year-old child rummaging through his parent's closet. For a pre-teen, closets hold potential treasure and forbidden mystery.

After moving around some old tools and a family scrapbook, however, Jeffrey discovered his adoption papers. From reading over the well-folded documents, Jeffrey came to the realization that his mother had not given birth to him. His father was not who he thought he was. The nine-year-old Jeff was in shock. In my office, the forty-year-old man began to cry and rock himself gently, enveloped again by the pain of that moment and the overwhelming feeling of betrayal.

The very next week, this bright gentleman was back with me to explore his issues just a bit further. But when, just to get the ball rolling, I asked him what we had spoken about the previous week, Jeffrey could not for anything remember what we had discovered. Even after I gave him the hint that we had uncovered how his childhood may have been different from that of other kids, my friend could not recall this revelation. It took almost twenty minutes and no small amount of sweating from Jeffrey for him to recall what he had so intimately reexperienced only a week earlier. Eventually, he would come to grips with his past and be able to grow beyond the trust issues that negatively impacted his family.

When it comes to certain painful memories, the brain does a great job of suppression. It does not mean that those memories are not there, however. In fact, their presence significantly affects our behavior. It just makes it hard to face them from time to time.

I can see now, in retrospect, that the themes of empowerment and recognizing that others observe what we do emerged from my early beliefs and experiences, including the story of Sergeant Murphy. More recently, Kids Kicking Cancer was inspired by the heroic life of our beautiful Sara Basya and, later, had its first student with Josh, the five-year-old boy from Texas who, after only five minutes of breathing instruction, didn't know the syringe had already been in and out of his chest. But even with those experiences, it took me many years to finally recall the face of the very first child whose utter terror of being in a hospital had so impacted me and surely had a large role in changing my life's mission into Kids Kicking Cancer.

In first grade, I was out of school for a long time with a sinus infection that just did not seem to heal. After a large dosage of penicillin, I only got sicker, a lot sicker. At my mother's insistence the doctor saw me again, but this time I had no reflex response. I was immediately hospitalized at

Montefiore Hospital in the Bronx. My doctor, Ann Botstein, had just presented a paper on Guillain-Barre Syndrome in Switzerland. She didn't imagine that she would be coming back to a new diagnosis that same week.

Guillain-Barre Syndrome is a rare disease, especially for a child. Usually following on the heels of an infection, it is an auto-immune disorder that turns the body against itself and destroys part of the nervous system. The result is weakness, paralysis, and sometimes death. In my case, my body grew progressively weaker until I was having trouble breathing on my own and required the constant use of an oxygen tent. I was getting hundreds of get-well letters from friends and family but reached the point that I couldn't even open the envelopes. Afterward, my mother shared with me that she had been warned that I had only a 2% chance of making it. That would turn out to be the same percentage the doctors quoted us before we brought our daughter to UCLA for her bone marrow transplant.

I remember the oxygen tent. I can still picture Lisa, the very sweet physical therapist who helped me to walk again as the disease weakened and my body strengthened. But I didn't remember much else until forty years later.

I was sitting beside six-year-old Jack at Children's Hospital of Michigan. Jack was having a spinal injection of chemotherapy for his blood cancer. This was our first time working together and Jack was very interested in using the breathing technique that martial artists use. He was responding well but for some reason I was beginning to get anxious. I noticed that the nurse standing by his head was leaning down on Jack's hands. "You're holding him too tight," I suddenly heard myself say, my voice rising inappropriately. This outburst startled the nurse, and I quickly indicated that everything was okay. But it wasn't. All of a sudden, I was the six-year-old child being held down and it was really hurting me. The memory of one particular spinal tap at Montefiore Hospital, when I was so weak that I was unable to speak beyond a whisper, was suddenly in my front of my eyes. I remembered being held down in a fetal position. Moving during a spinal tap can cause the needle to do damage to the central nervous system. The nurse near my head pressed my two wrists together and held them down against the bed with all her weight. She was really hurting me, a lot. I tried to beg her to let up just a bit, but I couldn't talk. I remember mouthing the words, "I promise I won't move—please—you are hurting me." She wasn't looking at my face and my voice was not making its way out of my mouth. It was terrifying. While my wrists eventually healed, the feeling of total weakness and victimization never left me. Three decades later, I walked into the infirmary of Camp Simcha and stopped a procedure that was overwhelming Josh, who was being held down so his port could be accessed for chemotherapy. "Wait!" I yelled. This time they did. He was my first student in the world of martial arts therapy. Kids Kicking Cancer was born that day. I finally had gotten the words out of my mouth. What had been so painful, I had removed from my active memory. It was still there; I just needed Josh to help bring it out.

We all have UFOs, our unidentified fears and obstacles. They can influence our lives, sometimes for good, but most of the time they haunt us and hurt us. Even when we don't remember, the memory is there.

Charles

A CIRCLE OF BREATH

> *Stress chemicals tighten our muscles and impact every part of our body. The challenge with getting really sick is that we become more stressed. Cancer patients in particular not only have stress but often therapies that make them feel a lot sicker. Nausea is a very common and potentially debilitating side effect of treatment. Using your breath to flow through the discomfort even in these circumstances can have a profound impact. By cutting down on the stressors, your breath becomes an important part of healing.*

Every chronic syndrome carries with it the memories that *sap* our being—resulting in stress, anger, and pain. These forces of negativity remain within our brains and influence what we experience and how we respond. Sometimes, as we have just seen, the memory remains hidden. Other times, the memory's impact is actively present.

I recently received a call about a young man in his early twenties who was going through his second round of chemotherapy. Charles has been dealing with a cancer that will not leave his body. At best, managing his disease will be a lifelong onslaught of chemotherapies with a regimen that commonly produces nausea. Although we are much more sophisticated today in dealing with that side effect, there are still people who become very sick from the chemo. Charles is one of them. He not only gets sick to his stomach upon receiving his four-hour infusions, but the very act of walking into the hospital begins to make him nauseous, an hour before even hooking up to his meds.

Every experience once placed into our long-term memory stays somewhere in our brains. Unless a person suffers from a closed head injury, some neuron, somewhere, is holding on to that experience. Pain creates a very powerful memory because the pain message is so extraordinary. As noted, the body associates pain with necrosis or dying. Usually something has to be going very wrong to produce that pain, so the human body is prepped on a very primal level to respond to that distress. Pain thus becomes a valuable tool for our everyday life; without it we would be in trouble. Quadriplegics, for example, must deal with the very serious issues of body sores that can become life threatening. In contrast, healthy people, even as they sleep, receive messages from their bodies to move because outer layers of skin cells are being overly pressured by a particular position. That pain message goes to the brain. The brain, even in the midst of sleep, says, "Move!" and we end up turning over one way or the other, saving that tissue from dying. The absence of pain for the quadriplegic keeps the body in the same position and causes serious sores. Unfortunately, all levels of pain memories stick together. Whether we would rate them as a 1, 2, or 10, they are all grouped in the same neighborhood. Experiencing a level 1 pain can thus easily be the trigger for the memory of a 10. It does not even matter how "real" the actual pain message is: the memory of the pain can quickly rise to the fore of our conscious experience. The best example of this is the "phantom pain" I described above. The discomfort that our children feel from a leg even after that limb has been amputated can be very great. The leg may not be there, but the memory of the pain from that limb is still present and profoundly accounted for.

Nausea is in the same category of pain. It is a powerful message that something is wrong. It gets our attention and remains a strong memory. Even very small reminders of nausea can cause that memory to flood our minds and then our stomachs with the worst feelings we have already experienced. The faintest smell, sight, or feeling can bring back that stress response, triggering the memory of the nausea. It can often go downhill from there (though uphill might be a better metaphor).

Charles became so afraid of his nausea that he began getting sick at home and needed to take Ativan (Lorazepam), a relaxant. Even so, his nausea was going from bad to worse. I joined Charles at his school for a twenty-minute lesson in our breath work and explained to him how he was getting mugged by the memories in his brain well before he was getting his chemo. Understanding the reality that we face is an important part of our taking control. Nausea can often feel like a heavy block inside of our stomach, rising upward toward our throats. The more we focus on that experience, the greater the nausea. We teach our children how to allow their breath experience to create a circle. In the martial arts, there is a form of breathing that allows the air to "come in" an inch above the navel. With Charles, I asked him to imagine that breath as a cool, calming light that was making piercing holes through the heavy feelings in his stomach. As we blow that light out, we are removing all the tightness that surrounds the place of nausea or pain. The imagery we project is of actually seeing that exhale as darkness or smoke. That breath then becomes cleansed as it makes the circle back to the center of our being, below the stomach, and we again inhale the coolness that penetrates the discomfort. At that moment, Charles was feeling fine, sitting in the school lounge. Practicing the technique while the patient is doing well is an advantage for when the challenge begins. This young man quickly experienced the calming effect from focusing on the rhythm of his breath.

The next day, Charles was to begin another infusion cycle. He and I met outside the chemo room and began to practice breathing, focusing on the cooling breath. This may have looked pretty normal to the other people walking in for their treatments, most of whom were probably breathing as well. (Not that I checked; it's just that insurance won't cover the procedure if you stop breathing.) But if every patient who walked into an infusion center knew how easy it is to redirect their breath and to make that part of their therapy, there would be a lot less need for anti-nausea drugs. As it turned out, Charles did not need his Ativan that day, nor the next when he was flying solo. His brain had learned that it could create a memory of Power and Peace, and he was already looking forward to teaching this to our other kids; that Purpose would be the reward for his effort.

We all have our own infusion centers, even if we've never been a cancer patient. We get infused with the chemicals of stress, anger, and pain. Our brain stores memories of being hurt in relationships, of being put down by those we expected to pick us up, and of being failed by the people we had relied on. When those synaptic connections emerge from the dungeons of our psyche, we can easily become filled with that emotional emesis that pushes out the people in our lives instead of pulling them toward us. Listening to your voice when it gets too loud, feeling the tightness in your neck, your shoulders, your chest, or your stomach, is your biofeedback call that someone or something is not flowing, and that your essence is being submerged in chemicals that are not the real "you." Taking that breath to relax your neck, shoulders, back, and stomach while blowing out the feelings of darkness does as much for all of us as it does for our young patients whose chemical invasions are part of their therapies.

Lani and Jennifer

TAKING A BREATHER

> *Few things stress the body more than when we feel deprived of oxygen to breathe. Pain, fear, and anger can often literally take your breath away. That pales in comparison to someone going through an asthmatic episode. Unfortunately, there is a vicious cycle. Feeling that we can't breathe creates great stress that in turn makes it even harder to breathe. However, the Breath Brake used by our Kids Kicking Cancer children is relevant even to asthmatics.*

We have seen the negative cycle that takes place especially when you get sick. If your brain registers nausea or pain, it will likely hit your stress buttons. The more stress you have, the greater the discomfort. Feeling worse now? Welcome to more stress. And this goes on and on. Breaking that cycle before it reaches a crescendo of disaster can be accomplished with the focused approach of your Breath Brake.

However, there are times that your very breath may fall victim to stress chemicals and other factors such as allergies or disease. When the body gets that feeling of suffocation, it may seem impossible to effectively use your breath as a tool for taking control. Millions of people whose breathing for one reason or another is compromised know this feeling all too well.

Noah and Cherie Levi are dear friends of ours who came to our house for a Friday night dinner not long ago. We were having a wonderful time together when their fifteen-year-old daughter, Lani, began to wheeze. An asthmatic, Lani took out her inhaler to promote her breathing. After a few minutes, she again started feeling constricted. Noah excused himself and took Lani outside to the cool air to catch her breath. A few minutes later they were back, and it seemed matters had improved. Unfortunately, it didn't take long for her discomfort to return. Noah stood up and apologized, saying that they would be heading home to give Lani her meds and put her to sleep. It was a regimen they were used to. I, of course, didn't want them to have to leave so early in the evening, and I certainly hated to see such a sweet young lady in distress. "May I sit with Lani for a few minutes outside?" I asked her parents. "Why not?" Cherie shrugged, and Lani and I went out to the porch.

As we sat there, I shared with her the story of Jennifer Taylor. Jennifer was seventeen years old when she was diagnosed with Hodgkin's lymphoma. She has had a rough journey with her evolving medical protocols but finally had some success with an experimental phase 1 drug treatment that had left her cancer-free for the last two years. She is very grateful to the doctors at Children's Hospital of Michigan for saving her life. Her treatment, however, did not come without a profound toll on her slight frame. Jennifer's lungs were damaged enough that she has to walk around with an oxygen tank. She doesn't let this keep her from her karate classes, though. No matter how bad she's feeling, Jennifer will do anything to make those sessions with us, even with her oxygen in tow. When she comes forward to demonstrate the power breathing we do in class, she tells everyone how vital it is for her to be able to do her Breath Brake when her lungs seem to be struggling. Jennifer is constantly teaching both children and adults how to use one's breath to relax the body even though a low oxygen level naturally tenses you up.

Lani listened intently, as if Jennifer had been sitting there with us on the porch. "You know what our kids go through," I told Lani. "If we can teach you the same breathing techniques that they learn to help your breathing, you could thank Jennifer for inspiring you. It would mean a lot to her. Are you up for a try?" It was clear that Lani was very motivated, but she was still having some difficulty with her breath. We needed to relax her and slow down the alarm that was going off in her head. "Sit back in the chair," I told her. "Let's go through a meditation together." I began by trying to get Lani to focus on the coolness of the air she was inhaling and the warmth of the breath she was blowing out. The very act of focusing on her breath lent a calmness to her breathing. I asked her to imagine a sandy beach washed by the gentle waves rolling in and then bubbling out. It was clear from her posture that her frame was changing and her breathing returning to a relaxed state. When we came out of the meditation, we spoke about her breath and the enormous fear that comes over her when she feels her oxygen compromised. Every memory of her brain begins to shout. The overwhelming triggers of fear well up inside her at the smallest indication of constriction in her airway. She responds with the stress chemicals multiplying the feelings of tightness and of her lack of oxygen. To combat this, we began working on a very calming Breath Brake that she could use to relax that stress while creating a gentle flow of breath in a circular motion that she could imagine in her mind. In twenty minutes, Lani had mastered a breathing technique that recentered her breath and relaxed her body. In a half hour we were back at the dinner table with our families. Lani was beaming. And not just because she was now breathing freely: she also knew she was going to be able to help the children of Kids Kicking Cancer by using their techniques in her life. Six months later, I received a beautiful note from Lani. "I can't thank you, Jennifer, and all the children of Kids Kicking Cancer enough," she wrote. "Ever since I learned how to focus on the circle of my breath, I have not needed my inhaler."

This is not to say that every asthma sufferer will never again need medicine, or that the Breath Brake is the elixir for all of life's problems. The point, rather, is that when a person has difficulty breathing, it is usually not possible for the human mind to look at the situation with detached academic interest. We're not Vulcans, after all. On the Starship Enterprise, Mr. Spock could be diagnosed with a rare mutating virus and merely respond with a raised eyebrow: "Fascinating." Those of us without pointy ears, however, have to accept the human condition. We will very naturally dress ourselves in fear and kindle memories of stress, anger, and pain that will ride our systems into a frenzy of negative responses. But understanding the mechanism that *saps* us allows us to intervene, to retake control of our bodies and thus of our lives. It starts with the power of our breath. Allowing that breath to simply relax your muscles is the first step toward joining the circle of heroes. We begin to take control. We thank the kids. They have less pain, and we have a more powerful life.

Kevin and Yossi

WHEN YOUR SIGN ISN'T CANCER

Today we understand the connection between pain and fear: it's a vicious cycle. The pain leads to fear that then multiplies the pain until it becomes overwhelming inside our brains. When the point of stress is acute, the voice of pain is very loud. Calming that voice requires us to speak first, then louder and faster, until we can take control of our stressors.

I was on call one warm summer afternoon when my cell phone went off with an urgent message from our Kids Kicking Cancer emergency switchboard. The operator on the other end wasted no time: "It's Kevin from Brooklyn. He's in a lot of pain." "Put him through," I said as my pulse quickened. A second later, the earpiece on my phone was filled with a primal and penetrating scream: "I can't!" Kevin, one of our sickle cell patients at Brooklyn University Hospital, was in the first throes of a vascular occlusive crisis (VOC). There are very few experiences as painful as when the misshapen hemoglobin of a child's body begins to engorge the blood vessels with no place to go. "Help me, I can't!" He was sobbing and his pleas were coming rapid-fire. We teach our therapists that intervention with that level of pain crisis is something like riding a runaway horse. As the horse is galloping away in fright, pulling back on the reins is counterproductive. The rider has to push the horse a little bit faster and then very gradually pull back to take control. In response to Kevin, I made my voice a bit louder and faster until I was able to get him to take that breath. "You can do it, Kevin. Take that breath." Then: "Come on, Kevin, you are very powerful." Then: "You are a powerful martial artist. You can take control." Then, slower: "Good, you're doing it. Let's focus that pain out of your body. Blow it out! You can do it, Kevin." In about ten minutes, Kevin was in his safe place and he was doing a meditation that embraced him and calmed his body. Twenty minutes later, his Mom picked up the phone. "I can't believe this," she told me. "Kevin fell asleep." Maybe not so surprising, though. I was a pulpit rabbi for almost twenty years. Nobody puts people to sleep better than I do.

Sickle cell disease isn't cancer, but in many pediatric centers sickle cell patients are treated by the same hematologists. We began taking sickle cell patients into Kids Kicking Cancer because at several of our hospitals, they would see our little heroes in their karate uniforms and want to join the program. Their crises can be very stress-driven and the level of their pain can be extraordinary. We now treat hundreds of sickle cell children throughout the United States and Canada. The mission of Kids Kicking Cancer is "to ease the pain of very sick children, while empowering them to heal physically, spiritually, and emotionally." The sickle cell population certainly fits right in.

Over the years, we have worked with many different populations of children in pain. They all receive our uniforms, which on the back have the logo of Kids Kicking Cancer, a circle of children's karate uniforms. Together the circle creates a star. The white background and the configuration of the star makes it seem that a light is shining from the middle of the image. The logo's message of inspiration is not limited to children battling cancer; our message has resonated in all types of facilities. One of the most moving stories we have witnessed is about an eighteen-year-old boy who was being treated for a significant brain trauma injury at a hospital where we work in Ossining, New York. This young man had an extremely difficult time doing his physical therapy. It was thus significant that the very first time he stood up by himself was to put on his karate uniform. A star of light, indeed.

As our Heroes Circle continues to grow, we are frequently asked to expand our therapy to many different categories of pediatric issues. Once I was called to the University of Michigan's Burn Center to visit Yossi Menora, who had been a passenger on a small two-engine airplane piloted by his grandfather two days prior. Yossi's grandfather was an avid pilot who was preparing to fly four of his grandchildren, visiting from Israel, back from a holiday on Mackinaw Island in the upper regions of Michigan. Somehow, the plane failed upon takeoff and crashed onto a highway, breaking in two and turning into an inferno. Yossi's grandfather was killed immediately, along with Yossi's two sisters and a cousin. Yossi, who had been trying to rest in the back of the plane, was thrown from his perch upon impact. Although he survived, over 60% of his body was badly burned. Yossi still has flashbacks of the crash and the life-saving helicopter flight that transported him to the U of M hospital.

When my wife Ruthie and I first met Sima, Yossi's mom, her daughters' bodies were being transported back to Israel for the funeral. Shalom, Yossi's father, would soon leave to accompany his family to the funeral, and Sima would remain in Michigan to be with her son through his ordeal. Sima spent more time comforting us than we could possibly do for her. The hours seemed like minutes as we shared our own stories and experiences waiting for the first of several surgeries for Yossi to conclude. When I first saw Yossi awake, he looked more like a mummy from a museum than a thirteen-year-old boy. Hooked up to machinery that was keeping him alive, his young frame was dwarfed inside the bed. Sima was anxious that I would connect with her son. Given his intense situation, he had pretty much dismissed social workers, psychologists, psychiatrists, or anyone else who wanted to help him with his traumatic episode. Yossi was dealing with extraordinary pain. As the nerve endings seared by the fire began to regenerate, the messages they sent to his brain mingled with the tragedy of his family. Together, all this was suffocating his very being. Even if I could have gotten his attention, it was clear I would be competing with a lot of other stuff. "Yossi," I told him, "we have some mutual friends who asked me to visit you. However, I have to tell you right out, I have an agenda." I let him know that we teach karate to kids with cancer, but that we had never worked with a burn victim before. "You have been through hell and there is nobody better able to teach other kids how to do this than a young man who has been through it. I need your help." Something changed in Yossi's eyes. Even from within his bandages, the soul of a hero was stirring. No one could make any sense of what he had been through. But if he could somehow get beyond the valley of the shadow of death by projecting light and teaching others, then somewhere, someplace, he could find a purpose.

Yossi was an amazing student and he became a great friend. He used his breath to increase his range of motion even after the grafts made his limbs feel as if they were cemented to his body. He fought through the pain of the outside burns and the inside wounds of his soul with an amazing spirit. And having Gerard Butler in his cheering section didn't hurt. Yossi was a big Gerard Butler fan.

I had shown Gerry a picture of Yossi, all hooked up to his intensive-care machinery, and then asked our actor friend to give his fan a call. What had been a pain-strained voice turned very teenager-like after hearing the distinctive brogue of the Scottish film star on the phone. But it works in two directions: every time we get somebody like Colin Farrell, Jessica Biel, Hugh Jackman, Josh Hartnett, Demi Moore, Miley Cyrus, or Christian Bale (to name just a few) to speak to the kids, these adults articulate how much they learn from the strengths of our young heroes. Kevin Jonas Sr. shared with me that when he told his sons, the Jonas Brothers, about Rabbi G., they thought I must be a rapper. But now, when they tell our children know how much they (the Jonas Brothers) have learned from them (our mighty little warriors), it leaves an indelible impression. Nobody tells children how heroic they are more effectively than the people these kids look at as heroes, Hollywood stars and sports greats.

The day that Ruthie and I came to the burn center to bring Yossi and his mother back to the airport to return home, I knew that this young man was more than anxious about getting on a plane, even a large commercial one. His last flight did not end so well. I texted Gerard Butler, who was in South Africa filming a movie, to let him know that Yossi was leaving the hospital. Gerry called me immediately. Hearing gunfire in the background, my first thought was that either Gerry was in the middle of a war or visiting the Bronx neighborhood where I grew up. "No, they're filming a fight scene, but let me talk to Yossi. I have a few minutes." "Do me a favor," I said. "Call my cell in five minutes. He'll be in the car then. Let's surprise him." As we pulled up to the front of the hospital and picked up a very nervous passenger wrapped in spacesuit-like burn gear, the phone rang. "Yossi, it's for you," I said. When Yossi heard the deep warmth and love from his favorite star, every part of his body began to relax. In five minutes, this apprehensive burn patient became a kid again. He got on the plane knowing that he was inspiring the world. And from there, it took less than a year before Yossi found the first burn patient he could mentor. From Hollywood superstars to young boys and girls, it really is a Heroes Circle.

For Yossi, having a tool that allowed him to know that the pain would not overwhelm him was crucial to effectively using our therapy. Using your breath to begin to take control is a tool we can all use no matter what the pain. When the pain screams loudly, we just have to get even louder in our own way. As strong as the pain message may be, the power of the human spirit is stronger.

LESSON 24

Olivia

BLOW OUT THE PAIN

> *Most physical pain is a staccato message in your mind that can make your life absolutely miserable. Creating a circle of energy flow with your breath is a powerful message to your brain that can actually lower your pain. From our little heroes to your bad back, creating a continual circular flow is a very effective extension of the Breath Brake.*

Pain creates stress. Stress is the starter culture of fear. The perception of pain increases and contributes to a cycle that can wreak havoc on our bodies and our long-term health.

It is said that there are two types of Americans, those who have back pain and those who will have back pain. The notorious backache is a great example of how stress makes pain worse—often, a whole lot worse. Any time there is an insult to the body, the muscular skeletal system forges a primal response, tightening the muscles around the injury to protect if from further damage. That self-protective response often causes cramping and spasming, resulting in worse pain and a longer-lasting handicap. Of course, the memories of past pains make that process more intense, tightening the area and leading to a cycle of debilitation. The *Journal of the American Medical Association* estimated that the amount spent on back pain in the United States in 2007 was $86 billion. A great deal of that money went for analgesics and relaxants that do what the human brain is really very capable of doing itself: relaxing the muscles that are cramping much more than just our style. Even better, the breathing comes without side effects. The same cannot be said for pharmaceuticals.

When one thinks of pain, what usually comes to mind is either the staccato message of stabbing discomfort or the dull thud of generalized agony. Pain is so powerful that our focus seems to get stuck on the sharpness of the sensation. It is almost as if our very identity starts and stops on the nerve endings of that pain.

Of course, pain is the body's way of saying, "Warning!" As we have discussed, the body senses that some form of potentially life-threatening danger in that area has begun. This is obviously a priority brain message. Pain is "hot-wired" into our primal being as the protective fight-or-flight message of life and death. It does not have to be the only message in our system, however.

I know of a young man named Yoel who was a gunner in a tank that was called to the Golan Heights in the October 1973 war between Israel and Syria. His position was overrun by Syrian forces, and his tank, now greatly outnumbered, was hit by a missile early in the fire fight. Yoel did not have a second to check out the damage his tank had sustained; just staying alive required his full focus, and that meant destroying the enemy tanks in his range quickly and efficiently. Two hours later he was finally able to pull back. Only then did he notice that the earlier shell had torn through the side armor of his tank and mangled his legs. He immediately passed out.

It is amazing what the brain can do to push away one message of pain when another more immediate threat to life is present. All pain is in the brain. Even when it starts and ends at a particular injury, it must first travel through the brain to be processed as pain. How much attention the pain message gets has a lot to do with how our brain prioritizes the damage in light of other messages.

What we are learning today about the cycles of pain is that we have more control over the process than we may have thought. Relaxing the muscles can significantly lower the perception of pain. Lowering the pain further relaxes the muscles. Putting ourselves more in control of the situation creates a signaling of the parasympathetic system. Memories of traumatic pain become weaker, and rational strategies to create flowing movements channel away the staccato messages of agony. It starts with your breath.

Until 2010, Kids Kicking Cancer received major funding through the federal Centers for Disease Control and Prevention in Atlanta, but that expired with a vote in Congress to end all earmarked appropriations. It was around that time that I found myself doing a lot of Breath Brakes. There was much talk then about wasteful government spending that no one could defend, like the infamous "Bridge to nowhere," but it was nice that Larry King singled us out on CNN as an example of a government-supported program that actually saved money. Our senators in Michigan, Carl Levin and Debbie Stabenow, and our congressman, Joe Knollenberg, had all been very supportive of our program for years. Even the chairman of the Senate Appropriations Committee, Tom Harkin of Iowa, had our back, as it were, but unfortunately it wasn't enough. During one visit I made to Capitol Hill, Senator Harkin told me that he believed in our program. He himself had back trouble, needed surgery, had gone through occupational therapy, physical therapy, and who knows what else. "Nothing helped my back," he said, "until I went to see Dr. Sarno, who told me how to use my mind to release my back."

Dr. John Sarno wrote many books on a particular cause of back pain that he called TMS, or Tension Myositis Syndrome. Myositis is the muscle inflammation that can be caused by tension or stress. His focus was on repressed emotional stressors and the need for getting to the root emotional causes of back pain. It is important to know that stress not only inflames the muscles of the back but can do a downright nasty job of inflaming our heart muscles as well, accounting for a significant percentage of heart disease and stroke.

"Neurotics build castles in the sky. Psychotics live in them and the therapist collects the rent," or so the familiar quip goes. In the present context, this suggests that the process of releasing back pain and thus countering the constant clamping of the surrounding muscles may be a lot simpler and less expensive than psychotherapy.

On my desk at our Kids Kicking Cancer office in Detroit is a beautiful drawing of a healing breath created by one of our little martial artists, Olivia Thompson. The picture looks like angels with the words "Breathe in the

Light and Blow Out the Darkness" inscribed below. When the children of Kids Kicking Cancer focus on their breath, the wisp of air turns into a healing light that they envision channeling through their pain and illness. The light is so powerful that they don't want to let it go. It is the darkness of fear, pain, anger, and sickness that they are blowing out. Olivia maintained that breath and light even as a brain tumor was trying to snuff every element of life from her eleven-year-old body. Olivia's back hurt along with a whole host of other tribulations. She refused to give in to the pain, however. Olivia created a circle with her breathing that gave her spirit a power over her body that belied her young age. No matter what we are going through, we can keep that flow of light circulating through our pain and distress.

Pain is staccato, strangling, and attention-seeking. Creating a circle of breath that goes through the pain is an exercise that is quite simple to do. Our children know that when martial artists approach a target, sometimes the attack is straight and direct. However, other times we approach from the right or from above or perhaps from the left. Accordingly, we ask children to see which approach pokes the greatest holes in their pain. "Try allowing the light to puncture the ball of pain from the right, the top, the bottom," we tell them. We also ask them to work on resizing the light to create the most effective assault on the discomfort. Some children like to work with a laser-like power that makes small spaghetti holes through their pain. Others prefer to bring out the heavy strobes to blow through their adversary. The breath guides this healing light inward and pushes out the pain with the exhale. The brain rewires the pain experience, and the body learns that you don't have to be a victim of the messages of stress, anger, and pain. Our children can help you release the tightness of your back and the burden of pain and stress. Simply breathe in the light and blow out the darkness. If your breathing relaxes your muscles and allows the circle of breath to poke through your pain, you create your own powerful circle while joining ours.

ax

A CIRCLE OF THE HEART

> *The secret of our Heroes Circle is simple. You lower your stress, pain, and anger when you succeed at caring for others. The natural chemicals of peace within us are activated when we cling to social circles that create a positive energy. When you do for others, you are the greatest recipient. The more you are concerned with the pain of another person, the more you can proclaim freedom from your own discomfort.*

Max Ritvo is a student of poetry and literature at Yale and a professor of life at Kids Kicking Cancer. In high school he was diagnosed with Ewing's sarcoma, a rare cancer of the bone or soft tissue, and he went through a difficult regimen of interventions and treatments. He is also an accomplished martial artist. His mother, Ariella, a professor at several medical schools, knows way too much to not be overwhelmed by the challenges of her son's disease. She is also a dear friend and an extraordinarily beautiful person. Max was immediately drawn into the power of our mission and quite helpful in shaping several meditations that we still use. His cancer now in remission, he has served several years as a member of the national Kids Kicking Cancer board. More importantly, he has shared his unique breathing techniques with many others. All told, Max has made his way through this journey, including less than fully effective courses of chemotherapy, with a wisdom and strength usually reserved for the ancient sages and the tested heroes of mythology.

Samuel Stein was diagnosed with abdominal migraines in the seventh grade. He is an extremely smart young man who waxed philosophical about his frequent attacks of debilitating stomach pain and cycles of vomiting. He was very touched that Max took the time to teach him some of the meditations that had helped him through his chemotherapy. Sam also understood that by teaching him, Max was achieving a greater purpose for his own disease journey. Max was driven knowing that Sam was taking the time and effort to focus on his stomach pain because it was benefitting Max, too. We named this the Heroes Circle. Max and Sam were among the first to inspire each other with the themes of Power, Peace, Purpose.

Five years after Max and Sam successfully worked together, I received a call from a woman named Robin Lash. Her eleven-year-old son Yale was suffering from gastrointestinal attacks that left him doubled over in pain. These pains returned again and again, accompanied by vomiting. After the standard tests indicated no specific organic source, Yale was diagnosed with abdominal migraines. Robin had heard that Kids Kicking Cancer had a great track record reducing the pain in sick children. We met for a while, and Yale was a great student in the breathing and meditations I showed him. I asked that he call me when his next episode occurred to give us the opportunity to put our work into action. That call came less than twenty-four hours later. Robin and Yale were at his doctor's office for a regular checkup when Yale fell out of his seat and was writhing on the floor in pain. She called me as she was bringing her son back home to bed. I went to meet them there.

It is difficult to watch anyone in pain, but it's worse when the patient is a child. Yale was in bed and very uncomfortable. He reported the pain as a nine out of ten. "OK, Yale," I told him, "it's time for you to start using your martial arts power and begin to take control of this pain." We began a meditation in which Yale focused on the feeling of coolness when he began to inhale. He then noticed how it was a little bit warmer when he blew it out. We kept focusing on this slight difference in temperature between breathing in and breathing out. We then concentrated on traveling inside his head all the way up to the top of his skull, where he would allow every muscle in his scalp to begin to relax. Then he would descend into his forehead while visualizing a waterfall gently cascading downward, pulling the muscles behind his eyes and then his cheeks gently apart, flowing openly and gently through the bottom of his face. Muscle by muscle, Yale continued to descend in this inner journey, shedding the messages of pain from his stomach and continuing to relax every part of his body. We call this technique the Body Scan, and we use it in all our Kids Kicking Cancer classes, combining breathing and mind exercises to relax the body. The goal is to remove the tightness that accompanies the pain, and with it the pain itself frequently diminishes. An astounding 88% of the children who reported pain found a significant lessening when they finished the Body Scan.

Within forty minutes, Yale's pain descended from a nine to a six. In forty-five minutes, he was fast asleep. Until then, Yale's frequent episodes of pain and vomiting had resulted in missing the next three to six days of school. This time, Yale was back in school the next day. It was easy, of course, to expand our circle by connecting Yale to Sam. From Max to Sam to Yale, the Heroes Circle is a description of light channeled from person to person. As the children bring in that light, they are illuminating the world. You undoubtedly have many people around you who can use your wisdom and caring. The more you can give to them, the greater your ability to focus on the light and blow away the darkness.

Blake

REFLECTIONS ON A LAKE

> *The medical community has been behind the curve with regard to the human brain's power to control so many aspects of our health. There are numerous examples of how long it has taken doctors to accept the reality that the mind and body are intimately connected. For many physicians, it is easier to prescribe a pill than to treat the entire person. The evidence for the mind-body connection is quite impressive, however. I have learned from the children how even our body temperature can respond to the power of our thoughts.*

In 1996 I wrote a poem entitled "Blake's Lake." It was in memory of a twelve-year-old boy, Blake Kiven, who taught me a great deal about the power of meditation. He had gone through a difficult bone marrow transplant. It is not an infrequent side effect of that procedure that the new marrow filling the body will attack the cells of the host. In some transplants, doctors even attempt to promote a little bit of GVHD (graft versus host disease) since the graft may take on the leukemia. Unchecked, however, GVHD can eat away at the very body the transplant was meant to save. In Blake's case, he had a graft that was taking apart his body from the inside out. His skin was paper thin and his strength was ebbing.

Blake came to Camp Simcha from Glencoe, Illinois. The camp is located in the mountains of New York State bordering the winding Delaware River, a breathtakingly beautiful area. Even in the summer, the air at night can get a bit chilly. It was there that Blake demonstrated to me how the power of meditation can not only release our pain, it can even change our body temperature.

The first night of camp, I was called to Blake's bunk. Despite the application of a large number of blankets, Blake was shivering. He was a real trooper, but it was clear that he wasn't at all comfortable. Transferring him to the warm infirmary would have been an easy call. Something told me, however, that he needed to stay with his bunkmates. He had already had more than his share of isolation from his friends. So the plan now was to get Blake to take control of his shivering. Blake was very open to my attempts as I sat next to his bed. We first got Blake to focus on the warmth of the air he was blowing out of his body. Our Body Scan clearly left him more relaxed. Then we created an image together where we were sitting on the banks of the most beautiful lake. We called it "Blake's Lake." As we were watching the gentle waves on the lake continuing back and forth and the little bubbles that washed up on the shore, we were suddenly blinded by super-bright sunlight creeping out from behind the clouds. This was a powerful illumination that filled our heads with light and our bodies with the blanketing heat of its rays. Blake began to feel this heat washing over his shoulders and then the rest of his body. In twenty minutes, Blake had so warmed himself that we needed to pull away layers of blankets. With only two remaining, Blake fell asleep. He remained in his bunk with his friends. The next night, he was asleep after a fifteen-minute meditation. By the end of the two-week camp, he was able to do this meditation for himself. It was a technique that he used with great bravery through multiple surgeries and ongoing health struggles. However, even with the most advanced medical interventions, the price of each day of his life was becoming too much of a burden for his little body to bear.

About eight months after the camp season, I received a phone call from Blake. "I need to tell my parents I can't do this anymore. Is it okay for me to tell them that?" This was a conversation I was to repeat with too many young heroes through the years. "Yes, Blake, it is okay. You have done more than anyone could ever ask and you did it with the strength and focus of someone five times your age. No one could have asked for more. You can tell your parents that you can't go further." "Are you sure?" "They'll understand. They love you. We all love you."

Three weeks later I was privileged to speak at Blake's funeral. There were more than a thousand people there. Two weeks after that, I was so inspired by this young boy that I penned the poem describing our special place and the power of a young boy whose mighty presence could not be moved even in the face of the most vicious storm. This was a lake whose light continued to reflect on the world. The waves of that lake continue to flow back and forth. The power of those waves comes from the heavens.

Blake and his friends are world-class heroes. Even in their absence, they remain our teachers. From Blake we learned that we can even control the temperature of our body, and if we can do that, then we can control most of the pains we face. It's a lesson that the children of Kids Kicking Cancer teach to the world.

LESSON 27

Juanita

A LIGHT DIET

Obesity is just another casualty of stress. Anxiety affects what you eat and how you eat it. The more stressed we are, the more the body craves the worst junk food. The irony, of course, is that the more junk we eat, the more stress we create. The health of many people is thereby compromised by the widespread stress in our lives and the abundance of junk food around us. Using Power, Peace, Purpose, however, we can take control of our diets along with the rest of our lives.

By 2005 we had already seen the growth of the Heroes Circle concept from child to child many times over. It was now time to reach out to other groups of children. That year we began to have our children work with two very different populations: one was a group of overweight kids who had enrolled in obesity programs at a few New York hospitals, while the other group was students prone to extraordinary anger and violent outbursts, who were assigned to us by Detroit school principals. Both obesity and youth violence are significant public health issues that drain the resources of our medical infrastructure and schools. The Centers for Disease Control and Prevention was a willing participant in our study.

In each group, we taught the children that they are martial artists and that the stressors that can so easily control us can be conquered by our inner power. It all starts with a breath. For the obesity groups, we would explain how pain and frustrations take over our brains and say "Supersize me" when we walk into a fast-food place. (I always found it interesting that an Orthodox rabbi was teaching children how to walk into a McDonald's and take control of their lives.) Of course, this wasn't really about eating; it was more about letting the light pierce the heavy clouds of saturated fats.

We taught the children that martial artists are always aware that they could be attacked. Our greatest adversary, however, always lies within. No one can do as much damage to us as we can to ourselves. In our meetings with the children we gave them nutritional information, but none of the usual stuff about fatty foods or unhealthy treats. We taught them about power foods that could strengthen a body and empty foods that could weaken a body, even that of a martial artist. When our participants approached the counter at the fast-food joint, they needed to know they were going to get "mugged," but also that they had the power to respond as martial artists in training. The real key to the program, however, was introducing them to our very special world of Kids Kicking Cancer children. Our little martial artists are constantly being attacked by pain, fear, and anger. They regularly have to use their breath to focus themselves toward victory. Of course, our overweight fighters were made to understand that their personal victory over their pounds would make every one of their peers with cancer and sickle cell feel as if they were responsible for teaching that message. "You guys," we told our overweight group, "can help these children have a purpose in their lives. Could you do that for them?"

Juanita was barely twelve years old, with a beautiful angelic face that seemed out of place on a 250-pound body that was less than five feet tall. When I first met Juanita, I don't think she knew how to smile. The weight she was pulling around was measured in the stress of a child who did not have a mom or dad in her life. It was evidenced in her fights with her grandmother, who would desperately try to get her granddaughter to leave their tiny Brooklyn apartment and connect with other children. Her stress could be heard in her voice, which was sad and uncertain. Juanita had heard of both cancer and sickle cell anemia, but she had never thought about the pain that children with these conditions have to endure. It certainly didn't make her happy to hear that other children suffered so much, but it put her own life into perspective. What was more important, we made clear to her, was that our sickle cell and cancer children needed her. She could become a martial artist with the goal of losing weight to help these other children feel good and focus away from their pain because she was learning from them.

And that's what happened. Children with cancer and sickle cell disease experienced less pain because other children were learning from their techniques. Juanita and her friends in the overweight programs were working hard because they wanted to help these other kids with cancer and sickle cell. The circle was getting larger—but their waistlines weren't.

We were told that if the weight of the kids in our new obesity program just stayed the same, it would be a win. That's because as children get taller, even if their weight remains steady their body mass index decreases. But that's not exactly the way it worked out. At the end of twenty weeks, the girls *lost* an average of sixteen pounds. Juanita lost twenty, the best in the group. In that short time we saw many of these young women go from being fat, unhappy girls to martial artists with a purpose. Juanita began to smile. She started leaving her apartment. She wanted to help other children in pain. She had Power, Peace, Purpose. Although the funding for that particular program eventually ended, we saw clearly how easy it was to transmit our message to a different population.

In the Detroit Public School program, principals were more than happy to try to find a way to stem the violence in their schools. Studies clearly indicate that children who master some form of martial arts are less likely to get involved in violent altercations. Why? Because those kids don't have to prove anything to themselves or to others. To begin our program, each child was given a uniform and learned real martial arts. But perhaps even more important, they were also introduced to real martial artists: the little heroes of Kids Kicking Cancer. The impact was powerful.

One of the mottos in our organization is that there is no such thing as a problem. If our kids can go through what they have to deal with on a daily basis, then the rest of us can handle whatever comes along. Every "problem" can be reframed as a "challenge." If you're really good at reframing, then a "challenge" becomes an "opportunity." And so, if we remember that "a perfect God created an imperfect world, perfectly," then it's easy to see that there's no problem!

Mottos are great for teaching, but confronting a seemingly overwhelming challenge is the greatest learning tool. When we found out that the federal monies that were so important to Kids Kicking Cancer were going away, it sure felt like a problem. Two Breath Brakes later, however, we realized we had an opportunity.

There are many corporations that are heavily involved in charitable work, but in light of the federal and state cutbacks in public money, there is increased competition for private funds. We, however, had something unique to offer in exchange. Part of our mission in empowering children has always been to have them teach others whenever and wherever possible. Certainly the employees of corporations have plenty of stress. The more stress, the greater their health issues. The greater the health issues, the greater the breakdown in communication and morale and worker productivity. Safety goes down. Profits go down. But when our children get their inevitable standing ovation after making their presentations, their pain goes down and their morale goes up. People watching respond in kind. After the Breath Brake, employees' quality of life rises, as do their safety, productivity, and even their company's profits. Our kids certainly had something real to offer corporate America.

On July 19, 2011, our children received a "thank you" email from Jane Lloyd. Jane assists our friend and board member, Arthur Weiss, whose law firm, Jaffe, Raitt, Heuer, and Weiss, has been a wonderful advocate and supporter for many years. Jane is also a cancer survivor who uses the breath work that our children have taught at the firm. In her email Jane wrote that she had been scheduled for some follow-up surgery just that morning. However, when she got to the doctor's office her blood pressure was through the roof. They were going to have to cancel the surgery, which would have been more than a minor inconvenience. Jane asked for just a few moments by herself. She closed her eyes and began to take her Breath Brake until she could feel her body relax. In just a few minutes her blood pressure was down to 128/82. Our children inspired her. The nurses in the office couldn't believe it. "It was simple," she responded. "I have the best teachers in the world."

That same year, our Heroes Circle began to expand further than we could have ever imagined. We brought a group of our young heroes from

Memorial Sloan Kettering Hospital in New York to teach a seminar to Pfizer executives in New York. Three days later I received a call from Fanny LaMonica, a Pfizer marketing executive who had attended the seminar. "Would you come to Rome to do a seminar for the Pfizer Italy employees?" she asked. "We would be happy to have you come with your wife. We will put you up in a beautiful five-star Rome hotel." Since my previous experience with hotels had been at a Motel 6, I wrongly assumed that a five-star hotel was a step down. Fortunately, it didn't take much to twist Ruthie's arm, and soon we were teaching Pfizer employees in Rome. But the most important result of the trip was that Pfizer Italy was interested in beginning our first Kids Kicking Cancer program in Europe. We found a wonderful attorney, Michele Pizzini, a martial artist himself, who volunteered to incorporate Kids Kicking Cancer Italy, and Fanny agreed to chair the newly formed board of directors. They were soon joined by a most extraordinary individual, Dr. Mark Palermo, a Hopkins-trained neuropsychiatrist and accomplished martial artist who had been using karate therapy for children with autism in Rome. He completely understood the power of our program and became a close friend and leading mentor for our efforts in Europe. Our first program opened at Bambino Gesu, the Vatican's children's hospital. I had graduated from McDonald's to the Vatican—not exactly places where I had expected to teach back when I was in rabbinical school.

As we spread out through the world, we see more and more that we can use our breath to focus ourselves and lower our blood pressure, our anger, and our fears. With that very focus we can also control our weight and our lives. It's a valuable lesson the whole world can use.

Avrami and Mohammed

THE WORLD BECOMES SMALLER

> *Mindfulness is a type of meditation that allows the practitioner to become aware of everything one perceives in nonjudgmental fashion. By not focusing on anything in particular and not labeling any feeling, thought, or sensation as bad, the meditator is able to diminish the reactive stress response that can often throw us into a negative spiral. However, the technique requires an equal dosage of "remindfulness," something that will help us remember this control on an ongoing basis until our brain has been trained to defeat stress automatically. Our kids can help.*

With Kids Kicking Cancer having a successful start in Italy and then establishing a beachhead throughout Europe, it seemed only natural that we would seek to extend the program to Israel. Meir and Yael, our son and daughter-in-law, live on the west coast of the Holy Land. Meir is a young businessman but already expert at networking. He knows everyone, it seems, and he has the gift of persuasion. I also have many friends in the martial arts world in Israel. A branch of Sifu Sober's Tora Dojo martial arts instructors has grown there under the able direction of Arthur Gribetz. Meir and Arthur helped to assemble a team for us, and we soon got to work training a wonderful group of social workers, psychologists, and other assorted black belts on how to use their martial arts as therapy for children. A grant from the Coville Foundation in Detroit was a major boost. Several important pediatric centers were very open to our program, but we chose Alyn Hospital as the site of our Israeli pilot program in large part because their director of sports medicine, Uri Lahav, was a black belt whom we trained for several months. On the first day of our practicum at the hospital, Dr. Emanuel Kornitzer, the director of rehabilitation, gave us a brief introduction to the children we would be seeing. Every fifteen minutes a new child was introduced to us, and I assigned one of our martial arts trainees to offer the child one of the various techniques we had studied together.

Avrami, a twelve-year-old boy with a tumor on his spine, hobbled into the gym with his walker. His pain was clearly written in the creases of his young face. Dr. Andrew Chernick, a tai chi master, approached Avrami to engage him in his "safe place." As part of our therapy we help the child focus on a particular location that carries some personal meaning and comfort. That place is a fortress of security that a child can go to in his or her mind at any challenging time. It may be a garden or a palace with beautiful colors and wonderful sounds that we can walk through, taking us away from a frightening medical environment. Many children use the beach as their safe place, remembering a particularly carefree, fun time long before they were confronted with hospitals and treatments. Some of the children describe their grandparents' home. One little girl said that being on the shores of France with her uncle was her "happiest place in the world." Avrami was a little different from most kids. When asked what would be his safe place, he replied, after a moment's hesitation, "The study hall." That was where, in the middle of his school, he would love to go and open up his volume of Talmud to study, and so that was where our martial arts therapist would now direct him. First Dr. Chernick allowed Avrami to focus on his breathing and relax his body. He then asked him to imagine opening the large wooden doors that framed the entrance of the study hall. Avrami felt the contours of his seat and the softness of the cushion that padded it. As he sat down, he gently passed his hand over the leather binding of the ancient tome. This student, who sadly had spent way too much time out of school, opened up the book and peered at the letters of the law, those curling figures turned into symbols of light dancing off the page and swimming into his head. It was just moments before that he had been wearing a mask of pain, but now his face was bathed in a joyous light, beaming, emitting a glow of happiness that moved me so much that my eyes filled with tears. I turned toward the wall so as not to be observed and break the magic of that moment. This was power and it was peace. His purpose was evident to us all.

The next child who entered the gym was a little older. He was in a wheelchair. His name was Mohammed and his language was Arabic. His face transformed from pain to joy in the very same way. His light was no less bright nor any less powerful. He was using every part of his essence to increase the movement of his left arm. Every breath brought Mohammed more focus and greater power. It also brought more light, enough to illuminate the room. In fact, between them, Avrami and Mohammed were lighting up the world. The circle was becoming clearer. It did not matter if we were in Jerusalem or Detroit or the Vatican, if we were Jews, Christians, or Muslims. These children were replacing darkness with light and learning what they could do rather than being imprisoned by what they couldn't. They were journeying into their very essence. These young warriors were giving us a mandate to create a Heroes Circle that would join the hands of kids across the planet, all teaching Power, Peace, Purpose.

Thousands of adults in seminars across the globe have seen our children. Almost all of them have given the boys and girls a standing ovation that girds these children with an amazing strength; this in turn helps to refocus them beyond pain as they go back to the clinics and hospitals where they continue to receive treatments. These seminars give our children purpose. Judging from the testimony of our attendees and the hundreds of emails we have received, it's clear that the children have changed the lives of many people.

As I now travel throughout the public health world and lecture about stress and the multiple dangers to our health that it presents, I also see how simple it is to teach people in a one-hour session how to identify the tightness in their muscles and begin to take control of their stress with the Breath Brake. But ambivalence remains perhaps the most difficult obstacle to overcome when it comes to our health. We can teach people to exercise, eat properly, and much more. We can also inspire them in our sessions and leave them with greater motivation to take control of their lives than they have ever experienced before. I have already boasted that 97% of our adult participants in the Breath Brake seminars describe it as having had a "profound influence" on their lives. What I didn't tell you, however, was that it takes less than six weeks for that number to go down to about 18%. Our brains get distracted very easily—because the boss is too tough, the taxes are too high, the kids are too loud, and on and on—and so we lose focus and commitment. Just like that, we veer away from what's good for us and toward what *feels* good to us. So the real challenge is this: How do we keep the attention of those who have participated in our Breath Brake seminars one week, five weeks, ten weeks later?

To address this, we are developing a Breath Brake phone app. Your cell phone can sound an alarm at whatever interval you want. The alarm is the voice of a child announcing, "Time for your Breath Brake." Then, the users have the option to watch videos of the children teaching their breathing techniques or simply take that deep and calming Breath Brake on their own. After the user does so, he or she can record this on the touch screen, and the rising number of participants will register for the children to see wherever they are, on computer screens in their hospital rooms or on their iPads. Immediately they will be able to see that "Giuseppe in Rome" or "Fred in New York" is taking their Breath Brake. It's feedback in real time from around the world, and the children will have less pain knowing that people around the world are learning from them and are healthier as a result. Participants will do it for each other, a digital Heroes Circle. Integrating a focused breath into your life will, after a few weeks, train your brain to respond to the dangerous stress chemicals inside your body in a way that allows you to brake that downward rush. It will quickly become second nature in your head. The platform, however, will become the whole world.

Senator Carl and Barbara Levin have been wonderful friends of Kids Kicking Cancer for years. As the former head of the Senate Armed Services Committee, Carl has a profound concern about Post-Traumatic Stress Disorder among our military personnel, especially the rise in suicide among those who have returned from Afghanistan and Iraq. It was his idea to bring me to the Pentagon to talk to some of the Defense Department's own committees working on these issues. It's amazing to consider: our kids teaching the military how to use breathing to fight the stress of combat and post-combat trauma. Our heroes teaching real-life adult heroes is a perfect opportunity all around. In the meetings I have attended and presented at the Pentagon, I have met a whole crew of believers. As a result, many soldiers are now commanded into counseling. In the past, a soldier was far more likely to respond, "No sir, I am fine, sir" than "I would really like to share my feelings with you, sir." The Heroes Circle, however, offers another paradigm, and it's not simply "Soldier, you have a problem." It is also an opportunity to help a young child in pain. This much more closely fits the mold of positive response. Soldiers patrol dangerous outposts to protect these very children back home and can also help them by helping themselves. Just as the ancient samurai practiced meditative techniques to become better warriors, our modern-day warriors can do so, too. We are at our most powerful when we can come from a place of peace.

This book is the opening salvo in a Power, Peace, Purpose campaign intended to help millions of children across the globe gain purpose and conquer their pain while inspiring the rest of the planet. Young people suffering not just from the ravages of illness but also of war or abuse or poverty can join our Heroes Circle. Through a website that will protect their identities, they will be able to inspire people halfway around the world with daily messages or even hourly reminders of how to take a Breath Brake, how to stop, look, and listen, and how to pull and not push. At the same time, it will give them purpose. Purpose is an elixir. There are many groups today that can teach you how to stretch and relax, how to meditate and let go. Mindfulness is a wonderful exercise that helps many people live their lives more fully. Inevitably, however, we can easily become distracted and lose our motivation as we return to the daily grind, despite the best of intentions. The Heroes Circle is therefore not just about mindfulness but also "remindfulness." It is an applied technique of breathing and relaxation that reduces stress, not just on the day a person learns about it but going forward throughout their lives, because participants can be reminded of the techniques and at the same time thank the children for teaching and inspiring them.

The opportunities in our Heroes Circle are endless. Having adults donate their pounds to help children in pain can be another spoke in our growing circle in which our children mentor adults about power foods.

People challenged by addictions could be given purpose in their internal struggles. The gratitude expressed back to the boys and girls will continue to empower them with evidence of a world that is learning from them. It can be repeated across the globe millions of times a day. The beauty of the vision is its simplicity: a circle. One half of the circle is composed of millions of children with all different types of pain. Knowing that they have a purpose will change their ability to respond to their challenges. Arcing across the other half of this circle are the millions of people who desperately need to be inspired beyond the stress, anger, and pain of their lives. They need to recapture a perspective of what's important in life and what is not. These adults must learn how to breathe out the debilitating chemicals of "fight and flight" and learn to pull rather than push to reach their essence. The Heroes Circle grows because there is a primal need in almost every adult to respond to the pain of a child. We have also heard from children, even as young as five years old, that they need to know there is a reason they were put in this world, even if only for a short time.

Hanging on the wall in my office is the first Kids Kicking Cancer trademark. Our program about "healing with the power of light" received its official approval as a copyrighted trademark on September 11, 2001. That's the actual date on the document. Think about that in the context of what happened that morning. The entire government shut down, but someone stayed in the U.S. Patent and Trademark Office long enough to recognize our efforts to break through the darkness with the light of some amazing children. That was no accident: that person surely believed in what we were doing, all the more so on a day filled with tragedy. I also don't believe it was an accident that on the afternoon of April 15, 2013, my plane landed in Boston just five minutes before Logan International was closed because of the Boston Marathon bombings. I had come to town to lecture at Brandeis and Boston Universities on the topic, "Healing with Light in the Midst of the Darkness." There is so much tragedy in this world, but when we reach inward to the light of our souls and share it with others, we can illuminate the planet no matter how dark it appears. Who can teach this better than children like Avrami and Mohammed, a Jew and an Arab living in the Middle East, where the darkness of hatred continually seeks to choke out the light of goodness. A perfect God created an imperfect world perfectly. Not despite the threat of disease to their lives but actually because of it, they are dedicated to breaking through the stress, pain, and anger with the healing light of love and acceptance. When you can be truly mindful without the judgments of bias and negativity, then you learn to look beyond your stress-filled self and the anger it projects to those around you. It is then that we recognize the presence of God and the opportunity for greatness that has always been within our reach. We were just too stressed to know it.

LESSON 29

Klevis and Danny

MASTER TEACHERS

> *Our children have taught me that we are all connected to each other. When we choose to let go of our pain, anger, and stress, we can pull the world toward us. Our children are part of a circle that you can join as well. The focus of our united soul is the power of love. Together, we will encircle the planet.*

There is a young Korean singer who has a music video called "Gangnam Style" that has over a billion hits on YouTube. Probably a few million of those came from people like me who were just curious about what could be so profound as to draw that many viewers. But I have to say, if you haven't seen it yet, don't bother. It's not any more relevant to your life than the videos of children biting their siblings or of pigeons playing Ping-Pong. Some of those have over a million hits. There is another video on YouTube that I would recommend, however, called Klevis II, although at this writing it has only 913 hits. It is two minutes long and features a young Albanian boy named Klevis who was a patient at Children's Hospital of Michigan. In the video Klevis is receiving his black belt, somewhat prematurely because he was not supposed to live out the week. You can judge the video for yourself: Klevis's message is much more moving and life-changing than just about anything else you can watch.

Just six weeks before that video was filmed, Klevis went to South Bend, Indiana, with a whole group of Kids Kicking Cancer students to teach CVS managers how to "breathe in the light and blow out the darkness." He and his friends received a standing ovation. They always do. Klevis returned to Detroit with the knowledge that he was a teacher. He had transcended the incredibly difficult script of his young life with greatness. Rather than being defeated by his situation, he responded with Power, Peace, Purpose. This was what helped him deal with the news that he had reached the final chapter of his life. It was very soon after the seminar in Indiana that Klevis's darkness returned in the form of a full-blown relapse of his brain tumor. So there we were, as you can see on the video, awarding Klevis his black belt with his name embroidered on one end and the words "Master Teacher" on the other. The week of his black belt ceremony, Klevis was sleeping day and night and clearly was slipping away. When you watch the video, however, that's not the image you'll see. Klevis was so excited to get his black belt that one week later he got out of the hospital. His doctors couldn't believe it. He lived another six weeks. There was even talk about trying another round of chemotherapy. Unfortunately, it was too late. But it wasn't late enough for Klevis to learn that he really was a teacher. His life had a purpose and he fulfilled it with greatness.

Unlike Klevis, most of our children survive. For those that don't, the world has more light because of them. After Klevis died, many of the CVS managers sent notes to his mother through us. They were thanking her because her son was still teaching them. Their notes meant a lot to her, and to us.

In the beginning of 2012 we began a pilot program for children with many different disease and trauma challenges at Jerusalem's Alyn Hospital, a world-renowned rehabilitation center for children. Dr. Eliezer Be'eri, the chairman of the hospital's pulmonology department, was enthusiastic about the concept of martial arts therapy but a bit skeptical about how some of his patients could participate in a program like ours. "Rabbi G.," he said, "I have respirator patients, like Danny, who are so paralyzed they can't even talk. He can only communicate by blinking his eyes. He is deeply depressed. How can you teach karate to a child who can't even lift up his hands?"

I shared with Dr. Be'eri that Danny would be a great student in our Heroes Circle. In fact, I said, he could be an amazing teacher. We teach all our children that the real power of the martial artist lies within the mind and soul. We would help Danny to reach inside and feel that chi. Initially he might be able to do it for two minutes, then four and maybe five. We would work with him until he is able to do that meditation for a full ten minutes. With his eyes Danny would tell us, as he develops in his training, when he begins to feel that light inside of himself. One blink would mean that he is creating an inner place of peace within himself. Two blinks would represent when he begins to see a ball of light forming inside his head. Three would report that light spreading throughout the rest of his body. When he blinks four times, Danny would be letting us know that he is beginning to feel the warmth of that light. When he can progress to five blinks, Danny would be communicating that the power of his light is so great that he is able to take that light and project it outward to the world.

I also told Dr. Be'eri that we would videotape Danny in this progression, and edit it with the music he likes and at the pace that he can respond to, not only to reach his essence but to help him teach the world. It would be a powerful two-minute demonstration of Danny's meditation that we would post on a protected interactive YouTube website so that others could be inspired and learn from him. And I had no doubt what would happen next: thousands of people would share Danny's meditation and respond to this young man, thanking him for changing their lives. The beauty of the message is that it would be totally true. At the very same time, Danny would realize the amazing purpose that he maintains. This outpouring of love within a worldwide Heroes Circle would free Danny from the psychological incarceration of his respirator. What I've seen happen many times is that people write about how a meditation has lowered their anger, improved their blood pressure, allowed them to be a better parent, or helped them make changes in their lives they needed to make. Now they would be responding as well because an amazing young man has transcended the most challenging of situations. "Danny may have to be wheeled around in a special wheelchair," I told Dr. Be'eri. "He will never be able to walk. But that shouldn't stop him from flying." I still remember Dr. Be'eri's face. "Wow," he said. "That's so simple but it is so very profound."

As you, too, I hope, are inspired by the children in this book, sharing it with your community and following our children on our website, www.kidskickingcancer.org, you will become part of a growing circle that will be the platform for Danny and his friends to teach the world.

When we celebrated the transition from our pilot program at Alyn Hospital to a full-blown Heroes Circle program in January 2013, Dr. Be'eri was there excitedly describing the changes in the children he had seen thus far. Patients under his care were working hard to regain the skills of eating with a fork or going to the bathroom by themselves. These were difficult tasks but ones that did not naturally evoke a sense of pride or purpose. What was different about these children, however, after their introduction to the Heroes Circle, was that they began to recognize their value as teachers. All their friends could feed or dress themselves, but none of them could claim to be teaching the world how to overcome adversity. What was even more fascinating to Dr. Be'eri was the change in how the parents were now looking at their own children. It was a whole new level of pride, because the kids really were teaching others. Moms and dads of disabled children were now looking at their boys and girls with a new awareness of how uniquely abled they were to teach the world.

LESSON 30

Boris

NOT THE END

> *It is easy to be inspired by children who have faced death with the knowledge and power of their purpose. You don't need a book about dying, however; everyone figures out how to do that eventually. Power, Peace, Purpose is all about the challenge of living each day to its fullest. It starts with your breath and a commitment to focus on the power we are given every day. We constantly face the choice in our lives to respond to challenges with either our stress-drenched bodies or our very powerful souls. You can learn to respond to life's challenges with the light of your soul. Don't be afraid. Just remember: A perfect God created an imperfect world, perfectly.*

It was Boris Niyazov who first taught me about the power of light. He was fifteen years old when I met him at Camp Simcha. Despite his gentle years, lines of serious thought sculpted his handsome face. He was a veteran of not one but two bone marrow transplants to save him from a Ewing's sarcoma that had been painfully pressing against his ribs. Boris had come to the United States with his family from the former Soviet Union. Most of his acclimation to his new world, however, was in the hospital. He was anything but happy.

Camp Simcha is a very special place, one where it's really difficult to suppress smiles, joys, and laughter. It did not take long for some of the creases on Boris's face to dissolve into the happiness of just being a teenager.

At the same time, Boris, who was still experiencing multiple layers of pain and discomfort, was very eager to learn the martial arts therapy that I was offering. He was a great student and soon became a dear friend. Boris and I spent a lot of time together in camp. He was fascinated by religion, which he had not learned much about in his home country. After the two-week camp session, he would frequently call me to ask for advice on the proper way to respond to various life situations. One day, he called me and his voice was wrapped in even greater stoicism than usual. "Rabbi G., how do we prepare to die?" he asked. I was shaken and needed to take a focused breath. "What's up, Boris?" I said, my heart in my mouth. Without hesitation he said, "It's back and the doctors don't have anything else for me. I need to know how to prepare to die." I immediately suggested that we send his scans to Memorial Sloan Kettering, where we have friends who are the tops in sarcoma treatment. "No!" Boris answered. "You have to tell me how to prepare to die. It is too late for anything else."

What kind of advice does one give a sixteen-year-old on how to die? Somehow I found a theme that we would use often on this journey together. "Boris," I told him, "you don't prepare to die. You prepare to live. But you must understand that every day is life. When you get up in the morning and kiss your parents, hug your sister, smile at your friends, and thank God that you are alive, then you have made that day a life. You have also influenced the people around you who are watching you bring in that light and blow out the darkness despite your pain. You are an even greater teacher when you can do it under such difficult circumstances. But every day is life. God willing, you will do it one day and then the next. Every day is life."

Despite his initial reservations, Boris allowed us to send his scans to Dr. Leonard Wexler at Memorial Sloan Kettering. Lenny is a good friend, an angel of a person, and one of the top doctors in the world regarding pediatric sarcoma. He also had a protocol for Boris in mind. It worked wonders. The tumor began to shrink. Boris had a bit of a reprieve. This chemotherapy was working. He so much appreciated our help that he phoned me about nine months later just to say, "Rabbi G., God bless you!" My immediate response was "God bless you, Boris." Boris then got quiet, very quiet. It may have lasted twenty seconds, but it seemed like an hour. "You know, He has already," Boris finally said.

I was floored. Here was a teenager who had experienced a life of chemotherapies, transplants, hospitalizations, and ongoing pain. Yet he felt blessed. I couldn't talk. If this child felt blessed despite the mountains of challenges that had been his life, then how was I supposed to feel? At that moment, I remembered telling my students the story about Abraham and Isaac climbing up the mountain singing and dancing. I was overwhelmed and still couldn't speak. I finally was able to mumble that I would call him back, and then I just sat there in the quiet of my office, humbled by a seventeen-year-old young man.

Boris did well for another year and a half, and then his tumor returned with a vengeance. It occupied his body cavity from his abdomen to his shoulder blades. Even the great doctors at Memorial Sloan Kettering had nothing left in their arsenal. Boris was dying. He was now nineteen years old. I took the opportunity to visit him in the hospital or at his home in Queens whenever I was in town, and I would also call him on the phone. Again and again I promised him that I would tell his story. His heroism and strength would teach the world. Already tens of thousands have heard me speak about how this young man would breathe in the light and blow out the darkness even to the point of feeling blessed. This chapter is for the rest of the world.

Boris was at home when he went into a coma. He was slipping away. Very shortly afterward, Dr. Wexler, who can attest to this story, called me. "Elimelech," he said, "I just came from Boris's apartment. I want to let you know that Boris is going to die today." It wasn't a shock, but no one is ever really prepared to lose a loved one. I quickly called Inessa, Boris's sister. "Do me a favor," I asked. "Please put the phone by Boris's ear." "Rabbi G.," she sobbed, "it's too late. Boris has been in a deep coma for two days. He is not responding to anyone." Undeterred, I was emphatic. "Please, just put the phone by Boris's ear." She did. I could hear the very slow and shallow breaths over the line. "Boris," I began, "remember we said that every day is life. Now it is every second. Don't be afraid." I caught my breath. "Just look for a light. That light is a reflection of the beauty of your soul and God's love for you. Just look for that light."

Inessa took away the phone and Boris died very soon after. I couldn't attend the funeral, but at my first opportunity I came with our assistant camp director, Zahava Farbman, an expert in grief counseling, to visit Boris's mother. I have been with many parents who have lost children. It is easy to read their look of self-defeat and feel the rawness of their pain. But Mrs. Niyazov also had a question for me, and the importance of it was brimming from her eyes. "Rabbi Goldberg," she blurted out, even before we could sit down, "I need to ask you something. What did you say to Boris at the end?" The force of her question startled me. "Mrs. Niyazov, why do you ask?" "Boris was in a coma for two days," she began. "He was totally non-responsive to anyone. His eyes were closed. His eyes were closed until you called and then after you finished whatever you were saying, his sister took the phone away from his ear. Boris opened up his eyes. Then, he sat up. We were shocked. We tried to get his attention but it was like we weren't in the room. It appeared as if my son was looking for something. All of a sudden his face lit up as if he found what he was searching for. He then lay down and closed his eyes. And then he died. Please—you must tell me what you said to Boris at the end!"

What I say to you, dear reader, is that this is not a book about dying. It is about something much more difficult. It is about living. But our living can become so diminished when we allow the stress, anger, and pain of our lives to dominate our being. You can access a light that allows you to breathe out the toxic brain chemicals that can capture your soul and threaten your body. Today, most children and even adults are cured from their cancers; it is a battle we are winning. Even Sara Basya, Bernard, Chaya, Brendan, Boris, and the thousands of other children who are no longer with us did not lose their battles. They defeated their cancers by creating a light so powerful that it continues to illuminate our planet. They had long days to go with their far too short years.

You have now been introduced to thousands of amazing children in thirty simple lessons. In truth, those lessons can be reduced to three words: "Power, Peace, Purpose." Imagine your breath as a powerful light that you can bring into your very soul. Relax your muscles as you exhale and allow your breath to blow out the darkness that lives in your psyche, in your home or at your office. With that place of peace embedded inside you, look around your world. You are a teacher. Your children, family, and friends are watching. You will feel that power when you learn to pull them toward you rather than push them away. Don't be afraid. A perfect God created an imperfect world perfectly. You can choose to blow out the pain of your problems and see them as opportunities to reach a purpose of greatness. You can brake your stress and live greater.

This is your mountain. When you climb up that road singing and dancing, you will illuminate our world. The children of Kids Kicking Cancer do it every day!

Power. Peace. Purpose!

ACKNOWLEDGMENTS

The reader already knows that this book is first and foremost an acknowledgment of our perfect God who perfectly created our imperfect world. Although we may have different practices and customs, most of us believe we have one Father in Heaven. By recognizing His love for us despite the bumps we experience in the road through life, we create an opportunity to respond to our challenges with greatness. I hope that by presenting this message I may be one small vessel in His "exquisitely managed world."

In the scripts of our lives, we also meet many people who help to guide our response. To fully acknowledge all those people who have done this for me would require a book in itself. Nevertheless, I feel it is imperative to mention a few of those individuals despite the knowledge that I will leave out many who deserve recognition.

My parents, of blessed memory, like many of their generation, willingly endured great sacrifice for themselves while providing their children with every opportunity. In my parents' case, their sacrifice also came with constant love and support for me and my brother. Later in life, Ruthie's parents, also of blessed memory, were models of wisdom and devotion. My mother's brother Irv was my best man at our wedding, and he still fills that position today.

In the Talmud, a spouse is considered an extension of oneself. No one could better personify this idea than Ruthie. Ours has been an incredible journey together that I pray will continue so that we may expand our work in helping so many young lives. From the time that our daughter Ruchie and son Meir were very young, they were also immersed in our life's focus supporting the families of sick children. While this might have presented a challenge to some kids, their patience, sensitivity, and natural wisdom only grew, and they now pass this same understanding and caring to their own children. Ruchie and her wonderful husband, Rabbi Shmuel Berkman, have brought into this world our beloved grandchildren Chumi, Devorah, Motti,

Penina, Liba, Bracha, and Eli. They all perform our breathing techniques when something hurts them. My son Meir found his beautiful wife, Yael, in the Holy Land, and they have added the blessing of our new granddaughter Liana to our family. Our in-laws and their families have become as close to us as anyone could pray for.

Our extended family has been so very helpful in our mission as well. My older brother Jay remains a teacher to me, and he and his wife Judy, along with their children and grandchildren, are always very close to us despite the distance. Ruthie's sisters Brenda and Sharon, Sharon's husband Yaakov, and all their children and grandchildren are very supportive of us personally and of our work. A special shout-out to Joey, who is a real inspiration.

We have been blessed with active programs in over thirty locations across the globe. We would not be able to serve our children and families if not for the dedication and love of the people who provide the leadership, time, and money to sustain those programs in each location. To acknowledge all our board directors, committee members, martial arts therapy supervisors, and hundreds of volunteers, past and present, would take several pages. These individuals know who they are. Most of them would not want to be mentioned. They have my deepest love for all that they have given and continue to supply. That said, however, I do not want to leave the reader with the mistaken impression that I somehow have the capacity or talent to have created Kids Kicking Cancer by myself. That is not even close to the truth. Instead, I had the good fortune of finding an inner core of professionals who have shaped Kids Kicking Cancer International into the effective, focused organization that it is today. They have done so with great personal sacrifice and love, and they must be singled out. Marc Cohen and Cindy Cohen (not related) are my two right hands, Marc in administration and Cindy in our program staff. Gary Liebbe fell to us from Heaven, donating his time to be our chief financial officer at a very crucial juncture. Richard Plowden, our chief martial arts therapist, together with Peter Davenport and Michael Hunt, teach the children (as well as me) every day that we can conquer any darkness. Avital Mintz is superb at keeping it all together. Josh Schwartz has also been a great treasure, helping us get the message of our children out to the world. Beyond my support staff in Michigan, every location has individuals without whom, we would not be able to support the children. I am so appreciative of everyone who has come forward to lead our Kids Kicking Cancer chapters throughout the world.

I am thankful to Eric Schramm, the editor of this book, for his patience and diligence. Pennie Barbel, our graphics designer, constantly provides soul, talent, and incredible love in crafting her genius, as she did with the book's cover. I am very grateful to Reid Mclellan from Hello World who spent hours recording my voice for the audio meditations that accompany this book. Spencer Hall from Hudson Edits also donated days and nights applying his creative talents to merge the voice with beautiful music that he created just for us. The "Book Makers" who helped me to publish this work deserve special mention as well.

Our local Detroit community, including Rabbi Shmuel Irons and the Lakewood Kollel, as well as Rabbi Yechiel Morris and the Young Israel of Southfield, has been our home in every sense of that word. We have been blessed with many close friends who have been by our side through this entire journey. We are so very grateful.

Chai Lifeline and Camp Simcha showed me the impact that a well-run organization can have on the lives of children and families. I am privileged to remain close to Rabbi Simcha Scholar and our camp family.

I have great gratitude for the many experts in the medical community, both doctors and nurses, who have helped to train and mentor me, as well as for providing extraordinary response to the needs of our children. Drs. Peter and Laurel Steinherz, Lenny Wexler, Jeffrey Taub, Brian Berman, Mark Palermo, Aron Berkman, John Finlay, Carolyn Fein Levy, Shayna Zelcer, and Jerry Stein are just a few of the doctors across the globe who have taken great interest in our program and the children we refer to them. We are also very honored to have Martin Bluth M.D., Ph.D. as our U.S. medical director.

Our donors have provided us with the platform on which we stand today. They have supplied us with the treasure of their trust and love for our kids. Their generosity has directly lowered the pain of some amazing children. I feel very blessed to know that with their kindness, we have reached over five thousand children since we began our work. However, I remain challenged knowing that there are still so many hundreds of thousands of children in pain who can join our circle of heroes but whom we have not yet reached. I pray to our perfect God that we may be blessed with the resources to expand our Heroes Circle and reach these children, perfectly.

We look forward to the day when there are no more children in pain. But until that time, we are so very grateful to the moms, dads, and children who have joined our family and are surrounding this world with light. And finally, dear reader, my gratitude goes out to you. You are now part of this amazing Heroes Circle. Follow our children and never forget that a perfect God created an imperfect world, perfectly. No matter what, you can breathe in the light and blow out the darkness.

Meditations

*These meditations are the scripts for the
audio meditations that accompany each chapter.*

There is a great deal of science to evidence the positive health benefits of meditation. The thirty meditations in front of you provide a unique opportunity to train your brain to lower the chemicals of pain, stress and anger in your life while reducing the pain of some very beautiful children. By listening to this meditation, a message is sent through the book's website to the children of Kids Kicking Cancer letting them know that the world is watching and being inspired by them. When our children have purpose, they experience less pain.

If you have a smartphone with a QR reader, you can simply scan the QR code associated with each meditation and listen. There are many free QR readers available for download at your favorite app store. Without a QR reader, you can go to the books website - www.kkcbook.org and listen to any chapter meditation. When you see a place for the "Meditation Code", input the number "1613". If you don't know what a website is, you probably have no stress in your life, so don't start worrying about it now.

Introduction
~Taking Over the Controls~

To get to a place of optimism, we have to understand that our brain provides us with another voice. The sounds of stress, fear, pain, and anger can crowd out the strength of the voice of the soul. This introduction to our meditative techniques will allow you to begin to enjoy the voice of your soul that emerges from the sounds of silence. Place your phone over the QR box and download our introduction to meditation. Every time you hit the download button, the numbers go up in front of our children. You will begin a great journey of inner power, and they will have less pain because you give them the gift of purpose!

Many people harbor a misconception that meditation has its singular roots in the world of Eastern Spirituality. In fact, the tenets of meditation are present as early as the Bible. It doesn't require a lotus position or strange mantras. It's actually a recognition that there are two paths which travel through our brain. Each path has its own voice.

One voice is the sound of the body: it can be loud, disruptive, angry, overwhelmingly sad, frustrated, or jealous. It's a voice driven by the chemicals of our brain that pump stress through our body exactly as we see it happen to the animals of the jungle.

Because stress is a sign of necrosis or dying tissue, it really gets our attention.

Stress occupies a prominent space and can, without even trying, swirl our thoughts in a kaleidoscope of darkness that drowns out focus and light.

The other voice is the sounds of your soul. It is calm, powerful, and can be filled with an amazing light. The goal of all of the meditations that the little teachers of Kids Kicking Cancer use is to quiet the noise of the body, to create a light that can overcome the inner darkness of pain, fear, anger, stress. When you will feel this light, you will find the sound of your soul.

In the Bible, the Hebrew word for the soul is *neshama;* it is from the word *neshima,* or breath.

The pathway to the soul can be found by learning how to use your breath to quiet the noise of the body.

In the thirty meditations that we will learn together, you will discover the power of your neshama, the light of your soul. Each meditation will build upon the other, using similar phrases and tools allowing your mind to grow from one experience to the next, building an inner platform for the voice of your soul.

What will make this exercise different from any other meditation in the world is that as you gain access to your inner light, you will be allowing the children of Kids Kicking Cancer to know that you are learning from them. When you give them purpose, they have less pain. Every time you open up the website of their meditations, it lets them know, immediately, that they are teaching the world.

We call that "Power, Peace, Purpose."

Let us begin together and take the next three minutes to begin this journey to find the power of the soul.

Choose a comfortable spot, a chair or a bed, to either sit up or lie back. Allow your body to be straight. Uncross your legs and put your arms by your sides.

Try to eliminate distractions. Turn off noise and as much of the world around you. Eventually you will be able to meditate any place and any time, but for now choose that special spot carefully.

Try to keep your back straight but don't focus on that.

Try to breathe in through your nose, and then gently out through your mouth.

Whether you are a mouth breather or a nose breather, just pick what is comfortable.

Take in that deep breath, hold it, and then gently out your mouth. Feel the air go across your lips.

Now close your eyes.

Another deep breath in through your nose, and then out through your mouth.

Notice, as you breathe in, that the air is a little bit cooler, and it's a touch warmer as you breathe out.

As any other thought or feeling comes into your mind, let them fall away with your exhale and simply focus on your breath.

Feel the coolness of the air as you breathe in, and the warmth as you breathe out.

When other thoughts or sounds come into your head, that's very natural. Just put them down gently and return to the feeling of your breath.

Feel the coolness of the air as you breathe in and the warmth as you breathe out.

Let every sound, feeling or tightness in your body melt into the chair or the bed, and continue to focus on the feeling of the coolness of your breath as you breathe in, and the warmth as you breathe out.

Notice your body rise with the breath, and fall ever so slightly with the exhale.

Feel the coolness of the air as you breathe in, and the warmth as you breathe out.

Continue to experience the gentle flow of your breath, as every other thought, sound, or message of "I can't do this" (etc., etc.) slowly fall out of your head with each breath that you blow out.

Feel the coolness of the air as you breathe in, and the warmth as you breathe out.

Feel the coolness of the air as you breathe in, and the warmth as you breathe out.

Allow the air to flow through you, focusing on the experience of each and every time that you breathe in and then on each and every time that you breathe out.

Feel the coolness as you breathe in, and the warmth as you breathe out.

Now, let's take one deep, cleansing breath in, slowly pulling it up and up and hold it, and now gently blow it out.

One more cleansing breath in, and gently blowing it out.

Slowly open up your eyes.

As you just lie there or sit there, calming the voice—the other voices in your head—is the beginning of a process of emancipating all of the stuff that grabs us, and finding the power of our soul.

The minds of the children whose wisdom we share can be clouded with so many unhappy voices. There are so many sounds of pain, fear, angers, dismay, unfair, etc., etc. Every time that you click on a meditation, you are letting them know that they are teaching the world. As you bring in this light, you are helping them conquer their darkness.

The Material of Your Soul
~Finding Your Essence~

As we respond to the scripts of our lives, we are given the option to react with either the stress-driven behaviors of weakness or with great power. We refer to that energy as "light." The children use this light to push out the fears of disease and the hurt of being so different from their friends. This light is a powerful tool for everyone. Using the energy in this meditation is an opening into your personal place of power. It is an opportunity to find the material of your soul, your very essence, and use it in your life. Our children do it every day. So can you!

During this meditation we're going to ask you to begin to experience the fabric of your soul.

In the beginning of Creation, G-d said, "Let there be light." However, the sun, the physical source of light and heat for the entire solar system, wasn't created until day four.

What, then, was the light of Creation?

According to our mystical sources, this light was a spiritual energy that permeated the early galaxies with godliness and purity.

This radiation became embedded within all of the primal matter of the universe.

It is also within every one of us.

This is a treasure for us to find, to hold, and to use in our lives. It doesn't matter if you call it chi, ki, tenaga dalam, prana, neshama, spirit, or soul: the ability to feel that light and to use that power is very much a part of our training.

Let's use this meditation to focus on the light.

Find that place where you can sit in semi-quiet comfortably, allowing your body to relax into the chair, or, if you are lying down, feel your body fall deeper into the bed.

Close your eyes, take a deep breath, and gently let it out.

Take another deep breath and gently blow it out of your mouth.

And now as you inhale—preferably through your nose and out through your mouth—notice that the air is a little bit cooler as you breathe in and it's just a touch warmer as you breathe out.

Feel the coolness as you breathe in, and the warmth as you breathe out.

As any other thought or feeling comes into your mind, let them fall away with your exhale and the simple focus on your breath.

Feel the coolness of the air as you breathe in and the warmth as you breathe out.

Feel every muscle of your body gently fall into the chair or into the bed.

Feel the coolness of the air as you breathe in, and the warmth as you breathe out.

Don't be afraid that there are so many thoughts that come into our heads or sounds or feelings that interrupt the flow. That's very, very common and natural because we are constantly bombarded with thoughts.

Continue your feeling of breath. Gently breathing in the coolness of the air, and the warmth as you breathe out.

Some of our thoughts we recognize and some of them we call forth, and some of them seem to come from nowhere. It does not matter. Just let them fall.

As you continue to breathe, you can learn that you don't have to stop the thoughts to take control.

Simply focus on the coolness of the air as you breathe in, and the warmth as you breathe out. And as you exhale, gently allow those thoughts to fall downward.

Continue to the cool feeling of the breath as you gently breathe in, and as you exhale, blow out any thought or feeling, any sound, and go back to the flow of your breath.

Feel the coolness of the air as you breathe in, and the warmth as you breathe out.

Gently lie there or sit there with the feeling of each breath, and your ability to notice that little difference of coolness as you breathe in and warmth as you breathe out.

Now as you exhale, I want you to say very gently inside of yourself, without even moving your lips, gently say the word "Light."

Every time you breathe out, very gently, inside of yourself whisper that one word: Light.

Light.

Light.

Feel the coolness of the air as you breathe in, and the warmth as you breathe out.

Gently repeating in your head that one word, "Light," every time you breathe out.

Light.

Light.

Light.

Continue to focus just on that one word: Light.

Feel the coolness of the air as you breathe in, and the warmth as you breathe out.

Now with me, let's take one deep cleansing breath in, hold that, and now exhale slowly, gently.

Another cleansing breath in and gently let it out.

Just sit for a moment with that one word, Light.

Together we will learn how to feel that Light actually growing inside of yourself. And, to be inspired by our children how to use that light in our lives to quiet down all of the messages of pain and stress, and fear and angers.

And eventually how to teach the ones around us that that light is theirs as well.

The Power of Purpose
~ Why Are You You? ~

There is a tremendous power in purpose. We are all given darkness and challenges in our lives, to allow the treasure of our light to break through the murky envelope that can encapsulate us. This meditation focuses us on the realization that every moment is really the moment of your life and that you can use such moments to find your greatness

There is a tremendous power in purpose.

We are all given darkness and challenges in our lives, to allow the treasure of our light to break through the murky envelope that can encapsulate us.

Our children become so powerful because they know that they are teaching others.

In this meditation we will begin to feel the light of our own power and our ability to reach out and use this power to impact the world.

Make yourself comfortable. Try to keep your back straight, whether you are sitting in a chair or lying down. Close your eyes.

Let us return to the experience of your breath.

Feel the coolness of the air as you breathe in, and the warmth as you breathe out.

As you are gently and very calmly breathing, feel the movement of your diaphragm as it moves in and out with each breath.

Feel how your breath moves the clothing on your body.

Continue to experience the fullness of each breath.

Now as you breathe in the air, imagine the breath entering into your body as this beautiful light. You can see the brightness of this light reflecting off the breath as it enters your body.

Feel the coolness of the light as you breathe in and the warmth as you breathe out.

As you are falling into a state of total relaxation, any other thought or sound or feeling, just gently breathe out as you exhale.

Whenever that thought comes into your mind, gently breathe it out.

Imagine that you are sitting by the side of a very beautiful beach. You can feel the sand on your feet, and hear the waves of the ocean. You can smell the smell of the sea.

Feel the coolness of the air as you breathe in and the warmth as you breathe out.

From a distance you can hear the sounds of the birds and the other noises on the beach, but it is a very tranquil and beautiful place.

And as you are watching, sitting by the shore of the beach, you can see the waves gently wash up upon the sand, changing the color of the sand to dark and wet.

You can see the little bubbles gather together at the lip of the wave.

Feel the coolness of the air as you breathe in, and the warmth as you breathe out.

As you are sitting there and you have let every sound or feeling or thought gently flow out of your body, you watch the beautiful waves wash up upon the shore.

The wave rides up upon the beach, holds itself there for one second, and then washes back out to the ocean.

Watch the waves come up and down, and back and forth.

Each wave approaches the shore, almost like giant fingers, gently reaching and wetting the sands of the beach as they go up and down and up and down.

And as you're lying there feeling the movement of the ocean and the warmth of the sand, every cloud overhead begins to part and you can see the bright, warm, and hot sun peer down from the sky reaching inside of your head.

And as you look upward with your eyes closed, that orb of sunlight becomes greater and greater, filling your head with the most amazing light.

And that light begins to become warmer and hotter, and every time that you breathe out, the light gets warmer and brighter and larger inside of your head.

Feel the power of that light grow inside of your head.

And now, every time you breathe out, gently say the word in the smallest of whispers, without moving your lips: "Light."

"Light."

"Light."

And every time you repeat the word "Light," that ball of sunlight gets deeper and warmer into your being and it spreads down into your neck, and you feel it growing outward onto your shoulders into your back filling your chest, continuing downward.

Every time you breathe out, the light gets bigger and brighter inside of yourself as you gently repeat that one word, "Light."

"Light."

"Light."

Feel the light growing inside of yourself.

"Light."

"light."

Every time you breathe out, the light journeys deeper and deeper into your being, filling up your torso and your legs, your chest, through your arms and down to your toes.

Just by repeating that one word, "Light."

Light.

Light.

Light.

Feel this light throughout every part of your body, so warm and gentle. So comforting and so powerful.

Just keep repeating that one word, "Light."

Light.
Light.
Light.
Feel that light give you strength and meaning.

Take in a deep cleansing breath, and blow it out slowly.
Another deep cleansing breath and blow it out slowly.
And gently open up your eyes, continuing to feel that light that is within you.

Being the Master of Self
~Drawing from the Well of Being~

Our children become masters not only of the martial arts, but of themselves. They start by being able to identify the places of pain, fear, and anger—the knots of stress in their bodies—and then they can use their inner light to drive out the darkness. To master the following meditation is to become a master of yourself. Even when you get mugged by the chemicals of anger, fear, and pain you can take control. When you follow this path, you can see yourself in control rather than being controlled by the swirling events around you.

Our children become masters not only of the Martial Arts, but of themselves.

We start by being able to identify the places of pain, fear, anger—the knots of stress in our being—and then we can use our inner light to drive out the darkness.

We are not our disease. We are not our pain. We are not our weakness.

These meditations are wonderful tools that enable us to become masters of ourselves. This body scan is a part of every one of our Kids Kicking Cancer classes.

Find that quiet place, and just allow yourself to fall into the bed or the chair, wherever you are comfortable, and begin to feel the experience of your breath.

As you breathe out, close your eyes and feel the gentle wave of breath come through your body.

Feel the coolness of air as you breathe in and the warmth as you breathe out.

Establish a gentle wave of breath, with a tempo that feels very comfortable as you feel yourself flow back and forth with your breath.

Feel the coolness of the air as you breathe in, and the warmth as you breathe out.

And as you're sitting or lying in place, imagine traveling all the way up to the very top of your head—the place where your scalp and your forehead meet, and as you breathe out, feel every muscle in your scalp gently pull away, one from the other, falling downward through your body, gently relaxing, letting go.

Imagine as if there is a waterfall at the very top of your head, and as you breathe out every muscle in your forehead gently is enveloped by that water, flowing downward, relaxing the muscles in your forehead and the muscles behind your eyes.

Feel the coolness of the air as you breathe in, and the warmth as you breathe out.

Go to the muscles in the back of your head and behind your ears. When you breathe out, allow every muscle to release and to fall.

Focus on the muscles in your cheeks and your jaw, the muscles by your mouth. As you exhale, let every muscle gently pull away one from the other and float downward into that waterfall.

Travel to the muscles in the back of your neck and the sides of your neck as you allow the air out of your lungs. Feel them pull downward into that waterfall, every muscle from your head down into the back of your neck.

Feel the coolness of the air as you breathe in and the warmth as you breathe out.

As you breathe out, feel the muscles in the front of your neck gently descend downward until every muscle in your neck is now released and relaxed, almost as if your head is now weightless, surrounded by the cascading stream of your waterfall.

Feel the coolness of the air as you breathe in and the warmth as you breathe out.

Go to the muscles in your shoulders, as you exhale feel your shoulders just drop as every muscle relaxes and releases.

Go to your shoulder blades in your back. As you breathe out, feel your right shoulder and then your left shoulder gently flow downward.

And go to your vertebrae. One by one, feel the waterfall gently pull aside the tension of every muscle, flowing through your back, allowing muscle by muscle to release and relax.

Feel the coolness of the air as you breathe in and the warmth as you breathe out.

Let the waterfall stream downward through the muscles in your chest. As you exhale let every muscle in your chest flow downward, washing away any tightness.

Continue down to your stomach. Allow the waterfall to gently release every muscle, allowing your stomach to feel so very comfortable.

Go to the muscles of the lower part of your back. As you breathe out feel every muscle gently descend downward through the upper part of your legs.

Feel the coolness of the air as you breathe in and the warmth as you breathe out.

Continue down your legs, allowing the waterfall to erase any tightness or tension in your upper legs, going down through your knees and into your calves.

As you breathe out, feel the muscles by your ankles flow downward to your feet and out through your toes.

Feel the coolness of your breath as you breathe in, and the warmth as you breathe out.

With your eyes closed, scan through every part of your body. Look through your body for any place that remains tight, any feeling of anger or fear or pain.

As you breathe out, allow those places to gently wash away in this waterfall.

Scan through your body and feel its power and feel its light.

The places of anger, and pain, and stress, you can blow away. You can allow them just to wash out, because they are not who you are. Your essence is this incredible light that dwells inside of yourself.

As you breathe out, let every place of darkness in your body be washed away by the incredible power of your light.

Take a deep cleansing breath in, and breathe it out slowly.

Another deep cleansing breath in, and breathe it out slowly.

And gently, open up your eyes.

Power, Peace, Purpose.

Becoming One with the Light
~Unity Is Peace~

In this meditation, we combine what we refer to as the "Body Scan" with the ability to feel the power of our inner light, removing the obstacles from our bodies that interfere with our ability to experience the essence of our being. In the place of the lonely existential "why," this meditation creates a path of unity between each individual and the universe, helping us to recognize that each of our days can be complete and profoundly satisfying. You simply have to take the time to allow that message to guide you.

In this meditation, we combine the body scan with the ability to feel the power of our inner light, removing the obstacles from our body that interfere with our ability to experience the essence of our being.

Find a comfortable place—you can be sitting up or lying down —and begin to focus on the flow of your breath.

Feel the coolness of the air as you breathe in and the warmth as you breathe out.

Gently allow your eyes to close.

Feel the coolness of the air as you breathe in and the warmth as you breathe out.

When any other thought or sound or image comes into your head, simply go back to the feeling of your breath, breathing out any other thought or sounds.

Feel the coolness of the air as you breathe in, and the warmth as you breathe out.

Feel the flow of each breath as it enters your body and moves your muscles, up and down.

Imagine going all the way to the top of your head to scan through your body and release any place of tightness. Go to the scalp and allow every muscle to just fall downward, to relax and release.

Go to the muscles in your forehead and feel them erase, gently flowing downward.

The muscles behind your eyes, and behind your ears: as you exhale, let every muscle just gently relax and release.

Go to the muscles in your mouth and your jaw and just let them drop and fall.

Feel the coolness of the air as you breathe in, and the warmth as you breathe out.

Go to the muscles in your neck and with your exhale, allow every muscle in your neck to gently fall downward.

Feel the muscles in your shoulders release and relax.

Your chest, your stomach.

As you exhale, let every muscle, vertebra by vertebra in your spine, gently pull apart on the sides of the bones of your spine.

Feel the coolness of the air as you breathe in and the warmth as you breathe out.

Go to the muscles in your stomach and in your lower back and let every muscle just gently relax and release.

The muscles in your legs, traveling down to your knees and your ankles, and then through to your toes.

Feel the coolness of the air as you breathe in, and the warmth as you breathe out.

And as you breathe out, allow every muscle now in your body to gently fall through the floor, out your body, so there is no place of tension or anger or fear or pain.

Now that your body is devoid of any stress, anything that would withhold the power of the light from you, imagine from the center of your being, just below your stomach, an opening that turns you into a vessel, like a deep receptacle for the light from above.

As you breathe in, imagine this ball of light that is warm and healing and powerful gently descend into your being from the opening below your belly.

As you exhale, gently whisper, without moving your lips, that one word, "Light."

Light.

Light.

Light.

Feel the coolness of the air as you breathe in, and the warmth as you breathe out.

With every inhale, the light, that ball of light, gets warmer and more powerful. As you breathe in, that ball of light begin to extend upward toward your head.

Feel the coolness of the air as you breathe in and the warmth as you breathe out.

Feel every muscle of your body being warmed by the powerful light that spreads through you and brings you wholeness and completion. Because this is the light of your soul, your essence, and when you can breathe out the stress, the pain, the fear and the anger, you become that light.

Feel the coolness of the air as you breathe in and the warmth as you breathe out.

Now each time you breathe out, gently inside of your head, slightly moving your lips to the form of a whisper, every time you breathe out just say the words, "That light is my soul."

That light is my soul.

That light is my soul.

That light is my soul.

And every time you breathe in, feel that light extend and reach into every part of your being, creating a wholeness, a oneness, between your essence and your body, as you keep repeating that one message, "That light is my soul."

Feel the coolness of the air as you breathe in, and the warmth as you breathe out.

That light is my soul.

And now, just focus on the feeling of your breath, and the power of that light.

Quiet any other phrase or thought and just focus on the feeling of your breath.

As you breathe in, you can feel the coolness and as you breathe out, you can feel the warmth.

And now, "That light is forever."

That light is forever.

That light is forever.

That light is forever.

Take in a very deep, cleansing breath, and hold it, and now breathe it out slowly. Another deep, cleansing breath, and breathe it out slowly.

And gently open up your eyes.

Your essence, your power, your light is forever.

Power, Peace, Purpose.

Gratitude
~Thankfulness Leads to Joy~

Your brain controls every muscle in your body. Using your breath to relax your muscles connects you to an amazing light. In this meditation, you experience that light as a fountain of gratitude, which can create a more powerful perspective. This is an opportunity to gain a new appreciation of a world that holds incredible riches. Sometimes they are buried within your very own challenges.

Your brain controls every muscle in your body.

Using your breath to relax your muscles connects you to an amazing light.

In this meditation, we experience that light as a fountain of gratitude, which can connect you to the infinite.

Find your comfortable place, and just begin to experience the feeling of your breath.

Notice, as you breathe in, the air is a little cooler, and it's a tiny bit warmer as you breathe out.

Close your eyes.

Feel the coolness of the air as you breathe in, and the warmth as you breathe out.

Maintain that slow, steady, but comfortable breath. We are now going to use the inhale to tighten all of the muscles in your legs and your exhale to relax them in the opposite order.

Place your feet together. As you begin to slowly breathe in, squeeze your toes and push your feet together, one against the other.

Tighten the muscles in your calves, behind your knees and all the way up your thighs. More breath and—

Hold that breath. . . two, three.

As you exhale, relax your thighs, behind your knees, calves, and finally your toes as you blow out that last bit of air.

Take in a few calming comfortable breaths and let's repeat this one more time.

As you begin to slowly breathe in, squeeze your toes and push your feet together, one against the other.

Tighten the muscles in your calves, behind your knees, and all the way up your thighs.

As you exhale, relax your thighs, your knees, calves, and finally your toes as you blow out that last bit of air.

Take a calming breath—feel the coolness of the air as you breathe in and the warmth as you breathe out.

Continue to breathe calmly as we prepare to tighten up our midsection. Let's take a few more breaths.

Now, as we breathe in, tighten your buttocks and then your stomach and now your chest. More breath and—

Hold that breath . . . two, three.

As you breathe out, relax your chest, now your stomach and . . . finally your buttocks as you blow out that last bit of air.

Take in a few calming comfortable breaths and let's repeat this one more time.

Let's take a few more breaths.

Now as we breathe in, tighten your buttocks and then your stomach and now your chest. More breath and—

Hold that breath . . . two, three.

As you breathe out, relax your chest, now your stomach and . . . finally your buttocks as you blow out that last bit of air.

Continue to breathe calmly as we prepare to tighten up our upper body. Let's take a few more breaths.

Feel the coolness of the air as you breathe in and the warmth as you breathe out.

Keep breathing normally as we prepare to use our hands, arms, shoulders, and neck to bring us to the next phase.

Feel the coolness of the air as you breathe in and the warmth as you breathe out.

Now as you take a deep inhale, clench your fists, your arms going up to your shoulders and now your neck. More breath and—

Hold it . . . two, three.

Breathe out, relaxing your neck, your shoulder, going down your arms and finally loosening your hands. Blow out that last bit of air as your fingers fall away from each other and relax your breath, breathing normally.

Continue to breathe calmly as we again prepare to tighten up our upper body. Let's take a few more breaths.

Feel the coolness of the air as you breathe in and the warmth as you breathe out.

Keep breathing normally as we will use our hands, arms, shoulders and neck to go to the next phase.

Feel the coolness of the air as you breathe in and the warmth as you breathe out.

And now as you take a deep inhale, clench your fists, your arms going up to your shoulders and now your neck.

Hold it . . . two, three.

Breathe out, relaxing your neck, your shoulder, going down your arms and finally loosening your hands. Blow out that last bit of air as your fingers fall away from each other and relax your breath, breathing normally.

Feel the coolness of the air as you breathe in and the warmth as you breathe out.

Just continue to focus on the flow of your breath as you experience the control that you have over all of your body.

Feel the coolness of the air as you breathe in and the warmth as you breathe out.

We are now ready to use the inhale to tighten up our entire body all the way from your toes to the tips of your scalp.

Feel the coolness of the air as you breathe in and the warmth as you breathe out.

Take in a few normal calming breaths and imagine that the air is coming into your body from the soles of your feet. As the air will pass through each part of your body, it will pull up all of the muscles with it, creating a tightness that you will hold onto.

Feel the coolness of the air as you breathe in and the warmth as you breathe out.

Let's pull in that air from the very bottom—pull it up, your legs are tight, your stomach, shoulders, neck, now your face up, up, and a little more.

Hold it . . . two, three.

And now let it out slowly, relax your face, neck, shoulders, chest, stomach, buttocks, legs all the way down your feet. . . . Blow out some more. . . . Relax.

One more time all the way up, pull it up and tighten up, up. Up—a little more.

Hold it . . . two, three, and now slowly blow it out, going all of the way down, relax your stomach, legs, feet, toes, and then a little more. . . . Blow it out!

Feel the coolness of the air as you breathe in, and the warmth as you breathe out.

As you control the flow of every muscle and part of yourself, thank your body for responding to the needs of your life and allowing you the great pleasures of this world.

Feel the coolness of the air as you breathe in, and the warmth as you breathe out.

There are many children that we have worked with whose legs cannot walk, whose mouths can't talk, whose hands are incapable of lifting, and yet these children respond to life with a light that connects them to the infinite.

As you are lying there or sitting there, relaxed and focused, breathe in a light of gratitude.

As you inhale, feel the power of that light.

As you exhale, feel the rest of your body totally relax.

And that light represents the essence of your soul.

Place that light over your eyes and thank your eyes for being able to perceive a world that can know great beauty.

Let your gratitude flow with this light, to the Infinite source of everything.

Allow the light to descend to your mouth and cover your nose with the power of this light.

Thank your nose for being able to provide the smell of the pine trees and the beauty of nature, and your mouth to taste the spices and joy of food, and to sing and to talk to those whom you love.

Take this light and let it descend upon your heart.

And thank your heart for every beat of its muscles that sustain you.

And respond with gratitude to the source of this life, to the Infinite.

Take this light and place it in your stomach, in your intestines.

And with gratitude, appreciate the ability to bring in nutrients and food and to separate that which is harmful to us and that which gives us life and renewal.

Allow this light to descend upon your hands and then thank the source of the Infinite light for giving you hands that can feel and touch and produce and move.

Allow the light to descend upon your legs, your knees, your calves, your feet.

And thank the source of this light, this Infinite light, for providing you with the opportunity to walk, to jump, to sit, to move from place to place in a world that is filled with light.

Feel this light over your entire body, and thank the source of this light for allowing you to walk on this planet and make a difference.

Feel the power of this light, because even when we may be faced with parts of our body that can't talk, or that hurt, or that tighten with fears and angers, the ability to feel the light of gratitude gives us an opportunity to spread this light and give meaning to our finite existence, because ultimately we are connected to the Infinite light.

Breathe in the light, and blow out any darkness, any pain, fear, anger, and give gratitude to the source of this light that we are able to feel and to know the power of His light.

Flowing with the Universe
~Being an Important Part of it All~

In our very big world it is possible to feel very, very small. It is also within our reach to view the universe as exquisitely managed, and that you are an important part of this universe. This meditation will allow you to feel a part of the rhythm of the enormous universe. You can replace the stress of living in chaos with the peace of being part of the indestructible whole of Creation.

In our very big world it is possible to feel very, very small. It is also within our reach to view the universe as elegantly managed, and that we are an important part of this universe.

This meditation will allow us to feel a part of the rhythm of the enormous universe.

Go to a place where you can feel comfort, and allow your body to simply relax. Any other thoughts or feelings that come into your head are perfectly natural; just put them down gently and begin to create a flow with your breath.

Feel the coolness of the air as you breathe in, and the warmth as you breathe out.

Close your eyes.

Feel the coolness of the air as you breathe in, and the warmth as you breathe out.

And look through your body for any place of tightness, anger, of fear or pain. As you exhale let every place of darkness simply blow out as if a cloud of darkness is emerging from your lips that you can push away from yourself.

Feel the coolness of the air as you breathe in, and the warmth as you continue to breathe out.

As you relax and feel your breath, imagine inside of your head that you are being transported, standing in a beautiful meadow on a moonless, dark night, with no sign of life or movement around you. The wind gently blows upon you, but hushes even the silence.

As you walk around the meadow grass, you can feel the plushness and the beauty of the grass beneath your feet.

And you sit down on this warm night, in the cool but dry grass and you lay all the way back.

And in the midst of the total darkness you look straight up into the sky, and in this moonless panorama the lights of trillions of stars pulsate as each one is dancing in unison with the other.

You can make out the contours of the Milky Way and follow the stars of the Big Dipper. And as you find yourself lost amongst the beautiful stars of the sky, you can actually feel yourself floating upward till the stars and all of the galaxies are dancing around you. As you breathe in, the stars become a little dimmer as you pull in their energy, and as you breathe out, they become just a little bit larger.

In rhythm with your breath, the stars become smaller, and then as you exhale, larger.

Feel the coolness of the air as you breathe in, and the warmth as you breathe out.

Create the flow of yourself breathing together with the universe and feeling the unity of all things.

You are surrounded by light, light that has traveled such long distances, just to be able to present itself to you.

Feel the breath as you breathe in, and watch the sky. As you breathe out, the light of those stars becomes brighter.

Feel the breath as you breathe in and the stars and their energy as you breathe out.

As you are floating in the cosmos, you are in total synergy with the light of the Universe.

Feel the coolness of the air as you breathe in, and the warmth as you breathe out.

Every time you breathe out, the light of the stars become brighter, more vivid.

Feel the coolness of the air as you breathe in, and the warmth as you breathe out.

And now, as you exhale, let's return to that one gentle word, "Light."

As you see the beauty of the light of the universe, every time you exhale, gently say that word, "Light," inside of your head.

Light.

Light.

As you say the word "Light" in each exhale, the stars become brighter and more powerful.

When you breathe in, you can feel the energy of the stars coming into yourself. And as you breathe out, gently say the word "Light."

Light.

Light.

Light.

Light.

Light.

Feel yourself as one with the rest of an elegant, very large universe.

By connecting with your breath to the light of the cosmos, you can project yourself closer to the Source of all Light.

Light.

Light.

Light.

Take in a deep cleansing breath and hold it, and gently breathe it out.

Another deep cleansing breath, and hold it, and gently breathe it out.

And slowly open up your eyes.

Power, Peace, Purpose.

Directing the Voice in Your Head
~You're Better than You Think~

There are so many audible voices inside your head that can clog your mind and stop you from being everything that you can be. In this meditation you will learn to banish those voices. This guided imagery will allow you to recognize that those destructive sounds are created by so many messages that confuse and weaken your very being. Allowing yourself to breathe out the stress of negativity will create a very powerful center where you can feel the light of your soul and respond so very positively with Power, Peace, Purpose.

There are so many voices that can be heard inside of our heads that can clog our minds and stop us from being everything that we can be.

In this meditation you will learn to banish those voices.

Find a comfortable place to sit.

Experience the feeling of your breath as you relax your body.

Close your eyes.

Feel the coolness of the air as you breathe in, and the warmth as you breathe out.

As you inhale, feel the clothing that surrounds you move upward, and as you breathe out feel the clothing gently fall.

Feel the movement of your clothing respond to the flow of your breath.

Create a rhythm of gentle movement with your breath.

When any other voice or sound or feeling or thought comes into your head, gently blow it out with your breath.

Feel the coolness of the air as you breathe in and the warmth as you breathe out.

Imagine that you are sitting in a chair in a room that is filled with rows and rows of balloons. They are all the walls around you. The balloons are all different sizes and colors, but they are not happy-looking balloons. Instead, scribbled on the sides with ugly letters, one on top of the other, are words of anger and fear. The messages are about you.

"You're bad." "You're a failure, a big disappointment."

The words are evil and dark, malicious and angry. The balloons are closing you in on all sides and coming closer and closer. As they surround you, these balloons are banging into you.

It is as if you are being submerged by them, and you can't move because of them. And they are holding you down.

"You're stupid," "You're fat," "You're ugly," "You're no good," "You don't care," "You're not loved."

These balloons are brutal. Even though they are simply filled with air. They hurt you . . . a lot.

And they are always closing in, not allowing you to move on in your life.

Feel the coolness of the air as you breathe in, and the warmth as you breathe out.

As you watch yourself surrounded and drowning in the sea of angry words, you are going to purge all of those angry messages out of your head.

You will take control of your breath to take control of your life.

Feel the coolness of the air as you breathe in, and the warmth as you breathe out.

Breathe slowly and calmly. We are soon going to take in a breath that will be very sharp and powerful and place a laser-like beam of sharp power light in your fist.

Continue now, just breathing calmly.

Feel the coolness of the air as you breathe in, and the warmth as you breathe out.

As you breathe in slowly, feel the fingers of your right hand tighten into a fist.

Take in just a little bit more breath and hold it for a second.

Keep your fist tight as you gently blow out your breath.

Now, as you breathe in, imagine a very sharp pin of light being pulled into that fist.

Hold onto the weapon of light as you gently breathe out.

Calmly continue your breathing.

Every time you breathe, the pin like a dagger becomes stronger and more powerful in your hands.

Feel the coolness of the air as you breathe in, and the warmth as you breathe out.

Notice that the balloons that surround you respond to the power of your breath. Every time you breathe in you create a current that brings them toward you.

With your light, you realize that you can simply pop all of the balloons that seem so real and unmovable in your life.

As you breathe in, pull in the balloon of ugly into the light of your pin, and as you breathe out, watch it pop and disappear.

Breathe in the balloon of disapproval and pop it as you breathe out with the light in your hand.

Breathe in the image of ugly, and watch that word disappear as it pops as you breathe out.

The balloon of no good disappears as you exhale, popped by the power of your light.

The balloon of stupid disappears as you breathe out.

Failure, disappointment, anger dissolve into nothingness, shriveling away as the air escapes from their fractured shells.

Pull the balloon of evil into your pin as you breathe out: it pops into nothingness.

The balloon of bad, of not enough, of no good, of not caring—one by one with your breath as you enhance the light inside of your hands, as you breathe out you are destroying and breaking every negative message that surrounds you.

These are the balloons of thought that dwell inside of your head. These are the images that keep you pinned to the chair, afraid to grow, afraid to be, afraid to love, afraid to care. Afraid to give.

But by bringing in the light you can destroy every one of those images that your brain supplies to you.

One by one, you destroy the balloons of indifference, of sadness, of anger, of pain and of fears.

Until there are no more balloons left, only the most beautiful light that beckons you. With your power to join it, now you can stand up and in your mind imagine that you are walking with this light inside of yourself. The power of your breath that you bring into your soul and that you can now bring that light to a world where you are not bounded, you are not encapsulated, you are not inhibited by any of the images, any of the words, any of the thoughts that stop you from being you.

Take in a deep cleansing breath of light and blow out all of the darkness.

Whenever those words that hold you down come back into your head, don't be afraid. They are only air held together by almost nothing.

Bring in the light and blow out the darkness.

Another deep cleansing breath. Breathe in the light and blow out the darkness, and gently open up your eyes.

Power, Peace, Purpose.

Being a Partner in Our Healing
~Go with a Flow~

Medical treatments, especially in the world of cancer, can have very negative implications. However, the more we can maintain a positive image of the treatment in its destruction of disease, the more we are able to participate in the healing process. This meditation allows the listener to create a very powerful, positive image of the flow of medicine into your being. Your brain is called upon to see the destruction of the deadly cancer cells and observe the strong, healthy inner body that is slowly returning to its rightful equilibrium.

Medical treatments, especially in the world of cancer, can have very negative implications.

It is counterintuitive to take medicines that can make us feel sicker.

The infusion process is not much fun for adults and a lot less for children.

However, the more we can effect a positive image of the destruction of cancer and disease, the more we can participate in the healing process.

Creating the imagery of a healing process actively helps the body to heal.

Find your place of comfort; sit back or lie down and relax.

Let every muscle fall into the chair or the bed and feel yourself, just a little bit, letting go.

Close your eyes.

Feel the coolness of the air as you breathe in, and the warmth as you breathe out.

Let's begin to scan our body to find any place of discomfort, of tightness, or anger or pain.

Take in a deep breath, and blow it out slowly.

Let's return to the feeling of coolness as the air comes in, and the warmth as you breathe out.

Create a flow of breath that is comfortable and nurturing.

With your eyes closed let's travel all the way to the top of your head.

Allow every muscle in your scalp to just fall downward.

The muscles in the forehead, allow them to release, one from the other, gently falling away from you.

Go to the muscles behind your eyes, the regions of your nose and your mouth and your jaw.

As you exhale let every muscle in your face just float and fall away, allowing your face to totally relax.

Go to the muscles behind your ears and in your neck.

As you exhale, feel every muscle in your neck and in the back of your head relax and release.

Travel down to the muscles in your shoulders, the muscles in your chest, as you exhale, let every single muscle flow downward.

Go to the muscles in your arms all the way to your wrists and your fingers.

Allow every muscle to simply relax and release.

Feel the coolness of the air as you breathe in, and the warmth as you breathe out.

Go to the muscles in your back, starting from your right shoulder blades to your left shoulder blades.

Allow them to fall gently as they relax and release.

Descend to the muscles down your back, to the small of your back, and feel every muscle gently drift downward.

The muscles in your upper legs, allow them to just simply fall and relax, releasing every tendon and ligament, all the way down your calves to your ankles and out your toes.

Feel the coolness of the air as you breathe in, and the warmth as you breathe out.

Imagine the picture of tumor or cancer cells, as dark fish, ugly parasites eating away inside of your body, taking up valuable nutrients for your life.

These are the cells of cancer.

And as you're receiving your infusion of medicine, taking your pills or are receiving radiation, allow the medicine to enter your body as a flowing light.

Imagine this gentle flow of healing, filled with light and radiance.

Allow this healing light to begin to penetrate the world of the fish.

And these deep, dark fish begin to get nervous and rattle around as the ooze of this light begins to flood over them, covering them, enveloping them, and destroying them.

As the medicine enters into this arena, into this place, see the fish becoming weaker and sluggish, and eventually as they're covered with this ooze, begin to disappear in that place.

As the light flows around each fish, every parasite, every element of the illness becomes covered with the healing power of this light. As the healing potion drips down on the ugly fish within you, watch the skin of the fish begin to break up as the fish dissolves into little pieces.

Feel that light go through you until the fish eating away at you become eaten away themselves.

Watch them disappear.

Feel the coolness of the air as you breathe in, and the warmth as you breathe out.

Feel that power to take control of your life and wipe out the disease.

Even though right now you may feel tired or weak, allow the image of this medicine to fill you with a light and a power, and see yourself as happy and powerful and well.

As you cleanse your body of the evil, destructive cells, you can see inside of your body the healthy tissue and cells come back with life and radiate with light, filling yourself up with the healing.

Repeat this image as the medicine continues to go inside of your self.

Keep seeing this ooze take over and destroy the cells of tumor.

Smile.

Feel yourself surrounded by joy and love and healing.

Focus on the power of that light to destroy all of the darkness.

Feel the coolness of the air as you breathe in, and the warmth as you breathe out.

As you breathe in, your body floods with this light, this healing, this power.

And as you exhale, all of the darkness that appears like a cloud upon your lips, and you blow out that which is disturbing the light because the light is so much more powerful than the darkness.

Feel the coolness of the air as you breathe in, and the warmth as you breathe out.

Take in a deep, cleansing breath, and blow it out slowly.

Another deep cleansing breath, and blow it out slowly.

And gently open up your eyes.

Power, Peace, Purpose.

Stopping Stress
~The Breath Brake~

Every time you have stress, the muscles in your body get tighter. Using your breath to relax your muscles lets your brain know that you are going from a sympathetic, fight-or-flight stress response to a parasympathetic, "relaxation" response. You can actually train your brain to stop the chemicals of stress from continuing to pour into your body. This meditation will walk you through a very powerful breathing technique that you can use whenever and wherever you want. It can save your life!

Every time you have stress, the muscles in your body get tighter.

Using your breath to relax your muscles lets your brain know that you are going from a sympathetic—a "fight or flight"—stress response to a parasympathetic—a relaxation response.

You can actually train your brain to stop the chemicals of stress from continuing to pour into your body.

We use a "Breath Brake."

Unlike the previous meditations, I'm not going to ask you to close your eyes or try to put ourselves into a place of extraordinary relaxation. The Breath Brake can be done any time and at any place.

Number one, it begins with the observation that our body is tight. If we are not exercising or engaged in a similar activity, we should feel relaxed and flowing.

"Tight" means that we must be facing the chemicals of stress.

Number two is to take accept this battle to stop the stress. We can do this.

And we do that simply by lifting up our body with the breath.

You can do this standing or sitting.

Start with your head and chin slightly lowered to your chest. Let your shoulders droop down a little bit and breathe in a comfortable manner.

After one or two breaths use the inhale, preferably through your nose to lift up your head. Pull up your neck and your shoulders. Allow the inhale to pick up your chest and your stomach as if your body is being pulled upward by the power of your breath.

Pull that air up higher and higher and higher, until you find yourself lifting off your toes higher and higher up until your body is totally filled with air.

And when there is no more room, pull in a little bit more, and hold that for three seconds. As you exhale, now go in the opposite direction. As you breathe out slowly through your mouth, you allow your neck to fall, your shoulders to relax, your chest to fall, your stomach. Your legs and feet become totally relaxed and reconnected to the ground. And when all of the air is out of your body, then you blow out a little bit more and now relax.

Let's do it together. Try to keep your back straight. You can use your hands as the children do to lift up the air, or you can do it with your hands down.

Preferably we breathe in through our nose and out through the mouth, but choose whatever way is comfortable for you.

Let's keep it very simple.

As you're feeling tightness in your body, pull your head up with a breath, continue to breathe in, further, more, a little bit more, lift up your body slightly and when there is no more room—pull in a little bit more . . . two, three, and now exhale slowly, feeling the breath across your lips, lowering your neck, your shoulders, your chest, your back, your feet. And when there is no more air left—blow out a little more.

I then teach people to say two Hebrew words, "Baruch Hashem," which literally means *Blessed is the Name*, referring to the source of the infinite for God.

But the word *baruch* is like a *breicha*, like a pool, and in this breath and in this blessing, we accept that that which is being channeled through us in our lives is ultimately an opportunity for greatness. Please use whatever phrase you are comfortable with, but this phrase is powerful.

As we breathe out, "Baruch Hashem."

One more time, breathe in, but this time as you breathe in feel yourself filling with a great and powerful light. Hold it: now you don't want to breathe out the light; exhale the darkness. Any place of pain, and fear, anger—blow it out.

Let's do it together.

Bring in the light, span your body upward, and push out the darkness.

When there is nothing else left: "Baruch Hashem."

Power, Peace, Purpose.

Taking Control of Your Eating
~It's Easy as Pie~

Children undergoing chemotherapy often have no appetite. We emphasize to our little martial artists that they are in training, and eating is an important part of that training. For most people, of course, having no appetite is not the challenge. Fatty foods and unhealthy eating habits have created an epidemic of obesity, especially in the United States. This meditation will help guide you to become a healthier version of you. Seeing your ability to make smart choices will make it easier for you to imagine the body you really deserve.

Among children undergoing chemotherapy, the medicines often leave them with no appetite. We emphasize to our little martial artists that they are in training, and eating is an important part of that training. It makes a big difference.

For most people having no appetite is not the challenge. The opposite is more often the case. Consuming unhealthy foods or meals too rich in calories has created a plague of obesity, especially in the United States.

Here the brain plays a significant role in exchanging what we want for what we need, and often lying to us about what we truly desire.

Having the power to push out the messages of "Supersize Me" and introducing foods that make us powerful into our own personal training strategy can help you to take control over your life.

Let's do a meditation together that will allow you to see the image of your body, healthy and powerful. Knowing what you can be allows you the license to travel to that place and fully arrive. This is a great way to begin your own personal training curriculum.

Take a deep breath and blow it out slowly.

Close your eyes.

Let your body relax. Any other thought or message or sound that you feel or hear, just blow them out with your breath, relaxing your body and creating a flow.

Feel the coolness of the air as you breathe in and the warmth as you breathe out.

Start from the very top of your head and as you exhale feel every muscle in your head just fall and relax . . . and release.

As you breathe out again, feel the muscles in your neck gently flow downward, as if your head is weightless.

Go to the muscles in your chest, your stomach, your arms as you exhale, feel every muscle ripple downward, gently pulling apart one from the other.

Feel the muscles in your back gently flow downward; relaxing, falling, creating a comfortable wave flowing through your back and down your body.

Feel the coolness of the air as you breathe in, and the warmth as you breathe out.

Experience your entire body very relaxed.

Find the memory of your afternoon munchies experience. Remember inside of your head, that feeling in the mid-afternoon—snack time—with your brain telling you that it's time for the chocolate bar. See yourself, sitting at your desk responding to the expectation of a sweet reward. You see yourself standing and approaching the refrigerator. At the next moment as your hand begins to reach for the cake or the chocolate, command your hand to pass over the chocolate bar. Pull out an apple, an orange, a juicy pear. You are going to be powerful and choose the reward that will allow you to be whom you want to be.

As you eat, see the image of yourself eating that healthy fruit; feel the sweetness and the energy flowing to your body.

See yourself satisfied that you have taken control.

Be proud of yourself and your strength not to listen to the seduction of your brain that will make you weak.

Feel the coolness of the air as you breathe in, and the warmth as you breathe out.

Imagine yourself sitting down at the dinner table with your plate filled up with the seductive foods of weakness.

See yourself stopping midpoint into your favorite food, satisfied in your stomach with what you have eaten, and knowing that any other bite takes away from your power.

Create the image of yourself choosing the foods that are powerful and passing over the junk that saps your strength.

When the pang of need enters your brain for just "one more of this" or "an extra of that" or the reward foods that your brain tells you are great, in your mind's eye see the darkness and the unhappiness that surrounds these foods, that ultimately will cause you pain even though in the moment they feel so good.

Surround that cake, ice cream, soda with those clouds of darkness that weigh you down in life.

You are training. You can be different. You can be healthy.

And now see in your mind's eye that new you. See yourself being complimented by others. "You look great!" "How did you do it?" Hear yourself telling the others how you recognized that our brains can lie to ourselves and our stress can take control and make us weak. Let them know how children with cancer inspired you to breathe out that darkness and bring in the light.

Feel the coolness of the air as you breathe in, and the warmth as you breathe out.

Tell your brain that foods that don't have power are foods of unhappiness and darkness.

And see yourself pushing away those foods that are bad for you.

Power, Peace, Purpose lies within your reach. You can have it.

See your new clothing adding a layer of beauty and sophistication to a body that is filled with muscles and is strong and healthy and good.

See yourself training your brain to know what you really want, and to recognize all that you can be.

Feel the coolness of the air as you breathe in, and the warmth as you breathe out.

One more time, see yourself looking really good, and smiling at others as they notice. And hear yourself teaching those others how to breathe in the light of health and strength and power, and blow out the darkness that is created by the foods, by the snacks, by the stuff that you put into your body that only add layer after layer of darkness and unhappiness.

Feel the coolness of the air as you breathe in, and the warmth as you breathe out.

Feel the power as you breathe in, and the weakness as you blow it away and begin to take control over your life.

Take in a deep cleansing breath, and let it out slowly.

Another deep cleansing breath, and let it out slowly.

And gently, open up your eyes.

Power, Peace, Purpose.

Pain-Free Injections
~Deflecting the Point~

So many people, not only children, are deathly afraid of the prick of a needle or lancet that they must endure for some normal diagnostic test. The more we are afraid of the pain, the greater the discomfort. This meditation, which is practiced by children as young as three years old, will help you transcend the pain and fear of getting stuck. Being able to breathe through the experience of getting a shot or having blood drawn will actually lower the discomfort. Ask our kids!

I explain to the children that I am a little guy, and if someone bigger is pushing me and I push back, I am not going to get too far. However, if I pull him toward me, I can throw my opponent wherever I want.

Push is weak, pull is powerful.

When a pain message comes into our body, there's a very primal response to push out against it, but usually that only makes the pain worse. The tighter the muscles, the more painful the needle.

Let's learn together a process that the children of Kids Kicking Cancer use to take in needles and to push out the pain.

Let's begin by doing a simple meditation of relaxation and train your brain that you are able to conquer needles.

Take in a deep breath; breathe it out slowly.

Close your eyes.

Another deep breath, and breathe it out slowly.

Feel the coolness of the air as you breathe in, and the warmth as you breathe out.

Create a rhythm with the flow of your air, gently coming in and then flowing out.

Breathe in a way that is comfortable for you, but look through your body for any place of tightness, of fear, of anger, of pain, and when you exhale, feel that tightness relax as you blow out any pain, fear, or anger.

Move your body with the flow of your breath.

Feel the coolness of the air as you breathe in, and the warmth as you breathe out.

Imagine that you are sitting in the clinic waiting to have your blood drawn from a vein in your arm. Allow your eyes to focus on one place on the wall. It could be an interesting picture, or a bell, or a light. And focus on that one place as the nurse or the doctor walks into the room. When they begin their preparation, continue to focus on that one place, feeling the coolness of the air as you breathe in and the warmth as you breathe out. Remember to pace your breath to be slow but comfortable.

Any tightness that you feel coming into your body, pull it up, and breathe it out.

Feel your body move upward as you inhale, and down as you exhale.

As you extend your arm outward to prep for the needle, continue your breath.

And then, as they take the alcohol and rub the place to cleanse it, feel your breath coming a tiny, little bit faster . . . a very, very slight difference.

As the needle comes into your skin, turn your head toward the needle. Take a strong quick breath as you draw into your body any discomfort entering into your arm. At the very same time that the needle is entering your arm, take your free hand and put it near where the needle is coming in. As the needle comes in, use your hand and your breath as if you are pulling any discomfort into your body and totally taking control of it.

Continue to pull in that breath, bringing in any pain as if a cloud is going through you, and turn your head and your free hand to the opposite direction and breathe out that cloud as you are using your arm to push out any discomfort that you feel toward the opposite end.

If you continue to feel discomfort from the sight of the source of the needle, come back, pull it up, and then turn away and breathe it out the other direction, continuing to repeat the procedure until you are again very comfortable.

Let your hand control the pathway of your breath as your breath takes control of the direction of the pain until you have removed it from your body.

And now that you have done an amazing job, you can allow the nurse to know how you did this so that she can teach others.

Most people have some level of discomfort with needles, especially children in the hospital.

Join our little teachers to teach the world how to pull in the discomfort and blow out the pain, taking control even over the needle. Let everyone you teach know that you learned this from some amazing little heroes.

Power, Peace, Purpose.

Happiness
~The Best Medicine Around~

Miles was a young man who knew that he did not have many days left. He was also a brilliant thinker and an extraordinary writer. He described life with penetrating metaphors. This meditation focuses on the metaphor just described. It will help you appreciate every day of your life. With a fresh perspective, you will see the possibility of a new beginning. These words are dedicated to Miles Levin.

Miles was a young man who knew that he did not have many days left. He was also a brilliant thinker and an extraordinary writer.

He once described life with an analogy of a golfer who is dedicating a few hours to the range. The fellow starts with a whole bucket full of golf balls. In the beginning he hits ball after ball with abandon, until he notices that there aren't many left. Each one becomes more precious, until finally there is the last one. That one will always be so much more focused than any that preceded it.

This meditation is dedicated to Miles Levin.

Take in a deep breath, breathe it out slowly.

Close your eyes.

Another deep breath, and breathe it out slowly.

Feel the coolness of the air as you breathe in, and the warmth as you breathe out.

Experience your entire body loosening up as your torso picks up slightly with the breath as you inhale, and gently descends as you exhale.

Let your body flow with the feeling of your breath.

See your breath as light.

Breathe in the light, and blow out any feeling of darkness, anger, fear.

Breathe in the light, and blow out the darkness.

Imagine yourself surrounded by beautiful sunlight, and see yourself standing on a magnificent driving range. The grass is very, very green. The sky is painted with the deepest of blue.

You have your tee in the ground, and a large aluminum bucket brimming with golf balls sits by your feet. One by one, with joy you hit the balls. One and then another go sailing down the range. You are doing really well. You feel very happy.

And each ball that you hit disappears into the grass far, far ahead of you. But that is okay, because you have plenty left. And you continue to hit and to drive with abandon until you notice that the sun is not as bright as it was just a little while ago. The sky is not as blue and there are not that many balls left.

And so now you slow the pace, place the ball upon the tee, ready your stance, and you whack a ball.

And you do that again, but this time even more deliberate as you notice there are only three left.

And then another.

And another.

Each time carefully focusing on the drive, knowing that there aren't too many balls left.

And finally you are standing there looking at the tee and at your last ball.

And now the sun has almost disappeared and the clouds have created a very dark sky, and you wonder if you really took advantage properly of each ball that you hit.

And the thought frightens you. Will anyone remember the distances you had reached? Will there be any more meaning to the drives you have taken?

But then, all of the sudden, the clouds drift apart from each other and the sun begins to renew its warmth of the air, and you are given another bucket full of balls.

Now the sky is even richer in its hues and the grass carpet even more luxurious.

This time, every ball has meaning. This time you carefully look at each golf ball as another opportunity. Each drive wants to make a difference for someone else, each swing as a motion of meaning, one that will live on.

None of us know how many days are in our bucket.

But the opportunity that we have each day is a full lifetime, if we cherish it.

Happiness is the ability to hold onto that day and supply it with meaning.

And God willing, we do it the next day, and the day after, and the day after.

Focus on the light.

Feel the power of that light come into your very, very being.

Feel the coolness of the air as you breathe in, and the warmth as you breathe out.

And realize that you can use that light every day of your life.

The more you will share that light the more you will have . . . forever.

Take in a deep breath, and hold it, and then breathe it out slowly.

Take in another deep breath, and breathe it out slowly.

And open your eyes.

Power, Peace, Purpose.

MEDITATION 14

Bereavement
~Long Days~

 *Physical pain and emotional pain follow very similar neurological pathways. The implications on the body of long-term ongoing stress messages can be very harmful. There are very few things that create the depth of emotional pain more than the loss of someone we love. This meditation allows you to focus beyond separation to reach a place of connection and unity with that beautiful soul that still lives within you. It is comforting to know that we are all part of that oneness.*

Physical pain and emotional pain follow very similar neurological pathways. The implications on the body of long-term ongoing stress messages can be very harmful.

One of the biggest complaints I hear from other parents who have lost children,surrounds the well-meaning attempts of some friends, family, and professional support who wish to help these parents get beyond their mourning. The message that the parents are hearing, "It's time to move on," does not usually resonate in a positive way to people who have lost children.

It is just not natural for a parent who loses a child to "move on."

We explain to our parents who have experienced the loss of a child that they will always hold onto the light of their child's soul, but I know very personally that not being able to hold my daughter's hand will remain with me as an emotional pain for the rest of my life. Don't even try to force yourself to let go of those emotions.

However, no one really wants to allow the stress chemicals of ongoing grief to destroy our health or inhibit our ability to be a mom, a dad, a husband, or a wife.

Therefore, this meditation focuses on the light of the souls of these beautiful children, while allowing our bodies to relax and stop the chemicals of stress.

This is an equally effective meditation no matter what the source of pain of bereavement may be.

Put yourself in a comfortable place. Begin to feel the experience of your breath.

Take in a deep breath, and let it out slowly, and as you exhale, close your eyes.

Feel the coolness of the air as you breathe in, and the warmth as you breathe out.

Let's scan through the body, and reach all the way up to the very top of yourself. As you exhale, let every muscle in your scalp and your forehead gently fall downward.

Allow the muscles behind your eyes and all of your face to gently pull away from each other as you breathe out. Let every muscle relax and release.

Feel the muscles in your neck and your shoulders and your chest simply let go as you breathe out.

Feel the coolness of the air as you breathe in, and the warmth as you breathe out.

Go to the muscles in your chest and your stomach; as you exhale let every muscle just fall downward.

And now the muscles in your upper back, vertebra by vertebra, allow every muscle to gently pull apart one from the other.

Feel the coolness of the air as you breathe in, and the warmth as you breathe out.

Go all the way down your upper legs, your knees, out your calves, your ankles, and your toes. As you exhale let every muscle throughout your body gently relax and release.

Feel the coolness of the air as you breathe in, and the warmth as you breathe out.

If you look through your body, there is an emptiness but there is no more stress or tightness.

In your mind's eye, you look upward in the midst of the darkness: there is a great light.

Feel the coolness of the air as you breathe in, and the warmth as you breathe out.

And as you breathe in now, imagine in your mind that you are reaching all the way, all the way up to this amazing light, a Heavenly light, a powerful light.

And you can see within that light the face and the smile of the one you love who dwells only in that light. But it is a place more real than any other.

Feel the coolness of the air as you breathe in, and the warmth as you breathe out.

As your hands envelop that light and that smile, you realize that the light is not so far away and that you can bring that light inside of yourself. Breathe out all pain.

As you breathe in, let your hands extend all the way upward until the light begins to come toward you. Breathe out all darkness.

As you breathe in, your arms embrace this orb of light, and as you exhale, gently, gently, the image becomes even clearer still.

As you continue to embrace the power of that soul, the universe around you begins to radiate about you with the beauty of that light.

Feel the coolness of the air as you breathe in, and the warmth as you breathe out.

As you embrace the light, that soul ventures more and more inside of yourself until you have become one and the same with the magnificent light.

As you breathe in, the light lifts up your spirit and fills the vacuum of your being.

As you breathe out, you expel the emptiness and the darkness, because the distance between Heaven and Earth has been overcome.

Feel that light dwell within you. Feel its warmth and its beauty.

Continue to blow out any darkness, any place of pain, sadness, or the torment of guilt—the "should have," "I could have done this or that."

Blow all of that out so that you can remain at one with the light, the light of that soul inside of yourself.

Feel the coolness of the air as you breathe in, and the warmth as you breathe out.

Feel that light warm and grow inside of your being.

And now see the image of that light inside of your being, with that smiling, sweet face, filled with love contained within the very light of your essence. In the midst of yourself.

Heaven and Earth are not far apart.

Feel this light, allow it to warm you.

See yourself traveling with that light, with that connection, with that inner smile.

Identify the darkness, and breathe it out.

Breathe in the light, and blow out the darkness.

And now every time you breathe out, just repeat gently inside of yourself, that one word, Light.

Light.

Light.

Light.

Light.

Light.

This is the light of the soul.

This is the light that keeps you together.

Breathe in the light, and blow out the darkness.

This light is forever. It is part of you.

It will always be.

Take in a very deep cleansing breath, and blow it out gently.

Another deep cleansing breath, and blow it out gently.

Now open up your eyes.

Power, Peace, Purpose.

Loving Another
~Pulley, not Bully~

The children teach us that when we push we are weak; when we pull we are powerful. Think of the relationships in your life where you are pushing instead of pulling. Those are the relationships that don't work. Very often the reason that we end up pushing others is out of our own fears and insecurities. Sometimes, we just don't feel valuable enough. This meditation allows you to be present in a place in which you recognize your power to pull others toward you. When you recognize the power of what you have to offer others, then you will be so much better in guiding your relationships with this light.

The children teach us that when we push we are weak; when we pull we are powerful.

Think of the relationships in your life where you are pushing instead of pulling.

Those are the relationships that don't work.

Very often the reason that we end up pushing others is out of our own fears and insecurities. Sometimes, we just don't feel valuable enough.

If we can imagine the importance we add to the lives of others, then it is so much easier to pull someone toward us.

Thinking of ourselves as being successful in relationships allows us to become a more significant, "significant" other.

In English the word "or," as in "either/or," represents another possibility. In Hebrew, *or* means light.

We are going to use this term to help you feel this light and create an image of the possibilities that you can create in the most important relationships in your life.

Go to a comfortable place and let your body just fall into the chair or the bed if you are lying down, and begin to focus on your breathing.

Feel the coolness of the air as you breathe in, and the warmth as you breathe out.

Close your eyes.

Any other sounds or words, thoughts or feelings, that come into your head—just put them down gently and go back to your breath.

Feel the coolness of the air as you breathe in, and the warmth as you breathe out.

As you exhale let every muscle in your body just fall downward through the chair or the bed. Let everything just fall.

Feel the coolness of the air as you breathe in, and the warmth as you breathe out.

Imagine above your head is an extraordinarily beautiful and powerful light.

As you breathe in, imagine this beautiful light coming straight into your heart.

Feel the light get brighter and warmer in the cavity of your chest.

Imagine as you breathe in every breath fills your heart with more and more wonderful, beautiful light.

And that light responds to your breath as if it is your beating light. As you become more and more filled with this light, you want more possibility of light and love and pulling that special person toward you.

Every time you breathe out, mimic the sound of your heart with two words: "More *or.*"

More *or.*

You're asking for more potential of light and the possibility of love coming from your heart.

More *or.*

More *or.*

More *or*.

More *or*.

Gently keep repeating those two words inside of your head every time you exhale.

More *or*.

More *or*.

More *or*.

More *or*.

Feel the light continue to illuminate, coming from the depth of your heart, and as you repeat the words "More *or*," see the light coming forward, coming toward whom you love. Use that light to pull them toward you, rather than pushing them away.

More *or*.

More *or*.

More *or*.

See the light come from your heart and radiate the face of someone whom you wish to pull toward your light and toward your heart.

More *or*.

More *or*.

As your light spans the distance between you and the other, it ripples through the waves of space so that your other can feel this light, and the joy that you have inside of your heart, until that other person will want to be attached to the power of your light.

More *or*.

More *or*.

More *or*.

More *or*.

Every beat of your heart radiates that powerful beauty. As your heart beats out the sounds of the rhythmic universe, your other comes toward you, pulled by the powerful light and the beauty of your soul.

More *or*.

More *or*.

More *or*.

In the place of pushing in fear, you have created joy and light that pulls that significant person in your life, your love, toward you.

As you embrace that light of another, you embrace the light of your heart and the beauty of your giving soul.

More *or.*

More *or.*

More *or.*

More *or.*

Sit with that feeling of holding that light together and smile from the depth of your soul because you can pull another toward you.

More *or.*

More *or.*

More *or.*

Keep repeating those two words.

More *or.*

More *or.*

More *or.*

Or.

Feel yourself wrapped up in the light of love, pulling in your other, creating a oneness.

A oneness of light together.

Feel the power of pull and it will let you take control over the weakness of push.

More *or.*

More *or.*

Breathe in a strong, cleansing breath, and blow it out slowly.

Another cleansing breath, and blow it out slowly.

And gently open up your eyes.

Power, Peace, Purpose.

Maintaining Perspective
~Stop, Look, & Listen~

"Stop, Look, & Listen" is a very quick but powerful meditation that can help get you to the other side of any challenge with success. If you recognize that you can lose control to your stressors even if you haven't been diagnosed with OCD, you can follow this meditation to begin to direct your life from a place of power. The first step in this process is to understand that stress and all of its impact on the body can be controlled. You can gain an effective, honest perspective on your life that will allow you to make those positive changes that you so very much want.

"Stop, Look, and Listen" is a very quick but powerful meditation that can help get you to the other side of any challenge with success.

The first step in this process is to understand that stress and all of its impact on the body can be controlled. You can brake the stress response.

Almost always, you will be able to notice one of the symptoms of stress jumping on you. The muscles of your body get tight because the fight or flight response activates your muscles to do just that—fight or flight. While this can wreak havoc on your back or neck, it also provides an opportunity to stop the stress progression and tell your brain that you are not in the middle of some life-threatening crisis.

Recognizing that your body is tight and that you're not carrying luggage upstairs indicates that there is other baggage that you are lugging that's more the stuff of Kryptonite than Samsonite.

As soon as you observe that tightness in your neck, your shoulders, your arms, your stomach, your head, then it's time to take your Breath Brake.

Breathing is the only part of the autonomic response that you can so easily control. By putting something that is automatic on manual, you can engage your "Breath Brake" and stop your adrenal gland from shooting out the chemicals of stress that are killing you.

Step number—I am feeling tightness in body.

Take a very slow deep breath, preferably with your nose. Bring in the breath as you pull up the air —slowly, slowly.

When there is no more room in your lungs, add just a little bit more with a quick and powerful inhale. Hold it. Your body is suspended all the way up —count to three (. . . two, three), and now exhale, very slowly through your mouth, relaxing and releasing every tightness in your body.

Every time that you have stress, those chemicals will tighten up your muscles. Feeling them, lifting up your body with the breath, and then relaxing the muscles in the exhale will tell your brain that you are not in stress mode. This is not a sympathetic "fight or flight" response. You have just told the command center in your brain to go into a parasympathetic or relaxation mode because you have taken control over the wheel.

Breathe normally for another twenty seconds and repeat the "Breath Brake," making certain to feel your muscles relax in the exhale. Continuing using the "Breath Brake," until you can feel that your muscles have relaxed. In the beginning it might take you two or three minutes. Your brain controls every muscle in your body. Relaxing those muscles with your breath can save your life.

After you have put a Stop! to the chemical flood of stress, it is time to "look."

Glance down on the floor all around you. Check the area around your feet. Look where you're sitting. If there are no major body parts lying around, then you are probably OK. If what you were "mugged" by is not going to require a run to the emergency room, then there is no reason to create emergency chemicals that will only make you sick.

Great! Now that you have stopped and you have "looked," now it is time to "listen."

The Chinese character for "crisis" suggests "opportunity." How is this particular challenge in my life an opportunity and not a catastrophe? How can you respond in a manner that will teach those around you? How can you use this moment as a vector to pull someone toward you, rather than push them away?

A perfect God created an imperfect world perfectly. How can I take this script and respond with greatness? Throw out this one question to your soul. Then sit back and listen.

Let us do the "Breath Brake" together as a meditation.

Find your comfortable place and relax your body into the chair or bed.

Feel the coolness of the air as you breathe in, and the warmth as you breathe out.

Close your eyes.

Feel the coolness of the air as you breathe in, and the warmth as you breathe out.

Travel inside of yourself all the way to the very top of your head. Now go up a little bit further and take a comfortable position outside of yourself where you can see your face.

Imagine the feeling of being mugged by your stress. Something about a test, an appointment, a meeting, a financial challenge, a disappointment, your children, spouse—any trigger that makes you get that "yuck" feeling of pressure. In your perch above your body, you can see your neck, stomach, your back tighten up. The creases of stress are written as knitted creases of worry upon your forehead.

As you watch yourself, you can actually feel the tightness in your back, in your neck, in your stomach, in your chest. Now command yourself, sitting there down below you, to take your body off of the automatic stress response and put everything on manual. Quickly fly back inside of your head and take control.

Let's take that Breath Brake together. Lift up your body with your breath and pull your torso up, and up, and feel your body extending upward. Pull up so that your stomach extends upward and you reach up with your legs. When there is no more room for any more air, take in a little bit more (. .

. two, three), and as you exhale feel your head come forward a little bit and the muscles in your neck relax, and your shoulders fall, and your chest and your stomach release, and when there is no more air in your body at all, blow out a little bit more.

And now check the floor. Look around you.

Anything dangling from your body? Organs all feel like they're in the right places in your body? Then you absolutely know that you can do this.

You have just switched off the 911 call inside of your brain.

And now listen.

Who will gain from your heroic response to this challenge?

Who will notice that you have replaced the creases by your eyes with the smile on your lips?

Who will benefit from the clarity of thought and the charity of your pull rather than the cluttered, flustered angry response of your stress?

Using the "Breath Brake" you will be surprised how quickly you can Stop, Look, and Listen to become an amazing teacher of life.

Our children do it every day.

Stop, Look, and Listen.

You have that power.

Power, Peace, Purpose.

Paradoxical Intention
~Fun Works~

Your brain has the power to make you feel that even relatively unimportant events are almost life threatening, representing crisis and insurmountable challenge. The more you become afraid, the greater the downward spiral of losing control will threaten you. This meditation provides a very practical technique to continue the process that you have learned in the last lesson. By creating a healthier sense of perspective, you can create positive, powerful outcomes in reaching your goals...

The brain has the power to make us feel that even relatively unimportant events are almost life threatening, representing crisis and undoable challenge.

Most of us remember that stomachache before a spelling test in fourth grade. We were convinced that we were going to fail and in fact we got a 100. And even if we had failed that test, chances are it would not have led to incarceration, execution, or worse. But at the moment, it was a crisis.

Our brains portray those challenging moments of our lives and make them a lot more overwhelming than they have to be because of our fears.

Victor Frankl, in his logotherapy, describes a very effective tool that helps us to put the brain in its place. It is called "Paradoxical Intention." This process allows us to make a joke out of the calamity that we face. It may not work as well with fourth graders, but I have seen with adults how effective it can be.

Let's say a person is petrified of public speaking. We'll train that individual to see themselves braced against a podium, making a presentation in front of a large audience televised to the world. In the middle of their speech, suddenly without warning, their pants fall to the ground. And yes, that is the day that unfortunately they chose to wear the briefs with that "Hello Kitty" insignia on it. You might as well add to the scene an unsatisfied audience getting up and throwing their iPads at you in utter disgust, or beginning to choke the person next to them out of sheer boredom.

Because the scene is so ludicrous, the brain is given an opportunity to reframe the fear into the reality that we are not really facing disaster even though there are stress chemicals that signal imminent destruction running through our bloodstream. Just as we did with our "Breath Brake," shifting out of automatic and manually controlling the gears is something that will make a giant difference in our lives.

Let's imagine the following very common fears—having a meeting in which it is very important for you to make a great impression. For some it may be a job interview; for others, a date.

Imagine that the interview goes awry and the HR manager decides to call in the state police because he has determined that you are an obvious menace to society. See yourself being led away in handcuffs for providing less than a brilliant answer or for fashioning a less than perfect perspective on how you can help that particular company grow.

The more we can recognize that our lives are not hanging in the balance, and that this is not a do-or-die situation, the more control we have over our brains, our stress, and our lives.

Let's do a fill-in-the-gap meditation.

Let's just sit for a moment, calm.

Focus on your breathing.

Feel the coolness of the air as you breathe in, and the warmth as you breathe out.

Create a flow of your breath so that any other thought or sound or message that comes into your head, we can put that down gently and go back to the feeling of your breath.

Feel the coolness of the air as you breathe in, and the warmth as you breathe out.

As your body begins to relax, let's evoke a stress response, contrary to everything we've done until now.

Think about the most stressful thought that you can have.

A thought that is holding you back from being the best that you can be.

Maybe it's a fear of public speaking, maybe it's a fear of asking someone for a date, maybe it's a fear of having an interview. Perhaps the fear of failing. Pick the first fear that comes into your mind.

Bring that fear into your mind and identify it to yourself.

Good.

Now imagine the most ridiculous outcome, the most unimaginable scene. Your pants fall down, or you're taken away in handcuffs. A SWAT team is called because you are talking too much.

Chuckle to yourself and see yourself letting go of the stress that allows your brain to lie to you.

You will be fine.

Make the script really funny. You will remember it.

And the next time you come into that situation, for example, getting up in front of a group to speak, take in a deep breath, blow it out slowly, relax your muscles, and think of that scene.

When you do, it will help you to reshape that scene, ultimately as one that is successful, one that you ace because you can do it. You did it in fourth grade; you are not going to stop now.

Power, Peace, Purpose.

Your Smile
~The Tooth Truth~

It's not unusual for you to be surrounded by people who automatically cause that stress response in you. Usually they hit the triggers or UFOs, the unidentified fears and obstacles in your head. This meditation will allow you to experience a new reality. Your inner light is expressed in the smile on your face. Using this energy, you can impact those around you in a very positive way. You become an amazing teacher. It is all within your smile.

Have you ever reached for the phone after reading the caller ID and then notice that your arm is tight?

Either your phone is way too heavy or whoever happens to be calling you is a source of stress.

It's not unusual for us to be surrounded by people who automatically cause us that stress response.

Usually they hit the triggers or UFOs, the Unidentified Fears and Obstacles in our head.

That simply means that every time when we were disrespected as a child or felt uncared for, unimportant, a drag, etc., those messages sit inside of our head.

And even after thirty or forty years later, when someone else makes that message, those old feelings create the same triggered chemical responses of stress as if it were yesterday. We do not respond to life only of the moment but to the amalgam of pains and fears that have been placed within us throughout all of our lives.

This meditation will help us identify how to respond to the sources of stress with Power, Peace, Purpose.

Let's put ourselves in a comfortable position, either sitting or lying down.

Allow the muscles in your body to shake loose, one from the other.

And take in a deep, deep cleansing breath. Hold it for three seconds and then gently blow it out.

Take another deep cleansing breath, one more time.

Close your eyes.

Pull your body up with the breath, hold it, and now exhale, feeling your shoulders and your back, your stomach, your head simply drop in place, relaxing each and every muscle.

Feel the coolness of the air as you breathe in, and the warmth as you breathe out.

Imagine you're sitting in the middle of a circle, like a carousel. Surrounding you are major characters who appear in your life.

Your family, your friends, the people you work with, the people you may work for.

Imagine that all around you are the faces of the people in your life.

As the carousel begins to turn, you look directly into their faces and they look back at you.

As the faces of your family pass you by, you notice that there are some who are not smiling at you.

As you go from person to person, amongst your friends there may be those who are not smiling at you.

As you go—much more likely—from person to person with the people whom you work with, you notice that there are those faces who are not smiling at you. You try to let go of each image, but it is hard.

All of the people who are not smiling at you are a source of stress.

As the carousel begins to turn around and around, take it off automatic. You take control. Stop it at the first person in your family who is not smiling at you.

Perhaps they are upset or angry at something you did or didn't do. Maybe they're jealous. Maybe they just don't understand you.

As they look right at you, you can sense a darkness projecting from their inner self at you.

Normally this darkness will trigger all different feelings of darkness inside of yourself. But not now.

Instead, you take a very deep breath in, and pull in a beautiful light that radiates above you. A beautiful warm connection to the source of all light.

Breathe in a breath as if the air is coming from the very top of your head.

With this next breath use that power to pull in this light that is above you.

And as you breathe out, imagine the clouds of darkness leave you.

Pull in the light and breathe out the darkness.

Pull in the light and breathe out the darkness, of negativity, of fears, of pain and of angers, and just blow it out like a dark cloud leaving your mouth.

Imagine as you look at that person who is not smiling, now that you've brought in your light and that you're in control, you open up your lips and you can feel the biggest smile come onto your face.

Walk away from yourself just for a moment just so you can see yourself smile.

Can you see your face?

Can you put on that face the most beautiful smile filled with teeth?

As you watch that smile emanating from your face, you produce this enormous light.

At first it is blinding but then it is comforting.

And you watch as that smile creates a trajectory of radiance and love onto the face of the person in your family who's filled with anger, or fears.

And you watch as the light from your face begins to bathe the face of your child, or your spouse, your brother, your sister, with your light. Whoever carries darkness needs your light.

With great patience you allow that smile to continue until eventually it washes away the darkness, and that angry face that was looking at you now erupts with the smile of light as well.

Feel yourself responding to the darkness of others with your own incredible light.

Feel the coolness of the air as you breathe in, and the warmth as you breathe out.

Allow the carousel to continue, until you notice that first person whom you work with, and perhaps feels disappointed, angry, upset that there's something that you did or didn't do to them.

Bring in your light, and blow out the darkness that you feel toward that person because you have been a mirror for his or her shadows.

Blow out your feelings of darkness, of fears, of insecurities; your own feelings of pain.

Bring in the light and blow out the darkness.

And again, you paint upon your face the most beautiful, wide, illuminating smile.

And you watch as out of your smile comes the intensity of a beautiful light, which is projecting onto the angry face in front of yourself.

And the light that comes from within with patience begins to wash the anger away from whoever is looking at you.

And you can see that your smile can wash away the angers and the fears and the pain of others.

Continue this one by one.

Pull in the light and breathe out your own darkness, and look at the faces of those around you and respond with the light of your beautiful smile.

Power, Peace, Purpose.

MEDITATION 19

~Appreciating Being Appreciated~

Do you ever feel alone or underappreciated? That no one knows your struggles or how hard you work? Your pain can make you feel very much alone. This meditation is a focus exercise to allow you to know, no matter who you are or what you face, that your struggles are important to the universe. What you do and how you do it is known, observed, and eventually imitated by those around you. Creating a positive energy within yourself impacts the globe that surrounds you without!

Do you ever feel alone, underappreciated?

No one knows the struggles that you have, how hard you work.

Nobody notices how hard we try and how often we have to cover over those feelings and thoughts inside of ourselves.

This meditation is a focus exercise to allow all of us to know, no matter who we are or what we face, that our struggles are important, that our challenge is being observed, but not from a place of criticism, but from a place of love.

What we do and how we do it does make a difference.

Find a place to sit or to lie down where you can be comfortable.

Allow every muscle in your body to fall into the bed or to glide into the chair and slightly pick up your body with your breath.

As you breathe in, feel the coolness of the air, and as you breathe out, feel its warmth.

Close your eyes.

Feel the coolness of the air as you breathe in, and the warmth as you breathe out.

Go to the very top of your head, and any place of tension or tightness, just allow to gently fall.

Go to the muscles behind your eyes and as you exhale let every muscle relax and gently pull apart one from the other.

Go to the muscles in your cheeks and behind your jaw.

The muscles behind your ears.

As you breathe out, feel every muscle in your face totally fall.

Feel the coolness of the air as you breathe in, and the warmth as you breathe out.

Go to the muscles in your neck and in your shoulders, and feel them melt away, gently falling downward.

Go to the muscles in your chest and in your stomach. As you breathe out, let every muscle relax and release.

Go to the muscles in your back and gently descend down your vertebrae, one by one, until you feel every muscle in your back relax and release.

Allow any tightness in your legs and your calves to gently fall away as you feel the coolness of the air as you breathe in, and the warmth as you breathe out.

As you're sitting there, you can replay in your mind so many times the feelings of discomfort.

That people are looking at you, that people are watching you, that they don't understand what you're really feeling.

And you only imagine that they're looking at you with such disapproval.

You feel different, so different, from everybody else around.

You only wish that it can be declared a sickness with a name on it so everyone would understand.

But truly nobody understands.

Your brain makes you think thoughts of all types of things.

Focusing on food, your weight, your mistakes, how you look, how you act, how you speak.

It makes you feel so different from everyone else.

But ultimately, you are being watched.

You're being watched not from a place of disapproval, not from a place of negativity, but from a place of great love, a place of light.

As you bring yourself back to that light, you impact the entire world because you are very powerful.

Feel the coolness of the air as you breathe in, and the warmth as you breathe out.

As you reach upward inside of yourself, you can see that there is an eye.

An eye that is peering out of the Heavens, watching and gently directing you to hear and feel and know the messages of light and of truth.

And you work so hard to continue to focus until you begin to feel the light that comes from the seeing eye above. That light enters into your head until you can feel the warmth of that light inside of yourself. To hold that light makes you realize that your struggle is so important because you refuse to be defeated by the darkness. You continue onward each day. You are being watched. Your very essence becomes a source of light for everything around you.

Feel the coolness of the air as you breathe in, and the warmth as you breathe out.

Your light is penetrating the vastness and darkness of the world because you refuse to be defeated. You are continuing with light and with strength.

You can see that your light is casting a glow upon the world because the eye above is reflecting your light onto those around you.

Reflecting on this light allows you to feel the power of your soul impacting the very Heavens.

Breathe in that light from above, and as you breathe out, the light returns through you and makes a circle with the rest of the world. It travels up and again reflects downward, all around.

Breathe in that light from above and allow that light as you breathe out to circle the world.

And now, as you sit with an image of a beautiful circle of light that surrounds you, gently repeat that singular word as a very quiet whisper from the core of your being.

As you breathe out, gently repeat the word "light"

Light.

Light.

Feel the power of that light.

Light.

Light.

Light.

Every time that you push out the feelings of darkness, of being different, of being judged, you breathe in a light that not only allows you to cope and transcend but a radiance that impacts the universe.

A perfect God created your imperfect world absolutely perfectly.

And as you respond with strength and with light despite the darkness, you bring with you an infinite light.

Take a deep breath, and blow it out slowly.

Another deep breath, and blow it out slowly.

And gently open up your eyes.

Power, Peace, Purpose.

Your Safe Place
~Better Oms & Gardens~

Just as you can store memories of pain, fear, and anger that feed the stress triggers in your life, you also have access to pleasant memories that can empower you. In this meditation, you create a path to a "safe place" in your memories, a location where you felt protected and nurtured. You can bring this safe place back to your active thoughts in order to help you achieve a positive response to the negative triggers of pain, fear, and anger.

Creating your safe place.

The same way we can store memories of pain, fear, and anger that feed the stress triggers in our lives, we also have many pleasant memories that can empower us. In this meditation, we will suggest the creation of a "safe place," Borrowing from the memories of your mind a location where you felt protected and nurtured can be brought back to your active thoughts in order to help you foster and grow a response of Power, Peace, Purpose.

Put yourself in a comfortable place. Begin to feel the experience of your breath.

Take in a deep breath and let it out slowly, and as you exhale, gently close your eyes.

Feel the coolness of the air as you breathe in, and the warmth as you breathe out.

Take a deep breath in and let it out slowly, and as you do take notice of the areas in your body which feel tight.

If the muscles in your chest, shoulders, or throat feel tight, you are most likely suffering with a bit of anxiety, perhaps some anger.

These feelings, though unpleasant, are incredibly normal and happen to everyone.

Even though everyone feels afraid sometimes, this does not mean that we have to let the fear take control of our lives and hurt our bodies.

Feel the coolness of the air as you breathe in, and the warmth as you breathe out.

Take in a very slow and deep breath. As you exhale, slowly feel your shoulders drop and your neck loosen.

Feel the coolness of the air as you take a deep breath in, and the warmth as you let it out.

Focus on loosening your shoulders and neck. When you have allowed all of the muscles in your neck and your shoulder to just droop downward, imagine yourself standing up.

Now, imagine that you find a new door where you are and behind that door is a large, beautiful walk-in closet.

You close the door behind you and you feel the quiet strength of the door.

The walls are made of cedar, and as you inhale you take in the earthy scents of the wood.

Now, you are sitting on the floor of the closet, but it is extremely comfortable because it is lined with quilts and blankets, and there are pillows and stuffed animals surrounding the edges. Your favorite toys of your childhood are lining the shelves.

Take a deep breath in, focusing on the soothing smell of the cedar, and the comfortable and plush floor.

As you exhale, try to feel the textures of the blankets and pillows around you.

They are soft and the toys are furry. They are comforting as they cradle you in your seated position.

The walls are lined with coats. There is fabric surrounding you, and warm earthy smells are filling your nose.

Take a deep breath in and, as you do, imagine the comforting smells permeating your body and settling into your chest.

When you exhale, imagine your breath coming out and mixing into these plush materials around you.

Take another deep breath in, and slowly and gently exhale, keeping the images of the smells and materials mixing together.

Feel your shoulders loosen with each exhale, and pay attention to the tightness in your chest.

Feel the coolness of the air as you breathe in, and the warmth as you breathe out.

Feel it loosen and leave your body, gently settling into the comforting materials.

Take another deep breath in, and hold it, and gently exhale.

One more time.

You are safe and warm and protected by the sweet-smelling walls of the cedar closet.

You are surrounded by comforting materials, and you can sink into the floor and feel cradled by the soft things beneath you.

Hold onto this feeling and, once again, breathe in this comfort, and exhale what is left of your fears, letting them gently fall through the floor of the closet.

When you are ready, open your eyes.

Power, Peace, Purpose.

MEDITATION 21

Defeating Deep Chronic Pain
~To See Your Inner Sea~

There are very few messages as powerful as the pain message in your brain. Pain is a sign of necrosis, of something going really wrong inside your body. When that penetrating alarm goes off, it is primed to get your attention fast. But many times the pain can be much worse than what it is trying to warn us about. This meditation will guide you through a pathway that can help you take control and transcend the negative messages of pain by creating a more powerful message of light that moves through us as the gentle waves of the sea.

There are very few messages as powerful as the pain message in your brain.

Pain is a sign of necrosis, of something going really wrong inside of your body. When that penetrating alarm goes off, it is primed to get your attention very quickly.

But many times the pain can be much worse than what it is trying to warn us about.

Frequently, the pain becomes the issue in itself.

However . . .

Despite the fact that pain is such a prominent message, it is not one that has to control your life.

In fact, the more you create in your mind pathways, breaking through that pain and using your brain to restructure the message of darkness into light, the greater capacity you have of transcending pain.

This meditation will create a pathway through pain. Even if you do not presently suffer from any particular discomfort, it is a great thing to learn for when you run into that occasional ache or pain.

Let's return to a comfortable place and try to focus on the flow of our breath.

Feel the coolness of the air as you breathe in, and the warmth as you breathe out.

Close your eyes.

Feel the coolness of the air as you breathe in, and the warmth as you breathe out.

Feel the flow of the breath coming in, and going out.

When other thoughts or sounds come into your head, gently put them down and return to the feeling of your breath.

Feel the coolness of the air as you breathe in, and the warmth as you breathe out.

Create an entranceway of the breath.

Imagine that you are bringing in the flow of your breath not through your mouth but from an imaginary opening one inch below where your place of pain and discomfort lies.

Imagine pulling up your breath through that place in the body, traveling up through that place of pain all the way up to your mouth. Now as you breathe out, slightly release and relax that place of pain.

As you breathe in, again allow your breath to travel through that place of pain, making small holes in the pain with your breath.

And as you breathe out, feel the muscles all around the place of pain, let go and relax.

Again, feel the cool breath gently poke holes through the pain and blow out that discomfort with your exhale.

Feel the coolness of the air as you breathe in, and the warmth as you breathe out.

Breathe smoothly and softly for the next few breaths as you gently let go of any image.

Feel the coolness of the air as you breathe in, and the warmth as you breathe out.

Now you will transform the cooling circle of your breath into a very fine but powerful light.

Imagine your pain like a dark black fist that lies inside of yourself.

And as you breathe in, one inch below the pain, feel the light pierce that fist breaking away chunks of that darkness.

As you breathe out, see the darkness, like a dark cloud come out of your mouth as you push it away.

Feel the coolness of the air as you breathe in your pain and the warmth as you push the pain out of your mouth.

Continue creating that circle of light, pulling the laser beam of beautiful light through the darkness of your pain and as you breathe out, blowing out this cloud from your mouth, pushing the pain out of yourself but breathing in a way that is gentle and calm and comfortable.

Pull in the light and breathe out the darkness.

Pull in the light and breathe out the darkness.

Continue the circle; the light you breathe in cuts through and pulls up the darkness with it, which you blow out, and then you go back again and replenish the light.

Pull in the light and blow out the darkness.

Feel the coolness of the air as you breathe in, and the warmth as you breathe out.

Change the width of the light.

Transform the thin laser beam to become a very thick light and pierce through the pain through this light, punching out a giant hole from the pain.

Bring up the darkness of that pain and breathe it out.

Feel yourself gently pushing away the tension and discomfort of that pain.

Breathe in the light and blow out the darkness.

Breathe in the light and blow out the darkness.

Change the color of that light.

See it become a very powerful red, burning a hole through the pain and push out the darkness.

Breathe in the light and push out the darkness.

Just focus on that red light melting through the dark discomfort.

Try a very vivid and cool blue.

Feel the coolness of the air as you breathe in, and the warmth as you breathe out.

Just focus on that blue light melting through the darkness.

Pull in the light and breathe out the darkness.

Pull in the light and breathe out the darkness.

Every time you breathe out, see the darkness of the pain blowing out from your mouth as your discomfort melts under the power of your light.

Feel the coolness of the air as you breathe in, and the warmth as you breathe out.

Pull in the light and breathe out the darkness.

Pull in the light and breathe out the darkness.

Now, instead of just one light beam, create five of them.

Four corners of the square and one going through the center.

Feel the coolness of the air as you breathe in, and the warmth as you breathe out.

Pull in the light and breathe out the darkness.

Pull in the light and breathe out the darkness.

Feel the coolness of the air as you breathe in, and the warmth as you breathe out.

In the martial arts we train to attack from the front, or the sides, or from the top or underneath.

Let's now change the angle of entry.

Allow your light to enter through the right side of that fist of hurt, breaking through the knots of pain and tightness.

Breathe in the light and blow out the darkness.

Another breath through the right side of your adversary.

Breathe in from the right side, and breathe out the pain.

Breathe in the light, and blow out the darkness.

Now come in from the left side, and penetrate the challenge from the other direction. Even if you now feel no more pain, continue to circle through that spot.

Feel the coolness of that light as you breathe in, and the warmth as you breathe out.

Vary the directions, the texture, the color.

On your own you can focus with it each time for several minutes, changing the colors and the shapes and the numbers of beams of light.

One last step in forging pathways of healing:

Allow the light to now take any shape, color, or pathway it wants. Just observe these lights as they create their own identity of healing and comfort through your body.

Feel the coolness of the air as you breathe in, and the warmth as you breathe out.

See if you can discern the different shapes and colors that penetrate and melt away any place of darkness, of pain, of tightness, or of fear.

Feel the coolness of the air as you breathe in, and the warmth as you breathe out.

And as you breathe out, see them pierce through the pain, pulling up any of the darkness that still remains, the darkness leaving your mouth as a vapor.

The more your brain focuses on breaking through that pain, the more you take charge of your life.

Feel the coolness of the air as you breathe in, and the warmth as you breathe out.

Feel the coolness of the air as you breathe in, and the warmth as you breathe out.

Keep focusing on the power of your light to break through the pain.

Keep maintaining that ongoing circle of breathing through that light and through that challenge.

Feel the coolness of the air as you breathe in, and the warmth as you breathe out.

Breathe in the light and blow out the darkness.

Breathe in the light and blow out the darkness.

Take a deep cleansing breath in, breathe it out.

Another deep cleansing breath in, and breathe it out.

And open up your eyes.

Power, Peace, Purpose.

Better Breathing
∽Respiration Inspiration∽

Breath is so natural that we take it for granted unless our breathing becomes compromised. Then the fear and the stress ride in, and the alarms that go off inside your head make it even harder to breathe. In this meditation we focus on using the power of your mind, your spirit, and your light to assist in respiration, allowing you to take control of your breathing.

Breath is so natural that you can take it for granted unless your breathing becomes compromised, and then the fear, the stress, the alarms that go off inside our heads are so profound that ironically the stress can make it harder to breathe.

In this meditation we will focus on using the power of our mind, our spirit, and our light to assist in the breath, allowing us to take control of our breathing.

Find a comfortable place, and let's get into a mindset of relaxation and focus.

Feel the coolness of the air as you breathe in, and the warmth as you breathe out.

Close your eyes.

Feel the coolness of the air as you breathe in, and the warmth as you breathe out.

Allow yourself to breathe in a way that is comfortable and pace the breath in a way that feels natural for you.

Feel the coolness of the air as you breathe in, and the warmth as you breathe out.

Go to the very top of your head, and feel every muscle relax and release.

Go to the muscles of your face, the back of your neck.

As you breathe out, feel them float downward.

The muscles in your shoulders, down your arms.

As you exhale, let every muscle gently float downward, relaxing and gently pulling away, one from the other.

Feel the coolness of the air as you breathe in, and the warmth as you breathe out.

Breathe in a way in which you can feel the comfort of the breath.

Breathe with peace, with incredible power, and energy that you bring into yourself.

Create a feeling that your breathing in and breathing out are connected. Your breathing out and breathing in are part of the same flow. Create this circle of the breath and feel as you breathe in, slowly but comfortably, that you can feel your body relax.

Feel the nourishment of the light that flows within you with each breath.

All fear within the breath dissolves with the circle of light that travels with the gentle circle of you breath.

Breathe in that light and blow out the darkness.

Continue to create that circle of breath, going through your body.

Pull in the light and gently blow out any darkness or fear, any concern, any discomfort.

Bring in the light and blow out the darkness.

Feel the coolness of the air as you breathe in, and the warmth as you breathe out.

Feel the coolness of the air as you breathe in, and the warmth as you breathe out.

Imagine yourself in a very beautiful place.

And as you breathe in, you can feel the cool but gentle wind upon your face.

As you breathe out you can feel the warmth of the sun-blessed breath.

Continue to make that circle of comfort with each breath, relaxing your neck and your shoulders as you breathe out.

Feel them gently fall and slide, relaxing one by one by one, every muscle in your vertebrae.

Feel the coolness of the air as you breathe in, and the warmth as you breathe out.

Bring yourself to that beautiful place of comfort and the place of extraordinary energy.

A place of peace.

And the more you can do that, you find your inner energy.

Feel the coolness of the air as you breathe in, and the warmth as you breathe out.

Sit with the feeling of the circle that flows within you and the gentle calmness of each breath that you control.

You are the master of your breath.

You are in control of your breathing.

Any time any other thought or feeling or sound comes into your head, just blow it out slowly and go back to the feeling of the circle of light of each breath.

Feel the coolness of the air as you breathe in, and the warmth as you breathe out.

Feel the coolness of the light as you breathe in, and the warmth that comes as you breathe it out.

Breathe in that light and blow out the darkness.

Feel your body gently moving with your breath.

Bring in the light and blow out the darkness.

Sit with the calmness of the power of your breath and feel it radiate through your body.

The light is your essence, the power of your soul.

Bring in the light and blow out the darkness.

Take a deep, cleansing breath in and blow it out slowly.

Another deep cleansing breath in, and blow it out slowly.

And gently open up your eyes.
Power, Peace, Purpose.

Transcending Head Pain
~Learning New Skulls~

All pain is in the head. If you stub your toe, the message goes from the bottom of your foot all the way through your nervous system to your brain, which translates it into "Ouch" and returns that sensation all the way down to your toe. To paraphrase Jack Lalanne, "No brain, no pain." This meditation uses the tools you have been learning to create a pathway of cooling light to penetrate and then dissipate the pain of a headache. All pain is in the head.

If you stub your toe, the message goes from the bottom of your foot all the way through your nervous system to your brain, which translates it as an "ouch" and returns that hurt feeling all the way down to your toe.

No brain, no pain.

However, when the head itself aches, it can be particularly troubling and sometimes so discomforting that it stops us from being able to function.

This meditation will supply you with tools to get ahead of a headache.

Get to a comfortable place even if you're not feeling so comfortable.

Uncross your legs and your arms and gently fall into the bed or the chair.

Feel the movement of your breath.

Notice that when you breathe in it is a little bit cooler, and when you breathe out it is a little bit warmer.

Feel the coolness of the air as you breathe in, and the warmth as you breathe out.

Close your eyes and allow any thought or sound or feeling, any sensation, just to gently drop to the ground as you breathe out.

Feel the coolness of the air as you breathe in, and the warmth as you breathe out.

Look through your body.

Any place of tightness, your neck, your mouth, your jaws, behind your ears, your chest, your stomach . . .

As you exhale feel every muscle in your body relax.

Feel the gentle movement as you breathe in. Notice how your body rises ever so slightly, just a little tiny bit with each inhale.

As you breathe out, feel your whole body fall that same, almost unperceivable amount.

Feel the rhythmic movement of your body as you breathe in, and the gentle falling as you breathe out.

Feel the coolness of the air as you breathe in, and the warmth as you breathe out.

As you look through your body and you allow every muscle to relax and release, imagine yourself traveling upward to your head where you feel discomfort.

As you breathe in, imagine that you're breathing in not just air, but a very cold ice-like light.

And you're breathing that light all the way through the place of pain and discomfort.

As you take in that breath, imagine the light push through and make holes in the place of discomfort, cooling and soothing the pain.

Take another breath in. As you breathe in, see that light make holes in the place of discomfort, and then gently release the breath.

Change the light to be several little beads of light, focused lasers, breaking through the black fist of pain inside of your head.

Breathe it in.

As you breathe out, feel the pain begin to wither.

As you pull on the light, breathe through the pain, and as you breathe out feel the pain relax inside of your head.

Choose a color for the light that feels comforting to apply to the pain. Imagine it push through every place of pain in your head.

Feel the coolness of the air as you breathe in, and the warmth as you breathe out.

Gently flow with that breath up and down, back and forth.

This time as you breathe in the light to the place of pain, allow the light to travel all the way to the top of your skull and make openings in the top of your head. As you breathe out, you begin to feel an ooze that drips downward, covering your pain. The ooze smothers the pain and begins to melt away the feeling of discomfort.

Feel the coolness of the air as you breathe in, and the warmth as you breathe out.

Bring in the light with your breath, to break through the pain from down below it with your breath, and as you exhale feel the ooze cascading downward, washing away every place of discomfort.

Feel the light break through the pain as you breathe in and as you breathe out,. Allow the slow ooze to wash away all of the little pieces that have been broken off by the light.

Feel the coolness of the air as you breathe in, and the warmth as you breathe out.

Pull in the light, and as you exhale allow the ooze to now drip on the sides of the inside of your head and all through your brain.

Allow this ooze to cleanse and to wash away any place of pain, of fear, of anger, of tightness.

Feel the coolness of the air as you breathe in, and the warmth as you breathe out.

Allow yourself to feel the cool, gentle, oozing waterfall pulling down any element of pain, or discomfort.

Bring in the light, and as you blow out the darkness feel any pain totally relax and release itself from inside of your head.

Feel the coolness of the air as you breathe in, and the warmth as you breathe out.

Continue the flow of air going up, and the feeling of the ooze gently flowing downward.

Pull in the light and blow out the darkness.

Pull in the light and blow out the darkness.

Just sit within that feeling of calm, allowing every sensation to gently fall and every tension to disappear with every breath that you take.

Feel the power of your breath and the movement of your body, gently pulling up the light and blowing out the darkness.

Flow with that breath and gently push out all of the darkness.

Take in a deep cleansing breath and blow it out slowly.

Another deep cleansing breath, and blow it out slowly.

And gently open up your eyes.

Power, Peace, Purpose.

Freedom from Back Pain
~Strengthening Your Core~

Back pain seems to be ubiquitous in our society. It's just a matter of time for most of us. Fortunately, strengthening one's core has been shown to help reduce the incidence of back pain. This meditation helps you to create a healing power that fortifies your core while helping your back to heal. You will be surprised how closely connected your brain is to every part of your body.

It is commonly suggested that there are two types of Americans: those who have back pain and those who will have back pain. Strengthening one's core has been shown to help alleviate incidence of back pain. Even using your mind to imagine the healing power of your core can bring you to a different place as well.

Find a comfortable place; try to keep your back straight, either sitting or lying down.

Begin to feel the coolness of the air as you breathe in and the warmth as you breathe out.

With every exhale, feel your body just relax and release.

Close your eyes.

Feel the coolness of the air as you breathe in, and the warmth as you breathe out.

Any other sound, voice, or feeling that comes into your head, just put it down gently and return to the experience of your breath.

Feel the coolness of the air as you breathe in, and the warmth as you breathe out.

Travel all the way to the top of your head.

Feel the muscles in your scalp relax and release.

And from the top of your head, as the muscles flow downward, visualize a beautiful waterfall, gently pulling its waters down through your head.

You can hear the sound of the water cascading down the cliff and watch the white foaming bubbles as it washes over the rocks.

Allow this waterfall to wash the muscles behind your eyes. You can feel every muscle behind your eyes relax and release.

The flowing waters inside of your head cascades down past your cheeks, your mouth, and your jaw.

Feel the coolness of the air as you breathe in, and the warmth as you breathe out.

Let the waterfall ripple down your neck.

As you exhale, every muscle in your neck is relaxed, flowing downward in the waterfall.

Go to the top of your shoulders.

As you exhale, let your right shoulder blade totally release and relax.

Another breath . . .

As you exhale feel your left shoulder blade gently flow downward as the waterfall expands itself through your entire back.

Feel the coolness of the air as you breathe in, and the warmth as you breathe out.

Allow this waterfall to cascade down both sides of your back.

And the waters become even stronger and more powerful, massaging every muscle in your torso.

Feel the coolness of the air as you breathe in, and the warmth as you breathe out.

Experience this waterfall traveling through any place of discomfort in your back.

This rapid stream brings its flowing healing from bubbling hot springs, richly endowed with healing minerals on its surface.

As you breathe in, the waterfall becomes more powerful, and as you breathe out, it rushes to the places of discomfort, warming and opening up any muscle that is closed.

Feel the coolness of the air as you breathe in, and the warmth as you breathe out.

Allow your back to totally relax.

And any place where there is still tension, as you exhale feel those muscles relax and release.

Feel the coolness of the air as you breathe in, and the warmth as you breathe out.

Allow the waterfall to penetrate down your legs, pushing away any tightness and discomfort and traveling all the way down to your toes.

Look through your body for any place of tightness, any place of pain.

As you exhale, try to blow out all of the discomfort.

Feel the coolness of the air as you breathe in, and the warmth as you breathe out.

As you are beginning to allow every muscle to relax and release, feel your power.

What is very important for the health of your back is to create a core of power inside of your stomach.

Feel the coolness of the air as you breathe in, and the warmth as you breathe out.

Turn off the waterfall and allow the last drips to fall.

In the place of that stream, the mist begins to clear and the sun begins to peer down from a cloudless sky.

As you are totally quiet inside of yourself, you watch that orb of sunlit heat coming closer and closer to you. However, in place of the giant star, this circle shrinks into a beautiful ball of light the size of a beach ball that stops right above your navel.

You are amazed as you watch how this ball of heat responds to your every breath.

As you breathe in, the light contracts even smaller, to the size of a volleyball. As you breathe out, the ball becomes a little larger again.

Imagine that ball of brilliant light hovering right above your navel.

Breathe in, the light contracts in; breathe out, it expands and becomes larger.

Breathe in, the light contracts in; breathe out, it expands and becomes larger.

You can feel the intensity of this warmth as you control the ball of light.

Breathe in, the light contracts in; breathe out, it expands and becomes larger.

Together, we are going to use our breath to pull that ball of light right into your belly.

We are going to take in a very calm and slow breath. Hold it and as you are slowly breathing it out, I will count to three. When I finish saying the word, "three," you will take in a very powerful and deep inhale, pulling the ball of light into your body.

First, just watch the orb hovering above your navel.

Breathe in, the light contracts in; breathe out, it expands and becomes larger.

Breathe in, the light contracts in; breathe out, it expands and becomes larger.

Now take in a very slow breath. Pull it up, up: hold it. Now slowly breathe it out.

One, two, three: now pull it in quickly, bringing the globe into your bell.

Now relax. The orb is no longer above you. It is in you.

You can feel its warmth and strength glowing inside of your body.

Every time you breathe out, that ball of light becomes brighter and warmer and hotter.

As you breathe in, gently contract your stomach muscles in, not in any way that's uncomfortable but very gently. Allow your stomach to contract with your inhale.

You can feel the ball contracting inside as well.

Breathe out and expand your stomach just as the ball of light is doing inside of you.

Breathe in gently, contracting with that ball of light.

Breathe out gently, expanding with that ball of light.

Breathe in, contracting with that ball of light.

Breathe out, expanding with that ball of light.

Just allow your stomach and the light to become one.

Breathe in, contracting the light.

Breathe out, expanding the light.

Breathe in, contracting the light.

Breathe out, expanding the light.

Feel the coolness of the air as you breathe in, and the warmth as you breathe out.

As you continue to simply breathe in a relaxed fashion, scan your back for any place in your back that may be uncomfortable or challenging.

As you breathe in, gently lift up your back ever so slightly. As you breathe out allow your entire back to relax and release.

Gently lift up your back with your inhale and let it all loose with the exhale.

Breathe in the light and breathe out any place of tightness or pain.

We are now ready to use the new powerful core of your body to support every muscle in your back.

As you breathe in, you are pulling out some of this powerful light in your stomach and stretching it out to the place of pain.

As you breathe out, you actually feel that discomfort begin to disappear.

As your breathe in, the light gets pulled like giant fingers massaging the muscles that hold all the pain. As you breathe out, feel the muscles gently fall apart from each other, supported from your core.

See the light as girders of power supporting every muscle in your back.

As you breathe in, feel your back being strengthened and healthy from the light of your core.

As you breathe out, you breathe out any pain or discomfort.

Breathe in, pulling up the fingers of powerful heat from your core, continuing to make loose the muscles that are massaged by that light.

Feel the power of the light as you breathe in, and the coolness as you breathe out.

Feel the power of that light as you breathe in, and the comfort as you breathe out.

This is the light that dwells within you. It is healing. It is warm. It is you.

Feel the coolness of the air as you breathe in, and the warmth as you breathe out.

Breathe in the light and blow out the darkness.

Breathe in the light and blow out the darkness.

Take a deep cleansing breath in; breathe it out.

Another deep cleansing breath in, and breathe it out.

And open up your eyes.

Power, Peace, Purpose.

Feeling Your Chi
~Energizing Your World~

Inside your very being, there is a soul complete with an energy that connects you to the Infinite. It doesn't matter if you call this life force chi, ki, tenaga dalam, prana, neshama, or spirit. All martial arts rely on the ability to feel that energy and use it in everyday life. With this meditation you will be invited to actually feel this energy within your hands.

We are going to take our meditation on light one step further to allow you to actually feel the fabric of this energy in your hands.

I am going to ask you to actually feel your chi.

Inside of our very being, the soul is complete with an energy which connects us to the Infinitely Supreme.

It doesn't matter if you call this life force chi, ki, tenaga dalam, prana, neshama, or spirit. The ability to feel that light and to use that power is very much a part of martial arts training.

But you don't have to be a martial artist to be able to create and identify the feeling of this power.

We're going to take a few moments to get to that place of light, and then in the middle of this meditation, I will ask you to vigorously rub your hands together and then pull them apart from each other and then hold them as if you are holding a large ball in front of your face.

You will leave your hands apart from each other, but they will be cupped in front of your face, as if you are holding a ball.

Let's see what the chi can feel like to you.

Go to a comfortable place.

And let your body fall into the chair or lie on the bed.

And begin to focus again on the flow of your breath.

Notice that when you breathe in, the air is a little bit cooler, and it's just a touch warmer as you breathe out.

Close your eyes.

Feel the coolness of the air as you breathe in, and the warmth as you breathe out.

Feel the coolness of the air as you breathe in, and the warmth as you breathe out.

Go to the very top of your head and feel the muscles by your forehead and scalp relax, gently pulling apart one from the other.

Go to the muscles behind your eyes, behind your ears, your jaw.

Let them all fall.

As you exhale, let every muscle in your face gently pull away one from the other.

Go to the muscles in the back of your neck, and feel those muscles loosen and relax.

Proceed downward to the muscles in your chest and your stomach and let every feeling of tightness dissolve as you exhale.

Any other thought or sound or feeling that comes into your head, gently put them down and go back to the feeling of the flow of your breath.

Feel the coolness of the air as you breathe in, and the warmth as you breathe out.

Proceed down to the muscles of your back, vertebra by vertebra. Let them just fall, gently pulling apart, one from the other.

Feel the coolness of the air as you breathe in, and the warmth as you breathe out.

Go all the way down your legs, to your thighs, to your knees.

Travel down to your ankles through any place of tightness.

As you exhale, let every muscle just ripple downward, flowing gently away, one from the other.

Feel the coolness of the air as you breathe in, and the warmth as you breathe out.

Now look for any place in your body that is uncomfortable or any spot of anger or tightness, fear or pain.

As you breathe in, pull in this tremendously powerful light, and blow out any place of darkness.

Breathe in the light, and blow out the darkness.

Now imagine sitting at the side of the edge of a beautiful beach, and you can see the waves washing upon the shore, up and down, up and down.

And you experience above your head the most beautiful, large, very, very bright light of the sun.

The sunlight is peering down and you can feel the rays of the light, even with your eyes closed, enter inside of your head.

Feel the coolness of the air as you breathe in, and the warmth as you breathe out.

And you notice as you're breathing in the light that it is continuing to grow inside of your head.

It is very, very powerful.

Every time you exhale, the light becomes even hotter and brighter.

Hotter and brighter.

Every time you exhale, repeat that one word inside of your head: "light."

Light.

Light.

Light.

Keep repeating that one word, "light."

And every time you say that word, the light becomes even brighter and warmer inside of your head.

Light.

Light.

The light continues to grow and become even brighter still.

Now rub your hands together.

And with your eyes closed, hold them in front of your face as if between your hands is a large beach ball.

And keep repeating that one word, "light."

Light.

Notice as you repeat the word "light," your palms and your fingers are beginning to tingle with the power of that light.

You can actually feel your hands getting warmer and warmer and hot as you are holding the power of this light between your hands.

Any other thoughts or sounds, just put them down gently and go back to the feeling of the power of that light that is tingling your fingers and your palms and making you warm.

Gently push your hands together just about half an inch and then gently pull it back.

A little bit together, and then apart.

A little bit together, and then apart.

You can almost feel inside of your hands like putty, as if you can feel the energy pulsating and being shaped within your hands.

As you exhale keep repeating that one word, "light."

Light.

Light.

Light.

Light.

Now take that light between your hands and push it back inside of your body.

Pull that beautiful ball of light into yourself, allowing it to wash throughout your entire body, creating health and strength and power and peace.

Feel that light washing through your body.

Push that light through your body and allow it to dwell within every part of yourself.

Healing and giving you power.

Just sit with the feeling of being awash in that light.

The light is so powerful that you can see your body disappear within the luminescence of that light.

And every time you breathe out, just say the word, "light."

Light.

Light.

Allow your whole being to be washed and embraced by the warmth and the health and the strength of that light.

Light.

Light.

Take in a deep cleansing breath, and blow it out slowly.

Another deep cleansing breath, and blow it out slowly.

And gently open up your eyes.

Power, Peace, Purpose.

Your Inner Warmth
∽ "Blake's Lake" ∽

This meditation is in the form of a poem, and it is dedicated to a beautiful little boy who was able to use the reflection of a lake and the power of the light that descended upon it to change not only the temperature of his body but also the lives of all those around him. This is the poem of Blake's Lake.

This meditation is in the form of a poem, and it is dedicated to a beautiful little boy who was able to use the reflection of a lake and the power of the light that descended upon that lake to change the temperature of his body.

This is the poem of Blake's Lake.

Blake's Lake
Rushing waters crashing through
The gentle silence shaken
Uprooting trees and pounding lees
The calm of nature taken

Where by its force no thing remains
Torrents tearing unrestraining
It strangles light that kissed the land
Nothing but darkness remaining

But as the coldness of that rage
Turns round and pushes through
It comes upon a gentle lake
With waters calm and blue

This loch stands firm, will not be moved
By the torrents of the stream
Its gentle ripples undisturbed
As the currents of a dream

Resign to me, you're just too young
Says the might of the rushing water
I've swept the boughs of mighty trees
In the path of my disorder

But the gentle pond will not yield its space
Its ripples will not churn
And despite the blaze of the storming wrath
Its waters will not burn

In fact, a calmness fills the space
The lake contains its fear
It gathers all that touch its banks
Caressing all that's dear

Small by its size not taught by years
It shares an endless source
That connects it to a strength above
That lets it run its course

And as the river rages by
Its torrents crash and thrash
Relentlessly providing pain
As the stinging of the lash

Mighty mountains crumble
Giant structures fall
But the waters of our gentle lake
Remain strong, proud, and tall

What defies this mighty siege
What power or what sage
Could give a force that can't be moved
To a lake of such gentle age?

Then in the midst of swirling darkness
The lake reveals its might
Within the very core of it
Is the most amazing light

This light has traveled many years
And endless paths of space
To find this spot of joy and tears
And alight upon this place

This light dwells within our very soul
It gives purpose to our life
It stands up against the storm-filled winds
Protecting us from strife

Our gentle lake is not afraid
It has conquered; it has won
No darkness can consume its light
It never has to run

And even when the storm prevailed
Crashing down with all its might
It could not move the water there
That was bathed in all its light

Thus when the stillness comes to me
In the middle of the night
My mind returns me to that lake
When it could no longer fight

I see the contours of its waves
As they alight upon the beach
I see the gentle smiling boy
As if he were still within my reach

And I close my eyes and see the light
Reflecting upon the lake
And know that the love-filled light that is his soul
Is still within our Blake

Altering Addictions
~An Easier Pill to Swallow~

The word "addict" comes from the Latin word dicta, which means "spoken," as in the word "dictation." An "addict" is "one who is spoken for." The voice that addicts hear inside of their brains is not really their own. It is not unusual for your brain to lie and tell you that what feels good is good—no matter how bad it really is. This meditation focuses on finding the inner light so that you can take control of your brain and your life. We use the metaphor of alcohol, but you can substitute any behavior or drive that threatens to rob you of your happiness.

The word "addict" comes from the Latin word "dicta," which means "spoken," as in "dictation." An "addict" is "one who is spoken for." The voice he or she hears inside of his or her brain is not really their own. It is not unusual for our brain to lie and tell us that what feels good is good—no matter how bad it really is.

This meditation focuses on finding the inner light, to take control of our brains and our lives. We use the metaphor of alcohol, but you can substitute any behavior or drive that threatens to rob you of your life.

The goal of the meditation is to reframe the brain and create a strong and powerful voice in place of the voice that can so easily destroy us.

Get into a comfortable place and feel the cycle and flow of your breath.

Feel the coolness of the air as you breathe in, and the warmth as you breathe out.

Feel the coolness as you breathe in, and the warmth as you breathe out.

Close your eyes and let every muscle in your body just float downward with relaxation.

Feel the coolness of the air as you breathe in, and the warmth as you breathe out.

Imagine the smell of the drink.

The whiff of the alcohol that quickly excites your brain and the feeling of completion and power when your lips pass the fluid, pass this liquid into your body.

See the bottle in front of you, glistening.

And know that inside of your brain, a craving arises that you must have the drink so much you can taste the alcohol before you can even touch the bottle.

Where is the bottle?

As you look around, you can see a little bit over to your right a beautiful full bottle that your brain is craving.

And as you reach out to bring it to your lips, it suddenly flies out of your hands and begins to project through the air, dancing away from you.

You look to the left and there is another bottle just as big and full as the other one and you reach for that one.

That one also flies away from your grasp. Each bottle seems to have a life of its own.

So you turn again and there is another bottle.

That one also flies away.

You keep jumping and trying to grab—a fourth one, a fifth one, and a sixth one.

And to your dismay, each one pulls away from you, dancing out of your hands. They seem to be playing with you, taunting you, controlling you.

So you begin to chase the bottles because you need the drink.

And just as you near one of them, it suddenly falls to the floor and shatters and there's glass everywhere.

But you must have another one. So you continue running.

And the shards of the first one are cutting your feet, but it doesn't matter. You have to have that bottle.

So you continue to run—and run—so frustrating, so much pain.

And you can hear the crunching of the glass, and the pain of the shards penetrating into your feet, but you don't care because you're so close to grabbing that bottle.

But that one, too, cruelly crashes down to the floor.

And then one and then the next one, and the others: there is glass all over you and not a drop to drink.

But you see there is one left.

And you jump at it and you grab that one.

And you fall to the floor, cut up with all of the pieces of painful glass, and you roll over and you bring the bottle to your lips.

But as soon as it begins to pour down on your mouth you realize that it is nothing but the most awful, toxic, burning acid that is burning your insides.

And it is awful and you try to spit it out.

And you look down at your body as the fluid that you spit out makes even greater pain on the cuts and the wounds that you have from head to toe.

Because you have been running after the bottles.

And then you see another whole bottle.

And it is standing in the air right in front of you.

And as you look and feel the pain of your body and the pain that you have caused to so many others, you take the bottle and you turn it over and you watch as the last drop of the liquor falls to the floor on the glistening glass.

No longer are you going to be cut and destroyed.

You have the power to take control.

See the image of determination upon your face as you stand upright and take in a deep breath of light.

And as you breathe out, the glass begins to disappear all around you.

Feel the coolness of the air as you breathe in, and the warmth as you breathe out.

And the darkness of the red blood begins to dry and then to disappear as well.

And your wounds begin to close.

And again you bring in another breath of light even more powerful than the last and you blow out the darkness.

And even though you can hear your brain yelling, "I need that, I want that!" you can feel the light of your soul drowning out the sounds of that pain with the power of love and light, saying there is only darkness in that bottle.

And you hear your real voice say:

"I will live with the light."

And as you stand even taller and breathe even deeper, the power of that light begins to well up inside of yourself, healing the wounds of your past and that pain of others.

And you make a commitment to spread that light and to teach others who are still running after the elusive joys of the poison of the bottle.

Feel your power as you replace the darkness with light.

Listen to a new voice, the sound of your soul that is so much more powerful than the screeching lies of your brain.

And as you stand up and proclaim with the power of your light, "A perfect God created this imperfect, extraordinarily challenging part of your life, absolutely perfectly."

And when you stand up to that challenge, you are very powerful.

With me, inside of your head, just repeat those words:

I am very powerful.

I am very powerful.

I am very powerful.

I am very powerful.

Take in a deep breath, and blow it out slowly.

Another deep breath and blow it out slowly.

And open up your eyes.

Power, Peace, Purpose.

Increasing Movement beyond Pain
~Ligament Liberation~

This meditation is a unique thought process for rehabilitating your body with the power of your inner light. In this meditation, you use breath to move your body and your body to move your breath. If you are having challenges with your range of motion, this meditation will be a great aid in your physical therapy. Together, the energy of body and breath will help you to heal and gain control over your movement and life.

This meditation is a very unique thought process to rehabilitate your body with the power of your inner light. We will use the breath to move the body, and the body to move the breath. This is a very cool meditation for anyone. If you are having challenges with your range of motion, bring this to your physical therapist to create the best trajectory and range of movement that will help your therapy. Together the energy of body and breath help to heal and gain control, increasing your mastery over movement and life.

Find a comfortable place where you can sit and just let everything relax and fall into the chair.

Feel the coolness of the air as you breathe in, and the warmth as you breathe out.

Close your eyes and focus on the flow of your breath.

Feel the coolness of the air as you breathe in, and the warmth as you breathe out.

Feel the coolness of the air as you breathe in, and the warmth as you breathe out.

As you exhale, let every muscle in your face and behind your ears and in your neck gently float downward, almost as if your head is now weightless.

Feel the coolness of the air as you breathe in, and the warmth as you breathe out.

Focus outward from your shoulders to your arms and into your chest; as you exhale let every muscle fall gently downward, as if your arms are gently hanging on your body.

Feel the coolness of the air as you breathe in, and the warmth as you breathe out.

Any other thoughts or feelings or sounds, just put them down gently and go back to the flow of your breath.

Feel the coolness of the air as you breathe in, and the warmth as you breathe out.

Go down from the muscles in your chest all the way to your stomach and hips, as you breathe out let every muscle relax and release, gently flowing downward.

Go to the muscles in your legs, down to your toes, and feel every muscle relax and release.

Feel the coolness of the air as you breathe in, and the warmth as you breathe out.

Place your hands gently, one on top of the other on your chest.

Place your right hand on top of your left hand.

Feel the coolness of the air as you breathe in, and the warmth as you breathe out.

Feel the flow of your breath as your body moves up and down with each breath.

Feel the gentle movement of your breath within your body.

Gently flow with the movement of breath inside of your body.

Feel the coolness of the air as you breathe in, and the warmth as you breathe out.

The energy of your breath is very great.

Let your head gently fall forward so that your chin is resting almost on your chest.

As you breathe in slowly, feel your head lift all of the way up: hold it.

Now as you exhale, allow it to float downward again, in tempo with the very slow breath.

Breathe in and pull your head up with the breath.

Breathe out and pull your head downward with your breath.

Feel the breath control the movement of your head.

Imagine the breath as a cable of light.

As you breathe in, the cable is attached to the back of your head, pulling it up.

As you breathe out the light is attached to your forehead, pulling it down.

Your breath in pulls your head up.

Your breath out pulls your head down.

And now in tempo with your breath you will continue to move your head, but as you breathe in, the energy of your breath pulls your right hand outward parallel to the ground as far as it can extend comfortably.

Breathe in and feel your arm being pulled all the way out slowly. Hold it . . . two, three.

Breathe out and feel your arm being pulled back to your chest.

And again.

Breathe in and feel your arm being pulled back as far as you can go comfortably. Hold it . . . two, three.

Breathe out and feel your arm being pulled back to your chest.

Relax and breath comfortably, just experiencing the feeling of your breath.

Feel the coolness of the air as you breathe in and the warmth as you breathe out.

Place your left hand on top of your right hand as they are both lying on your chest.

Feel the coolness of the air as you breathe in, and the warmth as you breathe out.

Imagine the power of your breath can move your arm.

At the count of three you will slowly inhale and experience the energy of your breath pulling out your arm.

One, two, three.

As you breathe in, feel the air pulling your left hand all the way out, out, out on the side of your body.

As you breathe out, see the energy of your light pull the hand back all the way to sit on top of the other hand.

Good.

Again.

Use your breath to gently pull out your hand.

As you breathe in, going as far back as you can, and then when you breathe in a little bit more and hold it, your arm goes even a little bit further back.

And as you breathe out, your hand gets pulled all the way back to your chest.

Feel the breath moving your hand.

As you inhale it goes out—a little more and . . . hold it.

Exhale goes back—gently, slowly, and relax.

Let's do that several times.

Breathe in, the light pulls your hand back.

Breathe out, and your hand is pulled back by the energy of your light.

Breathe in, and your hand goes out.

Breathe out, and you feel your hand being pulled in.

Feel the coolness of the air as you breathe in, and the warmth as you breathe out.

Take a few relaxing breaths and just sit there because you have felt the power of your breath moving your arm.

Now we are going to allow the power of your arm to move your breath.

This time, it will be your movement that controls your breath.

Let's start again with your head.

Allow your jaw to rest again gently near your chest.

As you lift up your chin, feel your head pull up the breath from your body.

Hold it.

As you gently lower your chin, feel your face pushing the light of your breath back down into your body.

Lift up your chin to pull up your breath.

Lower your face to push it back to your body.

Notice how it is the movement of your head that is controlling your breathing.

View your breath, the gateway to your soul. as something you can control.

Lift up your breath with your movement upward. Push it back down as you lower your head.

Excellent.

Relax for a moment and you will create the same experience, first with your right hand and then with the left. We will do this just with our arms and allow the head to rest.

Change the position of your arms. Bend your elbows and put them on the arms of your chairs with your fingers pointed upward to the ceiling. Cup your hands and place them a few inches from each side of your face.

Allow yourself to see the cables of light attached to your hands.

Feel the coolness of the air as you breathe in, and the warmth as you breathe out.

When I count to three, you will pull your right arm back down to your side just to where you need to increase your range of movement. As you move your arm you will feel your hand pulling out the breath slowly. You will continue pulling your breath out comfortably and then pull back a little more, creating one more quick breath in. You will hold it and then you will push your breath back into your body again with your hands.

One, two three.

Pull your right hand back pulling out the breath . . . a little more and hold it.

Now push back the breath into your body gently controlling the tempo of your breath with the movement of your arms.

But the air is really light.

So as you breathe in, feel your hands pulling in the light to your body.

As you breathe out, feel your hands pushing the light back in.

As you breathe in, pull in the light.

As you breathe out, push the light back in.

Relax, breathe normally, and you will do this one more time with your right arm. You will control your breath with your hands. However, this time we will return to our Kids Kicking Cancer paradigm of pulling in the light and pushing out the darkness. Practice and tell us which one works best for you.

At the count of three we will inhale slowly:

One, two, three.

Pull in the light.

Hold it.

Push out the darkness.

Pull in the light.

Push out the darkness.

Relax and breathe normally for another moment. Keep your hands cupped near your face with your elbows bent and you will do this one more time with your left arm. You will control again your breath with your hands.

At the count of three, we will inhale slowly:

One, two, three.

Hold it.

Now push back the breath into your body, gently controlling the tempo of your breath with the movement of your arms.

As you breathe in, feel your hand pulling in the light to your body.

As you breathe out, feel your hands pushing out any darkness.

Pull in the light.

Hold it.

Push out the darkness.

Pull in the light.

Push out the darkness.

Take a deep, cleansing breath. Blow it out slowly.

Another deep, cleansing breath. Blow it out slowly.

And open up your eyes.

When you reach into the light of your soul, you take control of your life.

Power, Peace, Purpose.

Falling Asleep with the Light On
~Defeating Insomnia~

 *One of the attributes of our master teachers is that they have the poise to accept and take control of their challenges as best they can. When the rest of us are challenged, we often find ourselves tossing and turning in bed at night, struggling to fall asleep. In this meditation, you are given a path to relax through the power of your mind, gaining nourishment and relaxation even if you're actually sleeping. Sweet dreams!*

Many, many people lie in bed at night, tossing, troubled, disturbed that they are not getting to sleep. Others get to sleep right away, and find themselves waking up in the middle of the night and then tossing and turning with that overwhelmingly sinking feeling, "I've got to get to sleep. I can't do this. Here we go again."

This meditation is a meditation on not sleeping.

Wait—not sleeping, that doesn't make sense.

But in truth, if we teach ourselves to simply relax our bodies and meditate and feel the floating process of just lying there without our bodies being stressed, there is tremendous nourishment from just relaxing and allowing ourselves to be in that place. Even if we are conscious, even if we are awake, we can get a great night of non-sleep as well.

This is not a meditation on going to sleep. It is a prescription of gaining nourishment from not worrying if you are actually sleeping.

And ultimately, if you sleep or not, you will be fine.

What is important is that you can relax yourself and allow your body to rest even if you are not sleeping.

Resting is the goal.

Don't worry about sleeping.

But if you fall asleep, I won't get hurt. Remember, I was a pulpit rabbi for twenty years. Nobody put people to sleep as well as I did.

Find a comfortable place to lie down, preferably without any other disturbing noises or sounds.

Feel the coolness of the air as you breathe in, and the warmth as you breathe out.

Close your eyes and focus on the cycle of your breath.

Feel the coolness of the air as you breathe in, and the warmth as you breathe out.

Allow yourself to just fall into the bed, and anytime you feel uncomfortable and you want to move, that is absolutely fine.

And any other voice or sound that comes into your mind, just gently put them down and go back to the feeling of your breath.

Feel the coolness of the air as you breathe in, and the warmth as you breathe out.

Travel all the way to the top of your head, where your scalp meets your forehead and let every muscle relax and release.

Feel each muscle pull apart, one from the other, gently relaxing and releasing.

Go to the muscles behind your eyes, and allow each muscle to flow downward, feeling your eyes relax.

Go to the muscles in your mouth, your jaw, behind your ears, and as you exhale let every muscle just fall and relax.

Travel downward to your neck and release every muscle that surrounds your neck.

Feel your neck just become very comfortable.

Every muscle is flowing downward.

Go to the muscles in your spine, going down your back, and feel every muscle, one vertebra by the next, every muscle relax and release.

Feel the coolness of the air as you breathe in, and the warmth as you breathe out.

Go to the muscles in your chest and in your stomach.

And gently feel each muscle fall downward into the bed, flowing downward, gently descending.

The muscles in your legs all the way down to your feet.

Feel every muscle gently cascade downward into the bed.

Look through your body for any place of tension, fear, anger.

Any thoughts, any feelings.

And as you breathe in, pull them all together, and as you exhale, feel them travel out of your body.

Feel the coolness of the air as you breathe in, and the warmth as you breathe out.

Feel the coolness of the air as you breathe in, and the warmth as you breathe out.

Now imagine that you're lying on a very comfortable floating lounge chair that is lying on the sand.

It is very comfortable and it has its own soft bedding inside of it, and the walls of the little float surround you.

Your head is comfortable, and you can feel the warmth of the sand underneath the float. It feels very, very good.

Feel the coolness of the air as you breathe in, and the warmth as you breathe out.

As you're lying on the sand by the shore of this beautiful beach, you can see the small waves of this little lake gently begin to lap up on the shore near your float.

As you gently turn your head to the side in your image, you can see the bubbles of the waves of the water beginning to form as they come upward onto the beach.

You watch the waves go back and forth, back and forth, back and forth, forming their little bubbles gently near your float.

You begin to feel your feet being lifted up by the water that flows back and forth on the lake.

And as the waves continue back and forth, they raise higher and higher, gently converging upon the sands of the beach.

And now you feel the bottom of your back being lifted up gently by the rising of the lake.

You can feel the waves against your back and now your shoulders, going back and forth, back and forth.

And as you continue to watch this beautiful lake begin to surround your float on all sides, you can feel it gently lifting you off of the sand.

And the lake is not very large, and it is certainly not deep. It is only a few inches of warm tranquil water, so you're very comfortable and you're feeling very safe.

You are totally calm, and as you feel yourself surrounded by the water gently rocking you back and forth, back and forth, you notice that the movement of the waves is in total harmony with the rhythm of your breath.

Back and forth; back and forth.

As the water surrounds you on all sides, you are gently carried to the center of the lake where you can see the most beautiful fish swimming to the sides of your little boat.

Gently going back and forth, flowing with the current of the lake.

And as you're floating you can see yourself as if you're floating on a cloud, surrounded by this beautiful lake, going back and forth; back and forth.

You feel the warmth of the light as it penetrates the Heavens, warming you and giving you wonderful comfort as you feel gently floating back and forth; back and forth.

You can feel a very heavy tiredness has fallen upon you.

But you don't have to sleep.

You just want to remain floating within that beautiful lake, floating back and forth; back and forth.

And every time you have a message inside of your brain that says, "I should move now" or "I am uncomfortable," every time you move, it makes you feel even heavier and more tired, but that is ok.

Just get back to the place of comfort and the feeling of your float, gently following the flow of the lake.

Floating back and forth; back and forth.

With every movement or sound around you, you feel an even heavier tired feeling, floating gently on that lake.

As the sun shines down on the water, all around you is the brightest, most beautiful light.

There is so much peace and calm inside of yourself that you begin to feel yourself disappearing into the light.

Every time you experience the flow of your breathing out, just repeat the one word:

Light.

Light.

Light.

Feel the gentleness of floating within the light, gently going back and forth.

Light.

Light.

Light.

MEDITATION 30

~World Filled with Heroes~

 *This meditation is the first one for the rest of your life. Knowing that you are part of a very special world in which you are learning from children how to breathe in the light and blow out the darkness will allow you to continue to give them the message of Power, Peace, Purpose. You are now very much a part of their lives, and they are a part of yours. In this world built upon love, there is no room for the darkness of fear, pain, and anger. It is a new world. Share it with those around you as you continue to live the lesson of how a perfect God created an imperfect world, absolutely perfectly.*

This meditation is a meditation of joy, of connecting, of being part of an imperfect world that a perfect God created perfectly, of finding the light and the power to respond to darkness and challenge by searching inside of ourselves for the essence of our soul, and in particular by being surrounded by the beauty and light and wisdom of the children of Kids Kicking Cancer.

Let's begin this meditation in a comfortable place.

Find a chair, a couch, a place where you can keep your back straight but feel very relaxed and at peace.

Take in a very deep, cleansing breath, and hold that . . . two, three, and now let it out slowly.

Another deep, cleansing breath, pull it all the way up and feel your head sit up with it, and hold it and then gently . . . close your eyes.

Feel the coolness of the air as you breathe in, and the warmth as you breathe out.

Feel the coolness of the air as you breathe in, and the warmth as you breathe out.

Look through your body for any place of tension, of anger, of pain.

And as you breathe in the light, this amazing, powerful light that surrounds you, that is above you, that is within you, hold onto that light and blow out any place of darkness or fear, pain, anger.

Imagine that you are standing by the side of a river.

And the river and its currents are fast and swift.

You see in the middle of the river a gate anchored securely on the floor of the rocks of the river.

And leading up to that gate is a walkway that will allow you to walk to the middle of the river.

The walkway is secure, cement, strong.

And you are able to walk all the way to the middle of the river.

Beneath you, the water is rushing but your footing is secure and strong.

At the end of the walkway you see steps, and although they begin to be covered with the waters of the river, the water around them is very, very peaceful.

And they allow you to step into the river and hold onto the gate that is strongly anchored from the floor of the rocks of the river.

At first the water feels a little bit cold, and when you breathe out it is a little bit warmer.

And then you can feel that you are submerged in the comfort and warmth as the waters of the river turn warm, as if to greet you.

As you stand there in the river you can feel the pressure of the water on your back and flowing hard around you, but where you are standing in front of you holding onto the gate it is very strong, and calm.

Feel the coolness of the air as you breathe in, and the warmth as you breathe out.

And you notice that the water itself is turning all different shades of beautiful blue and sparkles.

And as it rushes around you and as you feel the force of the water gently pushing your back, you allow that water into your being to wash away any fear, any anger, any pain, any stress, and it feels very good and powerful and comfortable.

Even crouch down a little so that the water is up to your neck and you can feel that water rushing through you, and every place of tightness and of darkness are washed away by the water.

And you feel very good and very comfortable.

Feel the coolness of the air as you breathe in, and the warmth as you breathe out.

And as you stand there, in this beautiful river, you begin to notice that the sparkling reflection all around you is getting brighter and brighter.

And you can feel the water even getting hotter, warmed by the beautiful midday sun.

And as you let go of all of the stressors that are in your life and feel the flow of your inner energy, you can see that the reflection of sparkles upon the water turn into the faces of beautiful children.

And the water begins to go down and you can see that the children are wearing uniforms, representing the force of the martial arts.

And the children are sitting as the water recedes further and further, and they are sitting on these beautiful cushions and smiling, reflecting a brilliant light into your heart and into your soul.

And inside of yourself you begin to smile their smile of triumph, of victory, of light over darkness and to feel that not only in spite of your imperfect world but very much because of it, you have been given an opportunity to wash away the darkness with the power of light.

As you sit there, surrounded by your light that joins together with the light of these beautiful children, you notice that the river is now bordered on banks with flowers that are growing, and butterflies that fly, pollinating light and love from flower to flower.

And you can see that your light is able to travel across the width and breadth of the entire globe, chasing away the darkness, and as you stand up and walk out of the river, thousands of children surround you and walk with you wherever you go because you'll be part of their light as they will be part of yours, and together all of us will bring this light to the rest of the world.

Take in a deep, cleansing breath, and breathe it out slowly.

And let us say, Power, Peace, Purpose.

HEROES CIRCLE CONNECTIONS

Kids Kicking Cancer Office
27600 Northwestern Highway
Southfield, Michigan 48034
248–864-8238
www.kidskickingcancer.org

Follow our children

Facebook: https://www.facebook.com/kidskickingcancer
Twitter: https://twitter.com/kidskickcancer
Pinterest: https://www.pinterest.com/kidskickcancer
Instagram: https://Instagram/kidskickcancer

To let the children know how they have helped to change your life, send them an email at:

youngteachers@kidskickingcancer.org (for children 6 and above)
littleheroes@kidskickingcancer.org (for children 3 to 5 years old)

In Canada

3465 Huntington Windsor, ON. Canada N9E 3M9
(313) 557-0021 / canada@kidskickingcancer.org

In Italy

Via Fulcieri Paulucci de' Calboli, 60 00195 ROMA, ITALY
italy@kidskickingcancer.org /www.kidskickingcancer.it

In Israel

HaAdmur MeRuzhin 3/32 Jerusalem, Israel 9387003; 058 730 0613;
israel@kidskickingcancer.org

ABOUT THE AUTHOR

Rabbi Elimelech Goldberg (lovingly known by thousands of children as Rabbi G.), is the founder and director of Kids Kicking Cancer, a nonprofit organization that teaches martial arts to children battling cancer as well as to those facing other serious challenges in their lives. The therapy techniques he has developed, using meditation and breathing exercises, have been very successful in decreasing the pain of pediatric patients. Rabbi Goldberg began the program in 1999, nearly eighteen years after losing his first child to leukemia. He holds a First Degree Black Belt in the Korean art of Choi Kwang Do as well as a clinical assistant professorship in pediatrics at the Wayne State University School of Medicine in Detroit.

Among many honors and commendations, Rabbi G. was awarded the 2004 Robert Wood Johnson Community Health Leaders Award, the nation's most prestigious honor in community public health, and in the same year he was the recipient of the Humanitarian of the Year Award from the McCarty Cancer Foundation. In 2012 he was featured in People magazine's "Heroes Among Us" page, and in 2014 he was named a "Top Ten CNN Hero."

Rabbi Goldberg received his rabbinical ordination from Yeshiva University, where he also graduated summa cum laude. He served for twenty years as a pulpit rabbi and police chaplain in Southfield, Michigan. He now lectures around the world on the subjects of spirituality and health, and has expanded Kids Kicking Cancer to Canada, Italy, and Israel. In addition to helping children deal with serious health challenges in their lives, Rabbi G. also conducts stress seminars at Fortune 500 companies, where 97% of adult participants have described the presentations as having had "a profound influence" on their lives.

Rabbi G. and his wife, Ruthie, have two married children and eight grandchildren.

CPSIA information can be obtained
at www.ICGtesting.com
Printed in the USA
FFOW04n1438020915
16405FF